INDIA EMPOWERED

INDIA EMPOWERED

Change agents speak on an *idea* whose time has come

WITH AN INTRODUCTION BY
SHEKHAR GUPTA

THE EXPRESS GROUP

PENGUIN VIKING

VIKING

Published by the Penguin Group

Penguin Books India Pvt. Ltd, 11 Community Centre, Panchsheel Park, New Delhi 110 017, India

Penguin Group (USA) Inc., 375 Hudson Street, New York, New York 10014, USA

Penguin Group (Canada), 90 Eglinton Avenue East, Suite 700, Toronto, Ontario, Canada M4P 2Y3 (a division of Pearson Penguin Canada Inc.)

Penguin Books Ltd, 80 Strand, London WC2R 0RL, England

Penguin Ireland, 25 St Stephen's Green, Dublin 2, Ireland (a division of Penguin Books Ltd)

Penguin Group (Australia), 250 Camberwell Road, Camberwell, Victoria 3124, Australia (a division of Pearson Australia Group Pty Ltd)

Penguin Group (NZ), cnr Airborne and Rosedale Roads, Albany, Auckland 1310, New Zealand (a division of Pearson New Zealand Ltd)

Penguin Group (South Africa) (Pty) Ltd, 24 Sturdee Avenue, Rosebank, Johannesburg 2196, South Africa

Penguin Books Ltd, Registered Offices: 80 Strand, London WC2R 0RL, England

First published in Viking by Penguin Books India 2006

This edition copyright © The Indian Express 2006

Introduction copyright © Shekhar Gupta 2006

All rights reserved

10 9 8 7 6 5 4 3 2 1

ISBN-13: 978-0-67099-949-1   ISBN-10: 0-67099-949-0

Grateful acknowledgements are due to Jayachandran for the illustrations and to Pamela Philipose, associate editor, the *Indian Express* for editorial support

Typeset in Sabon by Mantra Virtual Services, New Delhi
Printed at Gopson Papers Ltd, Noida

This book is sold subject to the condition that it shall not, by way of trade or otherwise, be lent, resold, hired out, or otherwise circulated without the publisher's prior written consent in any form of binding or cover other than that in which it is published and without a similar condition including this condition being imposed on the subsequent purchaser and without limiting the rights under copyright reserved above, no part of this publication may be reproduced, stored in or introduced into a retrieval system, or transmitted in any form or by any means (electronic, mechanical, photocopying, recording or otherwise), without the prior written permission of both the copyright owner and the above-mentioned publisher of this book.

Contents

INTRODUCTION xvii
Shekhar Gupta

LEADERS, POLITICIANS, POLICY MAKERS

EMPOWER RURAL INDIA THROUGH
KNOWLEDGE 3
A.P.J. Abdul Kalam

PAVE THE WAY FOR OUR POOR TO FIND
HUMAN DIGNITY 11
Bhairon Singh Shekhawat

OPEN DEMOCRACY AND OPEN ECONOMY 16
Manmohan Singh

JUDICIARY STRENGTHENED FROM WITHIN 18
R.C. Lahoti

EVERY INDIAN HAS AN EQUAL STAKE IN
INDIA'S FUTURE 23
Somnath Chatterjee

POWER FROM THE FEW TO THE MANY 28
Omar Abdullah

SANSKRITI, SAMRUDDHI AND SU-RAJ 30
L.K. Advani

PROGRESS MUST REACH THE LOWER MIDDLE
CLASS 33
Mani Shankar Aiyar

PEOPLE IN STRIFE AND THE IDEA OF INDIA 36
Ghulam Nabi Azad

SPREAD THE GAINS TO THE DEPRIVED 39
A.B. Bardhan

LEARN FROM MISTAKES, KEEP PACE WITH
CHANGE 42
Buddhadeb Bhattacharjee

EQUAL RIGHTS, NOT JUST RHETORIC 45
Dipankar Bhattacharya

GOOD GOVERNANCE A FUNDAMENTAL
RIGHT 49
B.K. Chaturvedi

GROWTH THAT CARRIES EVERYONE ALONG 53
P. Chidambaram

THE POTENTIAL OF PARTICIPATORY
DEMOCRACY 56
Sheila Dikshit

PROTECT THE RIGHTS OF CHILDREN 58
Priya Dutt

BHARAT AND INDIA AS ONE FAMILY 60
George Fernandes

THE AFFLICTED HAVE TO BE HEARD 63
Gopalkrishna Gandhi

STRENGTHEN THE SECURITY FORCES TO
CRUSH TERROR 66
K.P.S. Gill

DO AWAY WITH EXCLUSIVITY 69
I.K. Gujral

WHEN PEOPLE CHANGE THEIR OWN LIVES 72
Wajahat Habibullah

CONTENTS vii

PRE-EMPT SOCIAL CONFLICT 76
Bhupinder Singh Hooda

REGIONAL IMBALANCE DAMAGES THE WHOLE 79
Nitish Kumar

POWER TO THE DEPRIVED MAJORITY 82
Mayawati

NATIONAL CLEAN-UP BEGINS WITH THE
BUREAUCRACY 84
U.S. Misra

END THE SECULAR VS COMMUNAL DEBATE 90
Mehbooba Mufti

ENABLE ALL: INSTITUTIONS, INDIVIDUALS
AND FAMILY 93
Pranab Mukherjee

THE SUPPRESSED MUST ASSERT THEIR
RIGHTS 95
K.R. Narayanan

JUST FORMAL EQUALITY FOR WOMEN IS NOT
ENOUGH 97
Fali S. Nariman

EXPORTS AS KEY TO EMPLOYMENT 99
Kamal Nath

CLIMATE CHANGE AND RESOURCE
REGENERATION 102
R.K. Pachauri

EMPOWER WEALTH CREATORS, NOT
ACCUMULATORS 105
M.K. Pandhe

DECISIVE ACTION FOR THE NATION TO TAKE
OFF 108
Praful Patel

viii CONTENTS

THE WEAKEST AND THE POOREST MUST
EMPOWER THE NATION 111
Naveen Patnaik

A PARADIGM SHIFT IN AGRICULTURE 114
Sharad Pawar

EVERY REGION, EVERY RELIGION HAS A
STAKE 119
Sachin Pilot

BRIDGE THE INEQUITIES, LEVERAGE OUR
STRENGTHS 121
Vasundhara Raje

THE POWER OF THE FOURTH ESTATE 129
N. Ram

GOOD HEALTH FOR ALL 134
Anbumani Ramadoss

NOT MUSLIM INDIANS BUT INDIAN
MUSLIMS 137
Syed Kalbe Sadiq

YOUTHFUL PROMISE OF THE NORTH-EAST 140
P.A. Sangma

AN UNCOMPROMISING FOCUS ON LITERACY 142
Jyotiraditya M. Scindia

MAKE CORRUPTION A THING OF THE PAST 144
P. Shankar

SAARE JAHAN SE ACHCHA 148
Rakesh Sharma

TECHNOLOGY TO THE RESCUE 151
Kapil Sibal

AGRICULTURE CAN MAKE THE FUTURE 154
Amarinder Singh

CONTENTS   ix

FREEDOM FROM THE TYRANNY OF
CORRUPTION   158
Jaswant Singh

A NEW PERCEPTION OF INDIA   160
K. Natwar Singh

BULB, TAP AND TOILET IN EVERY RURAL
HOME   162
Raghuvansh Prasad Singh

LET THE DISEMPOWERED ALSO DECIDE   166
V.P. Singh

WOMEN'S VOICES FOR CHANGE   168
Sushma Swaraj

FREE ELECTIONS ARE THE HALLMARK OF
DEMOCRACY   170
B.B. Tandon

THE ELITE MUST QUIT THE IVORY TOWER   173
Mulayam Singh Yadav

STRENGTHEN THE BONDS OF OUR
COMMONALITY   175
Sitaram Yechury

ACTIVISTS, ACADEMICS, THINKERS

RESPECT FOR INDIVIDUAL DIGNITY   181
Meghnad Desai

A WORKING, PARTYLESS SYSTEM OF
DEMOCRACY   183
Nanaji Deshmukh

INFRASTRUCTURE FOR OUR TRIBALS   186
Mahasveta Devi

CONTENTS

HONESTY WITHOUT FEAR   189
Dhananjay Dubey

TEXTBOOKS THAT TEACH DIGNITY OF
LABOUR   192
Kancha Ilaiah

STEM THE BRAIN DRAIN, INSPIRE GROWTH   195
R.A. Mashelkar

INTELLECTUAL CAPITAL IS THE CHANGE
AGENT   197
G. Madhavan Nair

EXCITING RESEARCH OUT OF LABS INTO
UNIVERSITIES   199
Jayant V. Narlikar

PEOPLE IN CONTROL OF THEIR RESOURCES   200
Medha Patkar

SCIENCE AND TECHNOLOGY CAN DRIVE
SOCIAL CHANGE   204
S.Z. Qasim

TUNE IN TO THE VOICE OF THE DEPRIVED   208
Aruna Roy

NO TO BLAME CULTURE, YES TO COURAGE
AND CHANGE   211
Sri Sri Ravi Shankar

IN THE LINE OF DUTY   213
M. Shanmugham

ENSURE THE BEST, INSURE THE FUTURE   215
Devi Shetty

MAKE HUNGER HISTORY THROUGH GRAM
SWARAJ   217
M.S. Swaminathan

CREATE HEALTHY VILLAGES IN THE OTHER INDIA 221
Naresh Trehan

TECHNOLOGY FOR THE COMMON GOOD 224
Sadhguru Jaggi Vasudev

MADE IN INDIA, MAKE IT WORK FOR INDIA 227
P. Venugopal

CORPORATE VOICES

BE ACCOUNTABLE AND DEMAND ACCOUNTABILITY 231
Anu Aga

FINDING THE DHIRUBHAI WITHIN 234
Mukesh D. Ambani

EMPOWER LABOUR TO EMPOWER ITSELF 236
Subroto Bagchi

CHEER THE WINNERS 239
Rahul Bajaj

REVAMP EDUCATION FOR EXCELLENCE 242
Kumar Mangalam Birla

RESOURCE ALLOCATION IS THE PEOPLE'S PREROGATIVE 244
Michael F. Carter

INDIA INC AND LAST MILE CONNECTIVITY 247
Y.C. Deveshwar

AFFORDABLE AIR TRAVEL FOR EVERYBODY 252
Naresh Goyal

BUILDING WORLD CLASS PHYSICAL AND SOCIAL INFRASTRUCTURE 256
K.V. Kamath

INFORMATION PAGDANDI TO BRIDGE
DIVIDES 259
Kiran Karnik

A FOUR-WHEELER FOR EVERY FAMILY 262
Jagdish Khattar

NURTURE ENTREPRENEURSHIP IN VILLAGES 265
Naina Lal Kidwai

THINK NATIONAL, ACT LOCAL 267
Anand Mahindra

ENABLE THE SOFTWARE OF DEMOCRACY 270
Arun Maira

THE CORPORATE SECTOR MUST TURN AROUND
AGRICULTURE 273
Sunil Bharti Mittal

BIJLI, SADAK, PAANI, VAHAN 276
Brijmohan Lall Munjal

LEADERS MUST DREAM BIG 280
N.R. Narayana Murthy

MARCH AHEAD WITH A GLOBAL MINDSET 283
A.M. Naik

REDUCE THE KNOWLEDGE GAP BETWEEN THE
RULER AND THE RULED 286
Nandan M. Nilekani

GETTING READY TO WELCOME THE WORLD 289
P.R.S. 'Biki' Oberoi

FORTUNE FAVOURS THE PREPARED MIND 291
Deepak S. Parekh

EMPOWER YOUTH TO DRIVE INDIA'S
PROGRESS 293
Vivek Paul

CONTENTS xiii

AN EDUCATION WORTHY ENOUGH FOR
INDIA 296
Azim H. Premji

TECHNOLOGY WILL USHER IN CHANGE 299
Sam Pitroda

STABLE, QUALITY ENERGY: A DREAM COME
TRUE 302
Subir Raha

PEOPLE AS AGENTS OF CHANGE 304
Kiran Mazumdar Shaw

ISLANDS OF PROSPERITY IN A SEA OF
POVERTY 306
Venu Srinivasan

TIME FOR INDIA TO SHIFT GEAR 308
Ratan Tata

THE ARTS, SPORTS

DON'T WAIT FOR A CHANCE, MAKE IT
HAPPEN 313
Vishwanathan Anand

A LEVEL PLAYING FIELD 315
Shyam Benegal

PUT SPORTS ON THE FAST TRACK 317
Harsha Bhogle

TO COMPETE ON THE WORLD STAGE, THE
HUNGER TO WIN 319
Bhaichung Bhutia

ROADS TO INDIA'S PROGRESS 322
Kapil Dev

CONTENTS

DO JUSTICE TO OUR TALENT POOL 324
Anju Bobby George

LOOK AFTER ART, THE KEEPER OF A
NATION'S SOUL 326
Satish Gujral

IT IS MUSIC THAT BINDS A NATION 329
Bhupen Hazarika

LET THE NET GAIN COUNT 331
Shammi Kapoor

PUT A SMILE ON EVERY FACE 333
Shah Rukh Khan

GENDER NO DETERRENT 335
Sania Mirza

VILLAGE YOUTH MUST GET A PLATFORM 337
Dhanraj Pillay

FREEDOM TO MAKE UNBIASED CHOICES 339
Ganesh Pyne

AS MANY SPORTS CENTRES AS MALLS 341
Rajyavardhan Singh Rathore

WHERE THE MIND IS WITHOUT FEAR 343
Mallika-Kartikeya Sarabhai

KALA AND VIDYA ARE TWO FACES OF THE
SAME COIN 345
Gulammohammed Sheikh

REVENUE SHARING FOR SPORTING
EXCELLENCE 351
Milkha Singh

DEFINE YOURSELF BY WHAT YOU DO 353
Tabu

LOOKING FOR NEW ICONS 355
P.T. Usha

VOICES FROM THE ARMED FORCES

THE DISABLED MUST BE SELF-SUFFICIENT 361
M.P. Anil Kumar

DIGNITY, SELF-RESPECT FOR THOSE WHO
GUARD INDIA 364
Arun Prakash

SAFETY PRINCIPLE AS ARTICLE OF FAITH 367
J.J. Singh

STRONG, IN THE FACE OF DISASTER 370
V. Somasundar

LESSONS THE ARMED FORCES TEACH US 372
Shashindra Pal Tyagi

SEIZE THE MOMENT FOR A BRIGHTER
FUTURE 374
Yogendra Singh Yadav

LIST OF CONTRIBUTORS 376

SHEKHAR GUPTA
EDITOR IN-CHIEF, *INDIAN EXPRESS*

Introduction

Journalism of courage has always been the leitmotif running through the history of the *Indian Express*. Much before the newspaper chose to deliver this promise of fearless, uncompromising journalism—what the ad world calls the 'tagline'—this was all its founder demanded of people who worked for him. Solidly inscribed into our DNA, the practice of this promise evolved with the times.

So, during the freedom movement, journalism of courage meant the *Express* fighting the British when many other, richer, and apparently more powerful newspapers would rather side with the sahibs. During Quit India, it meant suspending publication rather than accepting censorship. A front-page editorial the late Ram Nath Goenka wrote then—one of the rarest of rare occasions he put his name in his newspaper—sets the agenda for us even today and for all time to come. Headlined 'Heart Strings and Purse Strings', it explained why he would prefer to suspend publication and take losses rather than accept the idea of censorship imposed by a colonial power.

A little over three decades later, the same principle was to come handy when the time came to resist censorship—and worse—from our own government of the day, during the Emergency. As his biography by B.G. Verghese, a former editor of the *Express*, tells you, Ram Nath Goenka never used the power of his newspaper. He always believed that an institution like this was not to be an instrument of power in his hands, but a medium of empowerment for the people of his nation.

Truth, knowledge, impartial and accurate information, he believed, were instruments of empowerment. For, these enable the citizen to ask the right questions, deny the rulers the luxury of avoiding having to give answers and bridge the gap between people and the establishment.

The idea evolved with the times. I was a journalism student during the Emergency and, after the shock of the first three months was over, you knew which papers had the spine to stand up for their beliefs, which ones did not. On my campus, as I am sure on many others, this is when the *Express* made its mark.

Soon, as you began to scan the *Express* for flashes of defiance, sometimes open, like blank spaces in place of edits that censors had stopped, and sometimes clever, like a tiny obituary in the classifieds that bemoaned the 'death of liberty, mother of hope, faith and justicia', it was easy to see why this paper was different.

I was among those fortunate ones who entered journalism, and in fact the *Indian Express*, just as the Emergency ended. For those of us, cub reporters then, it was a heady feeling when people pumped your hands in awe and said, oh, you work at the *Express*, such a courageous paper!

But courage, in those innocent days, had a simpler definition. Usually, it meant making sure you got the story others wouldn't bother to reach and telexing it back somehow in the days of poor communication. Or exposing a wrong and moving on to the next story, a heady hit-and-run that required courage, intellect, but did not demand that the story be taken to its logical conclusion, with redressal for the victims, punishment to the guilty.

Until the paper attempted to do just that under one more of my very illustrious predecessors, Arun Shourie, who discovered the instrument of the PIL to follow up on stories like the Bhagalpur blindings. From merely fighting an authoritarian state, the journalism of courage was now exposing and taking on its many limbs and instruments that were autocratic and unaccountable anyway. It was with this journalism that the *Express* then combined with the higher judiciary to empower some of the poorest and weakest sections of our society to seek justice.

India's mediascape was now changing rapidly. Newspapers were being seen more as mere products, the marketplace was being redefined, the rules of the game were being rewritten, and we were told the basic job of a newspaper was to entertain, amuse, even titillate. Also, that with the decline of the Congress, the politics of the country was too fragmented, instead of one establishment to take on, there were now several. Instead of the notebook, background interviews, anonymous sources, painstaking research, investigative journalism's new tool became the spycamera: switch it on, record the dirt, pack in both titillation and entertainment, hit play.

Yet, look at what this paper has managed to achieve amidst this noise.

Its series on the Vajpayee government's petrol pump allotments to its own led to large-scale cancellations and a Supreme Court mandated inquiry; its investigation on our largest bank-loan defaulters helped the passage of the Securitisation Act; its exposé on the defacing of glacial rocks in Himachal Pradesh resulted in a clean-up; and its persistence in first exposing, and then following up, the Satyendra Dubey murder led not merely to the arrest of his alleged murderers and a clean-up in the national highway project but also in the system moving closer to passing a whistleblower law.

There was, however, a great difference this time. In each case, action happened because others, the audio-visual media, NGOs and citizens' groups, Parliament and, most important of all, the Supreme Court, were willing to take up these issues. All they needed was information through '*Express*-type' journalism that wasn't just courageous but also incisive, credible, sincere, intelligent, dedicated and influential. The results are there to see.

Journalism of courage is no longer hit-and-run guerrilla warfare. It's a medium of empowerment by bringing to light information that either somebody in the establisment is trying to hide or something that others may not have had the integrity, intellect or courage to discover, print and then follow up until other institutions, from the media to the judiciary, join in and take the idea to its logical conclusion.

It is amazing how often, and sometimes how smoothly, such things can happen now. If you have doubts, look at the rapid pace at which things moved after *Express*'s first exposé that there were no tigers any more in Sariska. Ten days later, we found a similar story in Ranthambhore. The next week, the prime minister stepped in.

It is to celebrate this remarkable evolution of our society (and market!) that we initiated the India Empowered series. As the first few contributions, notably by the president and the prime minister show, empowerment through intelligent and incisive information is an idea whose time has come.

At this point, please allow me to dig a little into the memories of my reporting years. In February 1983, then as *Express*'s correspondent in the north-east, I broke the story of the massacre of 3,500 people in the village of Nellie in Assam. On a visit to Delhi subsequently, I was taken by my editors then to meet Ramnathji. 'You young fellow, you are doing a good job,' said the old man, always parsimonious with praise. And then he added, 'I liked that language in your story . . . taking a walk across is an act of courage. Must have been tough looking at so many dead and injured?'

Looking back 22 years, yes, it was an act of courage. As it was to drive to Guwahati airport, in a blood-stained white shirt, to hand over the roll of film from my Minolta to a Delhi-bound Indian Airlines pilot and then finding a telex machine in a strike-hit telegraph office to file the story at a time when STD was a luxury and fax not yet invented.

But even today, nobody has been called to account. That massacre, entirely of poor Muslims, has gone uninvestigated. Nobody remembers it, nobody complains that everybody got away. Today, if such a thing were to happen again, god forbid, there is sufficient institutional and political awakening in India to ensure it will not be so easy to forget, if not forgive, as *Express*'s coverage of the 2002 Gujarat killings (for which it got the International Press Institute award) has shown.

The difference between 1983 and 2005 is that then, information of a development like the Nellie massacre merely shocked you. Today, it empowers you to demand redressal, better governance, a better quality of life. That is why we believe that in today's India, our journalism of courage is an instrument of national empowerment.

So please enjoy the essays from across the country on the theme and the diverse points of view. Better still, join the debate.

LEADERS, POLITICIANS, POLICY MAKERS

A.P.J. ABDUL KALAM
PRESIDENT OF INDIA

Empower Rural India through Knowledge

A new situation is emerging in India. Very rarely in history have we come across such a constellation: an ascending economic trajectory, rising foreign exchange reserves, reducing inflation rates, global recognition of technological competence, the energy of 540 million youth, umbilical connectivities of 20 million people of Indian origin abroad and the interest shown by developed countries to invest in our engineers and scientists, including in new R&D centres.

Governments have been emphasising economic development by ensuring growth rates of 7-8 per cent annually, enhancing the welfare of farmers and workers and unleashing the creativity of entrepreneurs, scientists, engineers. This opportunity must be fully utilised to bridge the rural-urban divide, using knowledge as a tool. As such, I would like to focus on 'Empowering Rural India'.

This discussion will be in five parts. The first part cites experiences with knowledge centres working in the country. The second part presents a case for Village Knowledge Centres in relation to the integrated development of rural areas through Providing Urban Amenities to Rural Areas (PURA).

The third part deals with examples of PURA in action. The fourth part presents the working domain services for effective knowledge acquisition to the PURA complexes. The final part consolidates the flow chart of data needed for farmers, fishermen and the entire rural population in an integrated way for sustainable development.

It takes a village
In June 2005, when I visited Nagapattinam, I saw the Village Resource

Centre established by the Tata Tsunami Relief Committee in association with the M.S. Swaminathan Research Foundation at Akkaraipettai.

Speaking to the young members operating the system, I found they were helping locals by imparting education through computers, helping the self-help group members maintain their accounts, and providing weather and sea state forecast data.

While it was all very good, the important issue of providing a live database on various services to fishermen and farmers remains. This has to be a co-ordinated effort.

Recently, I inaugurated six Village Resource Centres in Ettimadi, Coimbatore district, Tamil Nadu, established by Amrita Vishwa Vidyapeetam in partnership with ISRO. They provide tele-education and tele-medicine to six villages in Tamil Nadu and Kerala through video conferencing.

I also understand the RASI Scheme of Tamil Nadu, implemented at Mellur taluk in Madurai district, is providing knowledge connectivity to villages. This enables local unemployed youth to set up village kiosks to provide computer literacy, Internet access through CorDECT Wireless system with a limited bandwidth and allows small value-added services through computers, with digital photographs as well as e-mail access.

This also helps villagers get birth certificates from local authorities and healthcare advice from the Madurai Arvind Eye Hospital through e-mail. I appreciate the efforts by these organisations for knowledge enabling the villagers at the Village Knowledge Centres (VKCs). These VKCs will act as a knowledge-delivery tool. How to equip the VKCs with knowledge and purpose in an integrated way, within a sustainable developmental framework, is the challenge.

Pure is as PURA does
Nearly 700 million Indians live in 6,00,000 villages across India. Connectivity of village complexes providing economic opportunities to all segments of people is an urgent need. We need to innovate to increase connectivities to the villages, making clusters out of them even while retaining their individuality.

The integrated method that will bring prosperity to rural India is PURA. This envisages four connectivities: physical connectivity through quality roads and transport; electronic connectivity through telecom with high bandwidth fibre optic cables; knowledge connectivity through education, skill training for farmers, artisans and craftsmen and entrepreneurship programmes.

These three connectivities will lead to economic connectivity through the starting of enterprises with the help of banks, micro-credit and marketing of products. We need to establish 7,000 PURA complexes in the country, encompassing 2,30,000 village panchayats.

For providing knowledge connectivity to PURA complexes, VKCs will act as frontline delivery systems. The VKC should provide the essential data required for the targeted population such as farmers, fishermen, craftsmen, traders, businessmen, entrepreneurs, unemployed youth, and students. It has to be acquired by visiting the village, talking to the rural people, by understanding their requirements and core competences.

Providing meteorological data for both farmers and fishermen has to be area specific, covering say twenty or thirty villages in the vicinity of the sea coast or farming area. Local relevance of information offered is essential.

Users have simple needs of information but it is often tough for system integrators because of the need to update data. Trained manpower has to be deployed to generate information that can explain in simple terms the meteorological data, weather data, marketing data on fish, agricultural and other rural commodities.

This data has to come from various connected institutions that provide service to the people on a timely basis. But the transformation of data into user-friendly information is the real challenge.

The main focus of the VKC should be to empower youth to undertake development tasks of villages and establish rural enterprises that will provide large-scale employment. So it is essential to skill enable and knowledge enable through academic institutions, industry, banking and marketing institutions. The VKC should act as a facilitator. Blended knowledge is better knowledge.

Nuts and bolts of connectivity

A low-cost multi-task handheld computer with GPS and wireless mobility should be developed and should reach fishermen and farmers. They should add value to this tool for their benefit to increase their earning capacity. Every VKC should have a computer terminal, wireless (Wi-Max) connection or fibre broadband or satellite connectivity to connect to the nodal centres for acquisition of knowledge and dissemination of updated real-time data.

Each PURA should have 'Nodal PURA Knowledge Data Centres', which should be the hub for all activities. These centres should be linked to the nominated domain service providing organisations in agriculture— including fisheries, cottage and small-scale industries and commerce, education and HRD, and healthcare. These domain institutions will have a mechanism to create continuously updated information systems needed to service the VKC.

PURA in action

I have visited many rural areas and seen working systems of PURA such as the Gujarat-BAIF model and the Vallam Periyar PURA model near Thanjavur. I have also visited tsunami affected villages of Nagapattinam and suggested the implementation of 'coastal PURA' to the district administration.

The Bharatiya Agro-Industries Foundation (BAIF) is an integrated village cluster development programme in two village clusters, Chonda and Lachakadi, in south Gujarat. Every summer, tribal people used to migrate to nearby towns. The BAIF model was installed in these two villages with the cooperation of the people and the participation of the state authorities. Water harvesting was undertaken. Every home was provided with livestock and also a market for milk. Simultaneously, orchards were established with various fruit crops such as cashew and mangoes, that are tolerant to drought.

Today, the tribal population is harvesting crops, packaging and carrying milk to different supply points. The project was implemented through self-help groups. The groups took the responsibility of helping weaker members, which boosted progress. The results were phenomenal.

Last year I visited the Periyar Maniammai College of Technology for Women and inaugurated the Periyar PURA Complex. Over sixty-five villages near Vallam, Thanjavur, in Tamil Nadu, have been transformed as a PURA cluster.

This PURA complex has all three connectivities—physical connectivity, with a circular road and interconnecting roads covering major villages, along with bus transport; electronic connectivity through Internet kiosks; knowledge connectivity through the academic background of the promoting agency—leading to the economic connectivity of sixty-five villages.

The centre of activity is the engineering college for women that provides electronic and knowledge connectivity. Periyar PURA has healthcare centres, primary to post-graduate education and vocational training centres.

This has resulted in large-scale employment generation and creation of entrepreneurs with the active support of 850 self-help groups. They have innovative water management schemes for irrigation and providing potable water for all village citizens.

All sixty-five Periyar PURA villages have only rain-fed irrigation. Two hundred acres of wasteland have been developed into cultivable land with innovative water management schemes, such as contour ponds and watersheds. Villagers are busy in either cultivation, planting Jatropha, herbal and medicinal plants, power generation using bio-mass, food processing and, above all, running marketing centres.

Due to shortage of rainfall in that locality, farmers were suffering from water scarcity for agriculture and for drinking. Periyar PURA developed six percolation ponds and five check dams to harness rainwater amounting to 2,73,000 cubic metres per year.

This water is supporting the irrigation of 300 acres of land through recharging open wells and borewells. It also supplies drinking water to the people. More than 5,000 farmers are benefiting from this programme.

Recently Periyar PURA has introduced a number of employment-oriented schemes for tsunami affected Nagapattinam villages and trained self-help groups in tile making, paper manufacturing, alternative building blocks manufacturing. This lone engineering college has empowered villagers through skill-oriented training, provision of finance and provision of market connectivity for their produce.

PURA on the coast
When I visited Nagapattinam, after reviewing the tsunami rehabilitation schemes, I proposed coastal PURAs, ideal for bringing sustainable prosperity to this region. The salient features of this PURA are the following:

- Physical connectivity: Construction of jetties and small and medium-sized boat-landing centres on the coast at intervals of 10 to 15 km. Each of these will have a good link road to the main coastal road. Second, establishment of community sheds for repair of nets, storing the nets and related equipment of the fishermen.
- Electronic connectivity: All the fishing villages in the coastal areas have to be linked with the district HQ through broadband fibre and wireless connectivities. Fishermen should be provided with broadcasting facilities through satellite radios and the HAMSAT network. Mobile phones with GPS facility may be provided for each boat for emergency communication.
- This will also provide the local fishing population meteorological and sea state data through SMS from the VKCs.
- Knowledge connectivity: The government should facilitate the training of fishermen in cost-effective yet safe fishing techniques, application

of technology for improving productivity, storage and preservation systems and marketing, banking and financing systems through the district HQ and connected VKCs. It must also provide adequate warning data for fishermen out at sea.

- Economic connectivity: These three connectivities will motivate and enable the local population to create cold storage infrastructure, fish processing and packaging and marketing for realising the value-added price. This will also provide alternative employment-oriented schemes during non-fishing days, and for people who are involved in agriculture and other activities.

Here I would like to appreciate the work of the Alaimagal self-help group, which in partnership with DRDA and NGOs has successfully got an export order of quality candles and other crafts products to the Netherlands. Such activities should be the objective of our rural development schemes.

So far, we have focused on 'live' PURAs in action and on VKCs. How do we get the periodically updated and relevant information to the VKCs, so that the best knowledge base is available to farmers, fishermen and craftsmen? Call centres for kisans.

I have studied a system currently used by farmers and fishermen in different parts of the country. This is the Kisan Call Centre (KCC), established by the ministry of agriculture in partnership with Telecommunication Consultants India Ltd (TCIL), an enterprise under the ministry of communication and IT.

The KCC offers three levels of interaction and support in agriculture, fisheries and animal husbandry domains, through national experts and corresponding directorates at the Central level.

In its one year of operation, the call centre has provided consultancy, information, assistance and guidance to over 500,000 callers from eight states. Anywhere in India, people can call 1551 as a toll free number to access the service. The top users are Maharastra and Tamil Nadu, followed by Uttar Pradesh and Rajasthan.

I have studied some of the typical questions answered by the call centres:

- From Warangal: In cotton, what are the suitable varieties to be taken and when can we avail the varieties?
- From Anathapur: What is the seed treatment of groundnut, with dosage?

- From Cuddapah: What are the ways to get citrus fruits ripened quickly?
- From Indore: In which market will I get a good price for my cotton produce?
- From Jalandhar: What is the method of controlling yellowing in a paddy nursery?

These questions were answered by KCC agricultural and fisheries specialists. This is the working system for providing domain services in agriculture, fisheries and animal husbandry.

Typical knowledge requirements in agriculture extend to soil, seed, water management, post-harvest management, productivity increase, crop insurance, banking and financial systems, education, healthcare and employment or entrepreneurial opportunities.

Flow chart for rural knowledge
As we have seen in the KCC example, similar domain service provider call centres are required in commerce and industry, entrepreneurial skill development and employment generation, travel and tourism, banking and insurance, meteorological forecasting, disaster warning, education and HRD, and healthcare. These call centres will act as service providers to the PURA nodal knowledge data centres located in the PURA complexes, which in turn will provide the area-specific and customised knowledge to the VKCs.

There have been many attempts across the country in taking information and communication technology (ICT) to rural areas. Each of the proponents of these efforts is passionately attached to the core idea and continues to pursue it even when it does not make economic sense or when it has proven not scalable or sustainable. Some of these efforts are successful only when centred on a creative leader.

What we need now is a serious and impartial review to decide on the best practices for nationwide deployment—a 'best of breed' solution for sustainable PURA.

Technology is the instrument for providing non-linear growth to our economy. Hence PURA driven by technology for sustainable rural development will bridge the rural-urban divide. Access to technology is the means to generate employment potential for sustainable rural prosperity.

Village Knowledge Centres are the essential component for realising our goal of graduating to a knowledge society and India's transformation to a developed country by 2020.

Higher the knowledge dissemination and its absorption by society, wider the perspectives of its citizens—leading to reduction in societal tensions and increasing cooperation and collaboration. Dimensions of political, societal and media thinking will also be wider and focused on relevant aspects of social and economic development.

BHAIRON SINGH SHEKHAWAT
VICE-PRESIDENT OF INDIA

Pave the Way for Our Poor to Find Human Dignity

In our Constitution, we made the solemn commitment to secure for all citizens justice, liberty, equality and, promoting among them all, fraternity.

To me, empowerment of India, therefore, implies further strengthening and deepening the roots of democracy; providing good governance to overcome under-development and the riddance of poverty, hunger and disease; building a fully developed and prosperous nation through sustained economic reforms so as to secure growth with equity and earning opportunities for a vast segment of our unemployed youth; providing opportunity in real terms to every citizen to fulfill his aspirations and ambitions; establishing an environment conducive to the pursuit of knowledge and learning at institutions of excellence—an environment of confidence, hope and motivation for the youth to build a nation of their dreams and vision and to enable the country to face emerging challenges in a rapidly evolving global order.

It is a matter of great pride that our country today enjoys the outstanding distinction of having evolved a vibrant and dynamic parliamentary system of democracy. India's experience of the last five decades is a story of the success of democracy in a populated nation that has shown how complex problems can be addressed within the constitutional and democratic framework. For sustained and successful evolution of democracy, it is imperative for us to overcome challenges of economic growth and development and be on the fast growth trajectory. Development that promotes people's welfare alone will strengthen and deepen the roots of our democracy.

I have been very concerned that challenges of growth and key issues of public governance and development be addressed in a non-partisan and apolitical manner with everyone's cooperation. As chairman of the Rajya Sabha, it has been my endeavour that such key issues are raised, debated and discussed in the Rajya Sabha in a focused manner so that constructive suggestions and recommendations for appropriate legislative and executive actions are evolved towards achieving the objective growth of the economy, public governance and public welfare. I have been voicing my concerns on vital issues in other public fora as well. I would like to share some of these concerns today.

Empowerment of the poor:
Focus on poverty alleviation: Our significant progress and development since Independence will be fragile and unsustainable if it is not inclusive of the welfare of our 26 crore brethren living in extreme poverty. In my view, democracy will survive and succeed only if it promotes welfare of the poor and the under privileged with little access to basic education, health care or shelter. I, therefore, regard poverty alleviation and welfare of the common man as the fifth pillar of our democracy.

Our Supreme Court has pronounced that the right to live with dignity is a fundamental right of every citizen. The poor have, therefore, to be enabled with access in real terms to basic services such as primary education, health care, drinking water, shelter and food security. Any development plan will have substantive meaning only if it includes comprehensive programmes of poverty alleviation.

It has been my firm conviction that eliminating the scourge of poverty and deprivation is the sacred duty of the government. Ensuring the welfare of the poor should be the first charge on the treasury of the State. I have believed in the Antyodaya philosophy of development, i.e., the focus of action being on the poorest amongst the poor. In the pioneering initiative taken in Rajasthan for alleviation of poverty under the Antyodaya scheme launched in 1977, action plans were formulated in every village to ensure economic uplift and empowerment of five poorest families in a year. This experience could be of some use and relevance even today in preparing micro plans for every village panchayat.

Governance at cutting edge level: Unfortunately, on account of corruption and inefficiency in management, public programmes have failed to deliver the intended benefits to the common man. Indeed, the poor have been cheated and robbed of the full extent of benefit that ought to have actually accrued to them under the PDS and other programmes meant for their welfare.

We need to make the delivery system of public programmes and schemes totally free of corruption. For this, it is necessary to establish transparency and accountability. Our parliament has recently legislated the Right to Information Act; we should effectively use the provisions of this law to disseminate and share with all concerned, information in respect of coverage of beneficiaries as also details of expenditure incurred under each of these schemes along with publication of audit reports on such expenditure. Establishing a mechanism for local vigilance on the public delivery system of goods and services will also go a long way in improving quality, efficiency and integrity of field administration.

The common man is also subjected to a regime of complex laws and complicated regulations, many of which he is not even aware of. Over and above that, he lives under the tyranny of the inspector raj. A rigorous review and simplification of existing laws, rules and procedures is called for to free the common man from transaction costs at each point.

Population stabilisation: We have the potential to become a great democracy only if we control the burgeoning population; otherwise, the fruits of development will never be real. Unfortunately, our efforts in this direction so far have not been adequate and effective. I believe we must create a strong will to mount a big national effort for population stabilisation; we need to build a social ethos where violating a small family norm attracts big social discount.

Judicial reforms: An independent and efficient judicial system is the backbone of democracy. The common man expects fair and speedy justice. We know that justice delayed is justice denied. We need a legal system in which courts ensure regular hearings, unpunctuated by frequent adjournments; a system where pursuing cases in courts does not become a luxury for the rich but something that inspires faith and confidence amongst the poor also.

The need for judicial reforms is a matter of urgency. The reform agenda should include setting up of special courts for the trial of corruption cases and also for other important cases of social concern; in such cases there should be day-to-day hearings in courts so that the guilty are booked and punished without delay.

Electoral reforms: Elections are an integral part of democracy. However, we are now witnessing the democracy of frequent elections. These have dealt a heavy blow to governance, political expediency overtaking genuine public welfare and long-term national interests. Frequent elections also generate a large demand for campaign funds.

It was in this context that I had earlier publicly made the suggestion that we should rid ourselves of the present syndrome of every-year elections. I believe that elections to the Lok Sabha and state assemblies should be simultaneous and, if possible, elections to panchayati raj institutions and municipal bodies should also be combined. This electoral reform will provide significant riddance from evils of caste-based politics of vote-banks, criminalisation of politics and the influence of money and mafia in elections.

The malaise of corruption: Our present environment of governance is polluted, ethical values are on the decline and corruption is all pervading. Our country certainly could have progressed much more but for poor governance and rising corruption which have been big roadblocks in national prosperity. Without rooting out corruption, we cannot have good governance. We need an effective and comprehensive attack on corruption. Those who do not adhere to ethics, falter and indulge in corruption ought to know that they will not escape the severest punishment. Unfortunately, the plethora of laws and enactments to control corruption have proved ineffective. Cases remain pending, under investigation or trial, for a long time; hardly any case results in conviction and that too, of only lower-level functionaries. This state of affairs has failed to create an effective deterrent against corrupt tendencies; it generates public cynicism while the extent and dimensions of corruption go on increasing every passing day.

The virus of corruption is not only a factor of social disintegration and distortion of the economic system but also goes to undermine the very legitimacy of political institutions. Our elected representatives in state legislatures and parliament should take the lead in ensuring effective action to combat corruption, to accelerate the pace of economic growth as also to strengthen the moral fabric of our democratic system.

Issues of values and ethics: Today it is a matter of concern that the institutions of governance in our democracy are increasingly suffering from a credibility gap and damage to their reputation and integrity. The declining standards of ethics in public conduct are the main cause of the erosion in people's faith. The foremost requirement, therefore, is to regain the confidence of society in the institutions of governance.

Indeed, many of our present ills are the results of a decline in our value system and loss of character. Forces of fierce competition in the technology driven era of globalisation have taken a heavy toll on our traditional values. We need to re-imbibe the *sanatan* values of honesty, integrity, compassion, care and cooperation. We once again need to establish our conduct based on truth and non-violence, peace and harmony. We need to promote a secular ethos that entails *sarva-dharm-sambhav*. That alone will promote social cohesiveness and re-establish the paradigm of the Indian ethos enshrined in our ancient maxim of Vasudaiva Kutumbakam. That will be India's unique contribution towards enrichment of the content of globalisation, which today has its focus only on trade and commerce.

These are the foremost challenges to face and overcome. Only then shall we build an empowered India. The need is to begin action in all earnestness, commitment and sincerity of purpose. Let us all work together, create a *lok jumbish* for building an empowered nation. I have abiding faith in the destiny of our nation and the bright future of the next generation. I am absolutely sanguine that we are bound to build an India that will do our posterity proud.

This will be, in the true sense, a fully empowered India in which none will be deprived and oppressed; everyone will be secure with dignity, equity and all basic necessities of life.

MANMOHAN SINGH
PRIME MINISTER

Open Democracy and Open Economy

A nation is empowered by its people. A people are empowered by their capabilities. People's capabilities are created by investments in their education, well-being and skills and providing them with opportunities for gainful productive employment. People are also empowered by the freedom they enjoy. A free press is an important element of our empowerment.

In the world in which we live today, no country can feel empowered unless all its citizens feel empowered. When a child, a woman, a person belonging to a weaker section or a minority community or group of any kind feels disempowered, we all lose something in us.

The well-being of each of our citizens empowers every one of us. We will empower our people by pursuing policies that will create employment opportunities and provide viable livelihood strategies. We will need to put in place effective arrangements for social insurance against old age and sickness, for the well-being and security of the aged and the disabled.

That well-being, defined in economic, social, cultural and all the other terms that define our social existence, is best ensured in the framework of an open society and an open economy.

Open societies enable the full flowering of our individual personality. Open economies provide the space for the fruition of our creativity and enterprise. Open societies and open economies empower those who live and work in them. Being an open democratic society and an open economy empowers India. Provision of effective social safety nets for the weak and needy will ensure that all sections of our population participate in processes of social and economic growth, making for a more inclusive society.

Some people think nations are empowered merely by their military prowess. They pursue mindless militarisation. Some think nations are empowered by their command over resources. They pursue greedy aggrandisement. Neither military prowess nor economic resources can by themselves ever empower a nation for any length of time. A nation is truly empowered only by the brain power of its people.

The creation, the dissemination and the utilisation of knowledge are what really empower both people and nations. India will be empowered when we can create a knowledge society and a knowledge economy within the framework of an open society and an open economy.

The battle against poverty, ignorance and disease is, above all, a fight for the empowerment of our people. The quest for a rapidly expanding economy, making full use of modern science and technology, is an integral part of the process of empowerment. The struggle to save our environment and protect all species empowers not just the present but all future generations. Ensuring ecological security empowers future generations of all species.

Such is the concept of empowerment embodied in the National Common Minimum Programme of our government. The creation of an equitable and free society that is prosperous and productive is our path to the empowerment of our people and thereby, our nation.

R.C. LAHOTI
FORMER CHIEF JUSTICE OF INDIA

Judiciary Strengthened from Within

India Empowered envisages empowerment of the people of India in consonance with the goals of such empowerment set out in our Constitution, which is the ground norm, the founding document and the source of democracy in India.

We the people of India solemnly resolved on 26th November, 1950, to secure to all its citizens justice (social, economic and political); liberty (of thought, expression, belief, faith and worship); equality (of status and of opportunity); and to promote among them fraternity (sharing the dignity of the individual and unity and integrity of the nation). The trinity of the Preamble, chapter III (Fundamental Rights) and chapter IV (Directive Principles of State Policy) constitutes the conscience of our Constitution. They together envision the establishment of an egalitarian social order guaranteeing fundamental freedoms and to secure justice—social, economic and political—to every citizen through rule of law.

Equality has to be accorded to all people irrespective of caste, creed, sex, religion or region. Our founding fathers while crafting the Preamble gave justice precedence over liberty, equality and fraternity by placing these philosophical terms in that particular order. Unless there is justice, liberty is meaningless. Justice and liberty together secure equality. There can be no fraternity unless there is justice, liberty and equality.

In the chain of philosophical thoughts underlining the Constitution, the most significant is the concept of justice. Duly honouring justice lays the foundation for the welfare and progress of society. It holds civilised beings and civilised nations together.

India is free but freedom as per the preambular goals is still elusive. Have any of these goals been achieved in its entirety? Has India awakened?

Having recently demitted the highest judicial office of our country and having served as a judge for about 17 years, I propose to examine whether India has been empowered by reference to the concept of justice.

It can be legitimately said that independent India has earned prosperity, power and landmark achievements especially in the field of science and technology. She is no longer an underdeveloped country. She has crossed into the circle of developing countries and is waiting to enter the magical fold of developed countries. However, we are not free from the evil clutches of poverty, hunger, violence, discrimination, casteism, communalism and unemployment which continue to plague us. This is compounded by the problem of inequities and inequalities.

27.8 per cent of the Indian population resides in the cities, and three-fourths of the unemployed are in the rural areas. If the growth rate of our economy is a commendable 9 per cent then why is 26 per cent of our population still below the poverty line? The real challenge before us is to overcome the imbalance in the distribution of our resources and outputs such that our national income and national growth no longer remain skewed and are 'democratised'.

A nation's development can be seen as a function of its investment in the social sectors to empower all sections of society and a strong judiciary is a key ingredient in the development of the social sectors. The judiciary today contributes towards the creation of a just social order in which all citizens enjoy civil, political and socio-economic rights. A judge does not merely interpret the law but he formulates new norms of law and moulds the law to suit the changing social and economic scenario to make the ideals enshrined in the Constitution meaningful and a reality. The formulation of a democratic republic does not involve only the vesting of political rights in the citizenry. Social and economic democracy is the foundation on which political democracy can be effectively established. The judiciary fully utilises the most important tool of social engineering that it wields; the law. And it is so used to create a just social order, without inequalities and disabilities and to provide opportunities for growth to all.

Our Constitution aims at securing not only legal justice, but also socio-economic justice. Our founding fathers realised that a political democracy cannot last unless there lies as the basis of it a social democracy. The fundamental duty of the judiciary is the establishment of a social democracy and to secure social and economic empowerment to all.

The system is rightly derided by saying that there is too much of law and too little justice. It is pointless to talk of an effective rights regime if the people lack the basic ability to access the justice dispensation system, both in terms of awareness and resources.

The political and civil liberties conferred by Part III of the Constitution of India are meaningless if the citizen is not, in the first instance, aware of the existence of such rights or does not have the capacity to pursue them, and in the second, does not have the economic means of exercising these rights and liberties. As an English judge cynically remarked 'The law, like the Ritz Hotel, is open to rich and poor alike'.

Rights and liberties exist in the letter of the law but it is the process of actualising these rights and making them meaningful that is the real task confronting us. These rights are required to be effectively implemented and they should not be allowed to remain mere pious declarations. For the common man, justice as a principle is of relevance only if it solves problems, furnishes concrete solutions and affords relief in practical terms.

There is a need to 'democratise remedies' for enforcement of these rights so that they become available to every citizen irrespective of caste, creed, religion or gender. More significantly, the legitimacy of the system depends on its ability to make an actual difference to the quality of life of the poor.

In its efforts to realise the preambular goals, the judiciary developed various innovative techniques in order to ensure that no section of the society was 'priced out' of the justice administration system. Public Interest Litigations (PILs) and letter petitions have been developed in order to take justice to the people.

The initial characterisation of socio-economic rights as non-justiciable posed a major challenge to proving effective access to justice to the marginalized sections. The basic needs of these sections of shelter, food, health, means of livelihood, etc. do not find avenues for redress within the formal legal system since these rights were caught in the constructed limitations of justiciability, the law and policy divide and the constitutionally drawn lines between enforceable fundamental rights and non-enforceable principles of state policy. This hurdle has been sufficiently overcome due to the enlargement of the scope of the right to life by judicial pronouncements.

Of the three organs of the State, it is the judiciary which is centrally placed to protect the democratic rights of citizens and marginalised groups. The executive and legislature are primarily concerned with national development at the macro-scale and construct broad-based policies. It is the judiciary which ascertains the actual impact of such policies on the lives of individual citizens and social groups in particular situations. But it is not only about the effective implementation of positive law, as it exists. There is a need to move on to the normative approach. Every legal system is based on some form of legal philosophy. Different social considerations and the changing spirit of the times necessitate a rethinking of the existing jurisprudence. In the discharge of its fiduciary duty towards society, the judiciary has embarked on this journey and has already made great strides. Keenly alive to its social responsibility and public accountability, it has liberated itself from the shackles of its traditional role, made innovative use of the power of judicial review, forged new tools, devised new methods and fashioned new strategies in order to bring justice to all and empower India.

The greatest challenge before the Indian judiciary is the tremendous docket explosion. The courts are flooded with cases and this has, consequently, led to immense pendency. The enormity of the crisis can be ascertained by a quick look at some statistics. The Supreme Court of India has twenty-six judges; there are twenty-one high courts with a total sanctioned strength of 719 judges; and there are a total of 12,360 subordinate courts functioning in India. On an average, in every year the Supreme Court of India decides about 40,500 cases out of 42,000 cases filed, the high courts decide 11,23,500 cases out of 12,41,000 cases, and the subordinate courts decide 1,32,22,000 cases out of 1,42,29,000 cases filed. In spite of such high disposal numbers, the pendency figures have been rising due to the increasing influx of cases.

The influx of cases cannot and should not be prevented but there has to be enhancement in the speed of outflow or new outlets have to be found. It is imperative that the judiciary is strengthened both quantitatively and qualitatively. In terms of numbers, there is an immense gap between demand and supply. The Law Commission in its 120th report (1987) had stated that in India there are only 10.5 judges per million population (which is now said to have gone up to 12-13) whereas countries such as the USA and UK have between 100-150 judges per million population. This is the primary cause for the staggering number of arrears burdening the courts. Recently the Supreme Court has desired that the number of judges should be increased in a phased manner in five years so as to raise the judge-population ratio to 50 per million. Any substantial progress in this direction would go a long way in reducing the burden of arrears on the courts.

Qualitatively the judiciary can be improved in three ways; development and use of judicial academies, information and communication technology (ICT) enablement and alternative methods of dispute resolution (ADR). During my term of seventeen months as the chief justice of India, I had declared 2005 to be 'The Year of Excellence in Judiciary' and had declared the above three imperatives to be my priority. The National

Judicial Academy along with fourteen state academies have been set up in order to impart continuing learning, training and education to all judicial officers. An emphasis has been placed on ethics and morality within professional education and training as the quality of justice dispensed by courts is a reflection of the quality of judges who sit in the courts.

In the wake of the boon of modern science, the Indian judiciary has to urgently re-equip itself and re-engineer its processes in order to harness the potential of the available ICT to enable enhancement of judicial productivity. The 124th Law Commission Report in 1998 had emphasised that the use of ICT in the judiciary is imperative for enhancing the quality of justice, reducing congestion in courts and securing timely disposal of cases. In October 2005 the National Plan and Policy for ICT enablement of the judiciary developed by the e-committee was released.

An absolute imperative to search for alternatives and supplements to litigation, which is the traditional mode of dispute resolution, has led to the advocacy of ADRs. The National Legal Aid Services Authority is working in the direction of creating awareness of ADR systems and providing training to all its functionaries. Although the statutory framework is already available, yet a national plan for effective introduction of ADRs, both within the mainstream traditional mode of dispute resolution and also as a parallel system, needs to be launched.

Let me conclude with a caveat that we must be ever mindful of. 'Yesterday is not ours to recover, but tomorrow is ours to win or lose' and therefore let us get together, stand united and make creative, cohesive and collective endeavours in order to realise our full potential. We must rise beyond the limitations of past trends and immediate pre-occupations so as to perceive the emerging opportunities and concealed potentials, such that India is awakened and empowered. Our future depends not on what will happen to us, but on what we decide to become and on the will to create it.

SOMNATH CHATTERJEE
SPEAKER, LOK SABHA

Every Indian Has an Equal Stake in India's Future

What does an empowered India mean to me? Can it mean differently to different people? Can there be a convergence of understanding on empowerment of a society like ours?

Even after 58 years of freedom, India still lives in different centuries. On the one hand is the India of the affluent, of those who have had the benefit of modern education and are intellectually and materially empowered, and on the other is the India of those who live under conditions of poverty, deprivation, squalor, illiteracy, ignorance, intolerance and prejudices.

We have not yet achieved the desired result of full empowerment of the socially backward sections. Caste-based social stratification is a reality we still have to reckon with. Similarly, gender-based discrimination is yet another major social issue we have to address. The women who constitute almost 50 per cent of our population are yet to have an effective share in the political decision-making processes, especially in our representative institutions.

Large-scale unemployment is another serious issue we have to grapple with. The working class, which is contributing significantly to the building of modern India, is not receiving its due recognition from the system as a whole.

More than one third of our citizens are yet to be extended the benefit of basic education. Only 6 per cent of the university education age-group, between 18 and 23, are actually taking the benefit of higher education in the country today. Nearly half a million of our villages are still without access to safe drinking water and dependable energy supply. The benefits of modern medicine and developments in the fields of science, information and communication technologies have not reached a substantial section of our people yet. Nearly 400 million of our citizens continue to live below the poverty line. The freedom that we talk about and all the achievements that independent India made in the last nearly six decades have no meaning for all those unfortunate citizens who still live unsure of their next square meal.

Socio-economic development is bypassing a significant segment of our population today. The absence of a credible social security system makes life uncertain even for those enjoying at least a minimum quality of living today. There is a wide gap between the opportunities available to the rich, educated and urban-centered people and the poor, illiterate or semi-literate, rural inhabitants and others disadvantageously placed.

There is a lot more scope for providing greater credibility to our democratic processes. People's problems and development have to be brought to the centre-stage of political discourse in the country. The unhealthy trends in the electoral arena have to be urgently addressed to win over people's confidence in the processes and institutions of democracy.

Democracy can be sustained in the long run only if everyone involved, particularly the leadership, the media, and the institutions, nurture it with care and commitment. If we consistently fail in keeping the promises to the people, they will lose faith in democracy as a viable system capable of addressing their concerns.

It is equally important to ensure that all institutions of governance, be it the legislature, the executive or the judiciary, remain sensitive to the hopes, aspirations and frustrations of the people and discharge their duties effectively and promptly. Unjustifiably long delays in the justice delivery system are a serious cause for concern today.

Once the people lose their faith in the system, no laws, no force can protect our system of government. These are the challenges that our political leadership and the civil society will have to address together in order to empower India and to make our freedom meaningful for all our citizens.

We need to recognise the fact that India lives in her villages. Long-term development of the country cannot be achieved without addressing the concerns of the agricultural sector which still constitutes the backbone of our economy. City-centric developments will not help in emancipating the substantial majority of our people who live in our villages and who have not been effectively touched by the developmental initiatives of the past.

One of the basic tasks that we have to undertake with top priority today is in the area of human development. An integrated development strategy linking social development with the economic development programmes involving the direct beneficiaries in the management and execution of all such programmes is, therefore, urgently called for. This can be achieved only through a strategy of decentralised planning and development.

Empowering India calls for transformation of our huge human resources into an asset. India has enormous unexploited potential as a 'knowledge hub' for the world. In fact, the rest of the world recognises this distinct advantage that we have. This has to be translated into a developmental agent for the whole country.

Education plays an important role in this. Only through universalisation of education, laying special stress on vocational education and on the education of the girl child, can we achieve true empowerment of our people. It is through education that we can equip women also to make their own contributions to the productive processes in society. Removing the factors that inhibit their full participation in various spheres of society is, therefore, a very important first step for their empowerment. We have to create conditions whereby our huge workforce is productively engaged in the task of nation-building. Initiatives like the Rural Employment Guarantee Scheme should become part of a national mission to achieve an empowered India.

Empowering the country would involve ensuring health for all, education for all, homes for all, jobs for all and security for all. This is the expected end result of democracy, which can be achieved only when the power structure is adequately representative of all sections of society.

Democracy is also about good governance. Only when the government is participatory, transparent, accountable, responsive and responsible, effective and efficient, equitable and inclusive, consensus-oriented and committed to the rule of law can we claim to be moving in the direction of good governance. The greatest challenge of good governance is to bridge the gap between the expectations of the people and the effectiveness of the delivery mechanisms. Corruption has no place in such a system. This can be achieved only through a leadership committed to the cause of the people.

Empowering India, therefore, would essentially involve bringing into the national mainstream, by taking the benefit of development, all those who have so far been kept out of it by social, economic, political and historical factors. It involves the establishment of a socio-political order in which no discrimination takes place on the basis of race, caste, creed or sex and where all citizens enjoy equal opportunities and at least an acceptable minimum quality of living.

It is about providing real substance to our democratic existence. The substance of democracy has to be assessed in terms of the impact it makes on the quality of living of the people. The new economic forces, unless monitored with a caring eye for the vulnerable sections of our society, have the potential to further impoverish the poor. Therefore, while applying new strategies for development, the social dimensions should receive adequate attention.

A fully empowered India will be a cohesive India. Intolerance, negativism, hatred and violence that have been generated in the country in the name of narrow, parochial, sectarian, religious and other divisive issues have been factors that inhibited our development. We need to be constantly on the guard against divisive forces raising their heads in the country.

An empowered India will be known for its inclusive and modern social order. In such an India, the State would be totally dissociated from the shackles of religious orthodoxy and use its power only to positively intervene in addressing socially dangerous and outdated customs and traditions and for bringing about social harmony and socio-political and economic stability.

Only when the basic needs of all our people have been catered to can we say that India has been empowered. For this we have to bring every section of our society within the purview of development and enable the people with the capacity to hold their representatives, the government and the bureaucracy accountable.

A socially, economically and politically empowered India will be scientifically and technologically advanced and industrially developed. It will be constituted of self-sufficient villages. Democracy will have taken deep roots there, it will be emotionally integrated, one in which every section of our population will begin to think that it has equal stake in this country and its future. It will be an India in which your social status will be decided not by your standing in the caste hierarchy but exclusively by your worth as an individual and as a citizen of this great country.

It will be free from the scourges of communalism, poverty, illiteracy, exploitation and unemployment, free from the feudal hangover, and with such a social system and economic environment as would provide plenty of choices for the fuller development of our human potential to ensure a dignified existence for all our citizens.

Such an India, in consonance with its traditions and ethos, will be fully committed to a peaceful, just, equitable, inclusive and co-operative world order and be able to play, from a position of strength, a decisive role in the comity of nations, helping provide a qualitatively new direction to the world.

OMAR ABDULLAH
PRESIDENT, NATIONAL CONFERENCE; MP, SRINAGAR

Power from the Few to the Many

India is the world's second most populous country. We proudly claim to be the world's largest democracy and are today counted as one of the largest and fastest growing economies in the world. Yet one cannot help feeling that as an empowered nation we have a long march ahead of us.

How can I envision an India Empowered when my home state is one of the most disempowered? The gun has snatched away the most basic aspects of our empowerment—our freedom to live free from fear, our freedom to study, our freedom to work, our freedom to celebrate, our freedom to mourn, our very basic freedom to choose.

Empower us by giving us a stake in our future. Let us feel that developments are taking place because of what we want rather than in spite of what we want. That is when we will feel truly empowered.

The same is true for large parts of the country facing a violent future—the north-east and Naxalite-infested areas to name a few.

J&K is a place the rest of India can learn a lesson from. It can form a vital lesson for an empowered India through one very important change—land reforms. J&K has one of the lowest levels of poverty in the country. This is because of the vision of the state's tallest leader Sheikh Mohammed Abdullah. His land-to-the-tiller reform ensured that every farmer owned the land he or she tilled. This is the bedrock of the reform that empowered the people of J&K from a social and economic point of view. Imagine what similar reforms can do for a state like Bihar, to name but one.

How would I like to see India empowered? By seeing genuine power transferred from the hands of a few to the hands of many. Genuine devolution of powers to the grassroots level as part of a transparent system that demands accountability will empower India. India is too large for the level of centralisation that we see. Too much power flows from Delhi. Power needs to be transferred from Delhi to the states and from the states to the villages. Instead of giving people a say in who will govern them every five years, give them a say in actual governance at the level where it directly affects them. That is an empowered India I would like to see.

We need to change the way we look at our country and our responsibility towards it. When was the last time we as Indians excelled in a team sport? We lack team spirit. We spend too much time thinking about ourselves and not enough time thinking about others. We need to instill in ourselves a winning spirit where second best is never going to be enough. We need to stop rewarding mediocrity. India empowered is an India where power flows from the people, where the people have team spirit and are no longer willing to accept anything but the best.

L.K. ADVANI
LEADER OF OPPOSITION

Sanskriti, Samruddhi and Su-raj

Words are carriers of meanings. But meanings, when culled out from equivalent words in different languages, often suffer from a phenomenon that is familiar to us: lost in translation. Thus, 'dharma' means much more than 'religion'. Similarly, 'power' means much less than 'shakti'. In India's philosophical and social traditions, 'shakti' has a profound spiritual connotation, and its use is permissible only for ethically good ends. 'Shakti' is even considered the empowering principle of the entire cosmos. In contrast, the meaning of 'power' is prosaic. And in today's environment, it is all too common that people take 'power' to mean 'satta' (political power). And since politics has acquired a certain undesirable, even ugly, connotation, its association with power—what is frequently called 'power politics'—has bred cynicism.

Therefore, the discussion on 'India's empowerment' brings to my mind three inter-related thoughts: Sanskriti (culture), Samruddhi (prosperity for all) and Su-raj (good governance).

I firmly believe that India's empowerment must be understood in its loftier sense, and not merely, as often happens these days, in terms of the attainment of a higher GDP growth rate or some other purely economic indicator. We should not confuse means with the ends. The idea of a 'Shaktishali Bharat'—India Empowered, if you will—must recognise that this great and ancient nation of ours is already the repository of so many hidden and unique strengths.

These strengths are mainly ethical, spiritual, cultural and intellectual in nature. These strengths are the outcome of the millennial journey of our civilisation and have survived numerous foreign invasions and the many vicissitudes of history. They are embedded in the lives of our ordinary people, in our family and community values, in our heritage of art and culture, and in our epics and in the immortal works of our seers and social reformers. Even when India was enslaved, and even when free India was not as prosperous as it is today, these strengths of India were globally recognised and they earned for India enormous goodwill and admiration among peoples all over the world. In diplomatic and strategic affairs discussions, these intangible strengths are described as 'soft power'. Thus, in terms of 'soft power'—in contrast to 'hard power' that is measured by nuclear stockpiles, force projection worldwide, economic might, etc. —India is already a highly empowered nation.

I am saying this not to suggest that science, technology, trade, investments and capacity to compete, and win, in today's era of globalisation do not matter for India. No, not in the least. Rather, in referring to India's spiritual, cultural and civilisational heritage, my purpose is two-fold. One, let us not be blind to, or belittle the value of, the 'shakti' that India already possesses. The value of this heritage is immeasurable, and its need in the future—both for India and some extent for the world at large—is going to be immense. Only a nation without an awareness of its own past, and a vision of its own for the future, will allow material prosperity to come in a manner that impoverishes us culturally, morally and spiritually.

My second reason for referring to it is that this cultural-spiritual heritage, diverse though it is, is the main source of our national unity. Therefore, a non-sectarian and non-communal invoking of the life-nourishing, unifying and truly empowering aspects of this heritage can unleash among our people latent nationalist energy, without which no nation can achieve big goals.

Some people wrongly, even wilfully, find fault with the BJP for describing culture as the unifying principle of Indian nationhood. I would like to emphasise that culture is not to be confused with any particular religion. India is a multi-religious secular nation and this is a matter of pride for all of us. India belongs to all, and all must belong to India. My party is opposed not to secularism, but to pseudo-secularism—to the tendency among certain parties to indulge in minorityism at the cost of both national interests and the interests of the minorities themselves. Indeed, if we are truly concerned about India's empowerment, we should progressively reduce, and ultimately do away with, the talk of 'majority' and 'minority' communities from the domain of public life. Every section of India must be empowered, for India to be truly empowered.

What is the way forward? I'll encapsulate the answer in just one word: Su-raj (good governance). Our forefathers won Swaraj (political freedom) for India. They had dreamed that attainment of Swaraj would lead to Suraj. That dream is yet to be substantially fulfilled. And that is the task before all the political parties in India today. A task to be accomplished through a spirit of cooperation, and with a firm understanding that exercise of 'satta' must be for the enhancement of 'shakti'—India's and every Indian's.

MANI SHANKAR AIYAR
MINISTER, PANCHAYATI RAJ, YOUTH AFFAIRS AND SPORT,
DEPARTMENT OF NORTH-EASTERN REGION

Progress Must Reach the Lower Middle Class

India empowered is Indians empowered. And if so much of our country still wallows in poverty and injustice, the root cause is that the independence of India is still to translate into the empowerment of most Indians. For, as Nobel laureate Amartya Sen has so definitively demonstrated, it is empowerment that leads to entitlements; and entitlements that lead to enrichment. The skewed distribution of the fruits of the impressive progress the country has made requires immediate course correction because economic progress in itself cannot be our national goal; that goal must be equitable progress.

The most significant outcome of independence has been the disempowerment of the earlier elite—the landed gentry—and the empowerment of a large and growing middle class as the new elite. This middle class has so entrenched itself in the body politic that it is substantially able to secure for itself its entitlements (and indeed, much, much more), and the consequent enrichment of this middle class has come to be both the proof and the symbol of the progress we have made. Increasingly, national goals and the national image are being defined and realised in terms of the aspirations and ambitions and value systems of this class.

However, one has only to step out of the shopping malls and cinema multiplexes to step into the teeming mass of humanity which constitutes the lower middle class, the poor and the utterly deprived of our country—Gandhiji's 'dumb millions'. Democracy has, of course, given the dumb millions a voice. And that is why, every five years, they strike back, almost routinely replacing one section of the ruling elite by another. It is the masses who determine the outcome of elections. But between elections, it is the middle class which determines the course and outcome of governance.

So, for economic progress to translate into equitable progress, the masses require the empowerment that has enabled the middle class to secure their entitlements and move as firmly as they have down the road to self-enrichment. For once it assured itself of its entitlements, the middle class positioned itself to build its personal future and determine the future of the country. Thus, the fundamental lesson of the last six decades of independence must be that if we are to spread prosperity to our people as a whole, we must revert to the Gandhian vision of participatory development through participatory democracy.

Rajiv Gandhi used to say that while we were, indeed, the world's largest democracy, we were also the world's least representative democracy. Consider just one figure: the number of MPs elected in India by close to a billion people is one hundred less than the MPs elected to the House of Commons by an electorate which is one-twentieth the size of ours! Rajiv Gandhi's initiatives for grassroots development through grassroots democracy, in both rural and urban India has so altered the nature of democracy today that we have close to 2.5 lakh elected institutions of local government spread through the length and breadth of the country. And, more impressive still, of the approximately 30 lakh representatives elected to these institutions, at least 10 lakh are women— an exercise in gender empowerment which in scale is without precedent in history or parallel in the world. Moreover, the most deprived sections of our society, the scheduled castes and the scheduled tribes, are not only represented in proportion to their numbers but a full third (and, in practice, a little more) are positions filled by the women of these communities.

Unfortunately, this silent revolution in empowerment is being virtually blacked out in the media. In consequence, it is either ignored by the middle class, especially the urban middle class, or paraded as a parody: horror stories of caste-based *khap* panchayats without clarifying that these panchayats are not the panchayati raj institutions of the Constitution; sneers about the 'decentralisation of corruption' as if the middle class have a monopoly entitlement to corruption; and jeering at the 'sarpanch-pati' rather than acknowledging the lakhs of women in the panchayats who are exercising their public office with the utmost responsibility.

Indifference and hostility in the already empowered sections of our polity and society do stand in the way of genuine devolution to the masses and their institutions. But it does not stop the trickle of devolution. And the fact that there are 30 lakh elected representatives out there demanding their entitlement to a share of governance is a countervailing force of growing importance in the power equation. Fortunately, Constitutional sanction makes panchayati raj irremovable, irreversible, ineluctable. Merely by being there, these institutions are slowly securing empowerment and being empowered.

The task at hand is to accelerate, widen and deepen this process of empowerment so that these 'institutions of self-government', as the Constitution describes them, become the 'principal authority for planning and implementation,' as has been provided for in the National Rural Employment Guarantee programme. That is the model to replicate and build upon in all development programmes, all the while remembering that one of the most significant observations of the Sarkaria Commission was that most people most of the time are mostly concerned with what happens in their own neighbourhood. Panchayati raj empowers the local community to determine its local destiny while remaining part of the larger destiny of the State and the Union.

It is, therefore, as much a requirement for equitable progress as it is for national integration.

GHULAM NABI AZAD
CHIEF MINISTER, JAMMU & KASHMIR

People in Strife and the Idea of India

India will be empowered only when politics returns to the ideals of Gandhi—dedication, service, truth and non-violence. During the freedom struggle and even in the first few decades after independence, politics was practised as a social service and not as a career. That is why we were blessed with leaders like Nehru, Patel, Azad and Shastri.

Our first prime minister died without leaving behind large material assets, he had donated his own inherited properties to the cause of the nation over the years. Shastri died a poor man. These men, who were the founding fathers of our democracy, instead of accumulating wealth had distributed even what was rightfully theirs. But then those days being poor and penniless was a badge of honour for politicians and leaders.

Today, all this has changed. The goals and objectives of politics have become only a struggle to attain power by hook or crook. Thus, much of our mainstream politics is now being run on regional, religious, caste and communal lines. There are people who get into politics to enhance their businesses or join the electoral process to foil the law-enforcing agencies from taking action against their criminal activities.

I think India can only be empowered when politics returns to its real goal and development and social justice become the driving force for politicians across the country. Unfortunately, this is no longer the main goal for most political parties. The reason is very clear: politics based on emotional rhetoric, whether it revolves around flaring communal passions, regional biases or caste divides, is very easy and needs little work.

Serious issues of development and social justice that touch the day-to-day lives of the common people requires a long struggle. Here, the performance of leaders is constantly reviewed while emotive politics has no accountability. Politics on the basis of regionalism, caste and communalism actually sharpens and exploits the ever-existing faultlines in our pluralistic society and politicians are never held accountable for any of their actions. It is politics based on fear of the other rather than focused on the tenets of progress. It is an easy shortcut to power. But negative politics always comes in the way of our development and hampers the process of our empowerment.

India as the biggest and the most vibrant democracy of the world can never be empowered when its leaders sacrifice the very idea of India to their own little regional, communal or caste vote banks.

We must set aside our little differences of caste, creed, colour and religion for the larger good of this country. Because if we do not wake up to the dangers of allowing our politics, especially electoral politics, to revolve around communalism, regionalism and caste, we might end up destroying the very idea of our democracy as well as the concept of India as a single unit where the differences of its people in its pluralistic society are a blessing, like various types of colourful flowers that make a garden, rather than a source of discontent.

We cannot hope India will shine if people with criminal backgrounds continue to use fear and muscle power to secure a place in august houses like the parliament and state assemblies and become our policy makers.

In fact, recent years have seen a sudden increase in criminalisation of politics and I think all political parties of the country need to set aside differences and think of a joint strategy to seal this trend, which is posing a serious and real danger to the very fabric of our democracy.

There are also people who aspire for public office for a vested interest. Their aim to run for office is exclusively to enhance their businesses and mint money.

For them, politics is an extension of their business and they use the powers entrusted to them not to empower the common people they represent but to safeguard their own business interests. This too has posed a very real threat to our system and created major road blocks in the overall development and progress of the country.

And as these elements do not have problems investing huge amounts to attain political offices, it changes the very contours of the electoral battlefield, making it difficult for genuine people with social service as their aim to join politics to even fight them. In several regions like Kashmir which have lagged behind in the development process, political aspirations of the people are being exploited for completely different reasons. These genuine problems which could have been sorted out amicably and peacefully have become hostage to politics of religion.

Instead of addressing real problems, religious sentiments are being fomented to keep alive the fires of conflict. Violence as a means to political communication now has put a serious hurdle in the country's road to progress. I think that the top leadership of the country will need to walk a step further to assure people that genuine problems, whether political or developmental, will be heard and addressed without the rattle of guns.

We need to empower the common public in places of strife like Kashmir and the north-east so that there's a sense of belonging to the idea of India. They must be made to feel part of a common journey, where people from every region, community, caste, religion march together to fulfill the dream of the forefathers of this country.

We need to return to the ethos and spirit of politics that Gandhi, Nehru, Shastri and many others of that generation practised. As we modernise and push ahead on economic and technological advancement, we need to return to the old but golden era of our politics when corruption, money-making, criminalisation and self-interest were unheard of in the lives of our political leaders. It is not just important to empower India but to keep alive the very idea of India.

A.B. BARDHAN
GENERAL SECRETARY, COMMUNIST PARTY OF INDIA

Spread the Gains to the Deprived

I think empowerment is the most important issue for speeding up India's progress towards a more democratic and better society. Without empowering the hitherto deprived sections—the Dalits, tribals, other backward classes and women in general—there cannot be empowerment of India. As long as there is part of India, shining at the top, and a vast India, dull and deprived at the bottom, development will be halting, skewed and partial. Science and technology are essential and can do a lot, but these are circumscribed by the system in which they operate.

With poverty, unemployment, illiteracy and disease haunting large sections of our people, India cannot rise to the heights that are its legitimate destiny.

The framers of our Constitution have clearly laid down 'That the State shall promote with special care the educational and economic interest of the weaker sections of the people, and in particular of the Scheduled Castes and Scheduled Tribes, and shall protect them from social injustice and all forms of exploitation.' Parliament has, therefore, provided reservation for these sections in education and in jobs. This has benefited them to some extent.

But after 58 years of freedom, can it be said that they have reached the level of others? The fact is that even after such a long period, the literacy rates for the SC/STs continue to be much lower than the rest of the population. While the general literacy rate is 65.38 per cent (2001), it is 54.69 per cent for SCs and 47.1 per cent for STs.

If this is the situation at the very base in terms of literacy, it cannot be better as we go up.

What empowerment can there be if they are not provided opportunities for education at higher levels? The commercialisation of education and hike in fees have denied them access to higher institutions, and the Supreme Court ban on state quotas in private institutions has more or less closed all avenues.

What is the fate of an illiterate person in the modern world, where at every step you are called upon to read and write, deal with complicated technology and so on? What price the empowerment of such a person? With one-third of India illiterate even today, it suffers from a grave handicap. China, which was as backward as India, if not more, 60 years back, took the first step by overcoming the illiteracy of its vast population.

Women suffer from discrimination in many respects. The gender divide in education stands out starkly. While the overall literacy rate is 65.38 per cent, it is 75.85 for males and only 54.16 for females. The difference is as much as 21.6 per cent. The discrimination against the female starts right from the womb of the mother. Female foeticide is so rampant that it has upset the demographic balance of the country.

For every 1,000 males born, there are only 927 females on a national average. The worst situation is among those communities which are more affluent and even educated. Isn't it the desire to perpetuate the family line and the family inheritance, here? It is a symptom of the preference for boys to girls in our society even today.

The gender parity index at the primary level works out to 0.91, i.e. ninety-one girls for every 100 boys in school. 39 per cent of primary school girls are out of school. The dropout rate is also much higher in the case of girls.

That being so, the dice is heavily loaded against girls, and also when they grow up, as women. Health-wise too, India accounts for 25 per cent of women dying during childbirth.

In the matter of education as well as health care, allocations made by the government are wholly inadequate. We spend only about 3.2 per cent of the GDP on education and about 1.3 per cent on health care. Unless there is more intervention by the State in the areas of education and health and in creating more employment opportunities for women, real empowerment of women will remain a distant goal.

The reservation of 33.3 per cent of seats for women in local bodies elections has laid a basis for involving them at the lower levels. But women and their organisations have been demanding 33 per cent reservation in parliament and state assemblies. It is a sorry state of affairs that for ten years this demand is in limbo because of opposition from some parties.

It has been seen that women are as capable as men, if not more, at the topmost jobs, including in politics and business. Yet, this has not brought a change in the outlook of the male-dominated society towards gender relations. This society allows individual women to rise to the top (rather, it cannot prevent this), but not the masses of women in the mass to rise to their due place. The Hindu Inheritance Amendment and the Domestic Violence Acts are steps in the right direction. But much more remains to be done for the girl child and her progress through life as a woman than expressing occasional concern.

Another obstacle to empowering the underprivileged sections is that they have been marginalised in the matter of owning productive assets in society. In the rural areas, it is known that the agricultural workers are generally landless, and they are mostly Dalits. That is also at the root of their poverty.

Tribals in forests cultivate small pieces of land for which no 'pattas' have been granted by the authorities. They are always threatened with eviction. So also in urban areas, where productive assets are owned by a small group of people. The fate of slum-dwellers in the cities is well-known. Even the ownership of houses and lands is generally in the name of the male head of the family, rather than joint ownership in the name of husband and wife.

The weaker and deprived sections today demand not only a few seats in schools and higher institutes, and reservation in employment, but real empowerment. The foundation for that is full access to education and health care, as well as basic improvement in their economic and social status.

This is not only a compensation for past and continuing discrimination and injustices through the centuries, but a necessary condition for India's empowerment. Certain steps undertaken in these years have raised India's position in the world. But we have a vision of the future India.

There is a gradual shift in the power centre from the west to the east. The 21st century should become Asia's century, with the two most populous countries, viz. India and China, in the forefront. The strategic concept of India, China and Russia has to be built up for ensuring peace and stability in Asia and the world. An India empowered is surely able to achieve this and advance towards a better social order.

BUDDHADEB BHATTACHARJEE
CHIEF MINISTER, WEST BENGAL

Learn from Mistakes, Keep Pace with Change

India's empowerment will come through two areas: natural resources and human resources. 58 years after independence, there are still so many unfulfilled tasks. We have to finish these, otherwise India cannot become an economic giant like China is today.

Take land reforms. Without advancement in agriculture, we cannot advance. We cannot be a strong country. And for that, what is necessary—and on this, we have failed all these years—are land reform programmes. Even when I had a talk with our prime minister, Manmohan Singh, I asked him about his vision. He told me, 'Look, if you go through the results of the last parliamentary elections, the changes that took place happened because of their failures in the rural sector.'

West Bengal was the exception, because we have done it. He told me that the government is initiating some programmes like the employment guarantee scheme. But if you don't implement land reforms, all this will only be cosmetic. Without land reform, no model will work, whether it is a green revolution or a yellow revolution.

Another pre-condition of India's empowerment is education. Without 100 per cent literacy, you cannot go anywhere. With a highly educated elite and a majority in darkness, we cannot advance. Finally, we can be proud of the intellectual power that India has as a Third World country. We have so many more scientists, engineers and technologists than any other Third World country. So, in brief, land reform, literacy, then advancing in science and technology using our intellectual power. If we can do this in a holistic way, India will be really an empowered India.

In West Bengal, 72 per cent of our agricultural land belongs to poor and marginal farmers. Some people raised doubts about whether small holdings help. Yes, they do. Together with our panchayati raj administration, our production of rice, vegetables, fish and potatoes is the highest in the country. The purchasing power of Bengal's rural masses is the highest in India. In other states, the growth in State Domestic Product (SDP) is centered around big cities and rural areas contribute very little. In our state, SDP growth is evenly distributed across the districts.

It's on this solid agricultural base that we have to build on our modern industries, iron and steel, chemicals, IT, biotech, agrobusiness. Industry, especially manufacturing, has to be given the necessary importance since you cannot create job opportunities without manufacturing.

Which political ideology is best for empowerment? Marxism has come through many tests and trials. In some places it failed, in some places it is working. China is now almost a miracle. Cuba could survive. Vietnam is also doing well. I stick to my ideology but not like in the earlier days. We have to learn the truth from the facts. We have to learn lessons from our mistakes.

Yes, we believe in materialism; yes, we believe in the fundamental contradiction between labour and capital, we believe in class struggle. We cannot give up all these ideas.

But we have to take into account all the rapid new developments taking place. And we have to reorient all our programmes accordingly. We have to learn from the failures of the erstwhile socialist countries.

So, we will stick to our ideology but we cannot stick to our earlier dogma. We are changing according to the situation. I like the word, not pragmatist but realist. Pragmatist is something that smacks of opportunism. I am a realist.

The Russians failed for many reasons. They could not join the world economy or world trade. Earlier, they had thought that Russia and the East European countries could set up a regional bloc. There was regional cooperation between the eastern European socialist countries and Soviet Union. And they thought that would be the alternative system. But finally it didn't work.

There was one problem. The Russians were cut off from the world economy. Secondly, they were a highly centralised command economy. As for China, they say, look, our basic economy is still under socialism, but we are encouraging foreign direct investment in certain areas, not all. For technology and transfer of technology.

They are doing it. They are allowing foreign investment, allowing private capital to go to certain areas. Therefore, in China there are many sectors working together: the private sector, state sector, cooperative sector, joint sector, including foreign investment.

For an empowered state, an empowered nation, we can't follow anybody's model. Even in West Bengal, we do not follow what the Chinese are doing. We are just observing, trying to understand the changes in their policies. But we have to learn lessons from them.

We should follow a policy of self-reliance and for that what we advocate is that in industry, the core sectors should be in the hands of the government, as far as Navratnas are concerned. It was a Nehruvian idea. We think he was correct and his idea is still relevant. The big undertakings that are the backbone of our national economy and earning profit should not be disturbed.

Then, if you are to allow foreign companies, they are most welcome. They are welcome for upgrading our technology, for creating jobs. We do not want any jobless growth. Unemployment is a big problem in India. Therefore, our import-export policies, our industrial policies should be based on these basic ideas: self-reliance and how to create job opportunities for people who have no jobs.

As far as West Bengal is concerned, our advantage is that a good number of our young people are well-educated, intelligent and have a world outlook. This generation will create the 21st century. And the cream of this generation, which is well educated, will have to lead.

IT companies are coming here for our human resources, for the intelligent boys and girls graduating from our engineering colleges. But others in rural areas do not get the opportunity to study in these institutes of higher education. If they get an opportunity to perform, they will.

So to empower them we are encouraging two new schemes. One is the self-help group, and the other are self-employment schemes. When we started this, the young people thought this is not a job. But now they have realised that something can be done through this model and they are doing well, particularly among the minorities.

Finally, empowerment's agents are the young people who are graduating from universities and colleges—they can change the face of West Bengal, they can change the face of the country. They have to have all opportunities for excellence, for reaching the level of talent that is global. My dream is that they get to do that here, in this state.

DIPANKAR BHATTACHARYA
GENERAL SECRETARY, CPI(ML) LIBERATION

Equal Rights, Not Just Rhetoric

India empowered must mean, first and foremost, empowering the people of India. Yes, my idea of India always begins with 'we, the people' and my definition of the people always begins with the working people and the oppressed. I think it is important to emphasise this at the outset because these people are often counted last or not counted at all. Large sections of them have been rendered invisible—they are probably counted only once in ten years when the nation counts all its survivors.

India does justifiably mean many things to many people—a multi-faceted stream of history, a unique cultural mosaic, an amazing treasure house of nature, a great nation, a mammoth state, and of late a huge and lucrative market. But a macho Indian state doing a tango with the marauder called global capital, and together riding roughshod over the lives and liberties of millions of dispossessed and dissenting Indians—that can never be my vision of an empowered India.

We are more than one billion strong. India can only get empowered by treating this population as the country's greatest asset and learning to take good care of it. If half of this population remains chronically hungry, under-fed and malnourished, empowerment is bound to remain just another empty word.

What can empowerment mean for a people for whom even potable water and elementary hygiene and sanitation remain a distant dream, an unavailable or unaffordable luxury? When malaria, tuberculosis and a host of other easily preventable and curable diseases are allowed to kill at will, and the shadow of 19th century colonial India looms large over its 21st century 'globalising' successor, the talk of empowerment can only sound like a cruel joke. And when starvation deaths mount in the same proportion as foodgrains rot in Food Corporation of India (FCI) godowns and the powers that be smugly trivialise and dismiss these deaths, the word empowerment only adds insult to injury.

The starvation deaths and peasant suicides spawned by the pro-market economic reforms have of course had their small revenge. They have forced a change of government and shattered the mega myth of 'India shining', leaving the official doctrine of economic reforms desperately looking for a human mask. Alongside disinvestment and Foreign Direct Investment (FDI), the new government has been compelled to pay at least some lip-service to the need for providing employment guarantee to the growing army of India's rural jobless. Yet the hullabaloo over the issue of finding the funds for even the most limited and diluted form of employment guarantee scheme legislated recently clearly shows that the official notion of empowerment still remains far removed from the basic agenda of livelihood.

Divorced from the material questions of employment, education, housing and hygiene, empowerment is often reduced to just another pious platitude. Our common wisdom tells us that 'health is wealth' and 'knowledge is power'. Can then there be any empowerment without equipping every Indian with a guaranteed right to health care and education? While the dominant discourse on empowerment prefers to remain silent on this score, the official policy and practice of increasing privatisation and commercialisation of health care and education is actually promoting mass disempowerment every day, every hour.

Bypassing the key issues of right to education and employment, many empowerment enthusiasts wax eloquent about the supposedly miraculous powers of information. Information is salvation, goes the new mantra. These 'information revolution' ideologues would like us to believe that sheer dissemination of information can obviate the need for a real and radical social transformation. They fondly hope that mass empowerment can proceed through the very structures and relations of social, economic and political power that have all along disempowered the majority and monopolised power for a tiny minority. But experience shows that just as real economic prosperity hardly trickles down through the market mechanism, real power too hardly travels down the corridors of information.

Experience also shows that information can play an instrumental role only when it is inspired by the emancipatory vision of freedom, justice and progress. Indeed, India empowered must put an emphatic end to the crude reality of feudal oppression and patriarchal domination. The burden of inequalities inflicted on our women has started telling upon even the numerical balance between the two sexes. The sex ratio is steadily declining and the decline is more striking in states that are rated high in terms of either green revolution or cyber revolution. The mythological elevation of women as goddesses in rituals and scriptures is complemented in real life by all kinds of violence and prejudice against women.

In India empowered, human dignity must cease to be an elitist, patriarchal or brahminical privilege and become an integral feature of everybody's everyday life. An empowered India must display much greater confidence and maturity in running its own domestic affairs. The gifts of nature and the heritages of history must find safe and careful custody.

The notion of secularism must never degenerate to the abysmal level of bankruptcy where one is asked to choose between the anti-Sikh pogrom of 1984 and the Gujarat genocide of 2002. The unity and integrity of India empowered must be able to walk barefoot without the jackboots of TADA or POTA. There must be no room for the kind of perversion that seeks to nationalise private beliefs like religion while privatising public goods like forests, rivers and seas. No leeway for the fascistic approach that advocates uniformity in place of unity, homogeneity in place of harmony, coercion in place of reason.

Such a state of affairs obviously presupposes a conducive and credible institutional environment in contrast to the criminal-politician-bureaucrat-police nexus that is fast becoming the common generic or genetic description of the dominant political mode in the country.

India empowered needs a judiciary that protects the people's rights and liberties and does not advise rape victims to marry their rapists or decree the communist manifesto as terrorist literature! We need a bureaucracy free from the colonial hangover of the 'brown sahib syndrome', comprising committed public servants and not corrupt bosses and babus.

And most importantly, we need a really vibrant and vigilant 'fourth estate' possessing the courage to defend the people and the truth in the face of the allurements and intimidations of state power.

Last but not the least, India empowered must play a more courageous and dynamic role in the international arena. We must never hanker after a superpower tag or an imperialist certificate of good conduct. On the contrary, we must be able to stand up and lead the international campaign against every instance of imperialist arm-twisting and aggression.

India empowered must never be viewed as a threat by its neighbours, but looked upon as a reliable friend by every country in distress. In short, empowering India is all about transforming today's India into a new and powerful people's India of tomorrow.

The point is not to embellish the existing power structure that discounts and even decimates the people, but engineer a new structure that respects the people as its designers, makers and masters. If this is what history calls a revolution, India certainly needs one.

B.K. CHATURVEDI
CABINET SECRETARY

Good Governance a Fundamental Right

Citizens have several rights specifically enumerated in the Indian Constitution. They have the right to equality, freedom of speech, right to life and liberty and now the right to education of children. The founding fathers of the Constitution debated over these rights and now these are part of the Constitution. But one area which did not receive attention initially was the citizen's right to 'Good Governance'. Effective implementation of constitutional rights is vital to provide meaning and substance to the written words and vision of our Constitution makers.

The civil service had several major responsibilities when the Indian nation was born. All these centered around the 'State' and its basic responsibilities. Maintenance of law and order, security of the nation and collection of revenue were the core functions of the administrative system. A citizen's right to good governance and the State's obligation to provide it was not a part of the initial agenda. The welfare of citizens was not central to the governance structure. It was not even at the periphery. The idea simply did not exist. All this has changed with the right to a better life coming to 'centre-stage' in governance. Infant mortality and mother's health, unacceptably high maternal mortality, absence of children from schools, mid-day meals and child nutrition, female foeticide and infanticide, good infrastructure, law and order, all are today central to governance. Efficient running of civic services—water, sewerage and health services—are citizen's rights which he can demand from the government of the day. Employment, minimum wages, new job opportunities are areas of priority for States. The citizen is now 'central' to the governance structure. A new right has been recognised—the right to good governance.

The civil service has been an integral part of the story of Indian development—fully involved in policy formulation, advising on alternatives, and implementing it. Many of these problems of development have no precedent and innovative solutions have to be found to address them. Skills of the highest order are required from this group of civil servants. Some of the most talented and brilliant minds have been working as its members. Engineers from the IITs, doctors, economists, students from the nation's best institutions, are all part of it today. A federal polity required an administrative system in which civil servants could contribute effectively working with Union and state governments. The experience of working in states provided the much needed local perspective while the government of India contributed a broader vision and a national identity. This provided the unifying structure and kept a check on fissiparous tendencies during the initial years of the nation's life. In our civil service, we have an invaluable resource for bringing about change and growth in our country.

In a country of one billion, 'empowerment' has no meaning unless it touches the economically or socially weak segments of the population. A series of legislations and changes in government policies, affirmative action including reservation in education and jobs has led to a framework for better provisions of education, health and employment for weaker segments of the society and deprived sections. More than one fourth of them, however, still do not have adequate income for two square meals for the family, a proper home and essential clothing. Unless their income levels go up, the objective of our development plans cannot be said to have been achieved fully. While 7-8 per cent growth in the GDP over a sustained period will certainly lead to larger employment and more income to some of these families, we need more direct measures such as the Rural Employment Guarantee Scheme, which is aimed at providing direct employment in various labour intensive development projects, and help generate additional incomes to these marginalised and vulnerable groups close to where they live.

Empowerment of society cannot be truly meaningful without a minimum level of good quality education, basic health services and child nutrition, a reduction of the unacceptably high levels of infant mortality, and the extremely high levels of maternal mortality—500 to 600 per one hundred thousand births. Nearly one crore children of a total of more than 20 crore are not in schools. An extremely small number completes ten years of education. Of these, girls constitute a disproportionately small proportion. It is essential that the dropout rate of young children be curtailed if education is to be meaningful. The Sarva Shiksha Abhiyan is a significant step in this direction. The provision of mid-day meals in all primary schools of the country has helped in two ways—by promoting nutrition and reducing drop-out rates. The National Rural Health Mission will further help in achieving better access to health services and lower maternal and infant mortality rates.

Many states have realised the contribution of e-governance in achieving good governance by bringing the citizen to the centre of service delivery. E-governance has, in many cases, restored the choice to the citizen as to the quality and adequacy of services he is entitled to expect from public organisations. Citizen-centric governance means government is for the people and the services are tailored to meet their requirements. The citizens' charter initiative already requires that government departments should lay down the standard of service which is delivered to citizens by each government organisation. It is simply a statement and an assurance of what a citizen can expect of the organisation and the remedial measures if the promise is not fulfilled. An assured quality of service delivery is vital to all service delivery mechanisms. Citizens in rural areas where infrastructure facilities are minimal, must have access to their land-ownership rights, details of common land provided in the land records and correct maps of their holdings. They should be able to transfer land with ease and without being harassed. Today, in Karnataka, Andhra Pradesh, Tamil Nadu, parts of Uttar Pradesh and several other states, land records have been computerised and are hence available with greater ease. In Maharashtra, registration of land transfers can be done with ease by citizens due to application of information technology and simplified procedures. Farmers can get information on prices in their mandis on a computer near their houses under the e-chaupal programme in Madhya Pradesh and earn a remunerative price for their crops. In Andhra Pradesh, the one-stop facility through kiosks with arrangements for payment of taxes, lodging of complaints, applications for municipal facilities, payment of some taxes etc. has helped citizens in accessing government services easily and with minimum harassment. The department issuing passports now assures time limits for renewal and issue of new passports. With the implementation of the DCA 21 computerisation project in the department of company affairs, starting businesses will become much easier. A new company could be started and registered in a few hours and returns filed online sitting in one's office. All this implies a paradigm shift in the way the government is perceived and the manner in which it functions.

Good governance also implies a corruption free bureaucracy. Citizens must be able to access all services such as registration of cases and their effective investigation, getting an electricity connection, municipal services etc., without having to part with 'extra charges'. Civil service reform is at the top of the government's agenda. The measures which are proposed to be introduced aim at ensuring a reasonable tenure of officers, holding them accountable for results and ensuring a more objective evaluation of performance. We would also like to promote professionalism in the civil service keeping in view the increasing complexity of governance issues and the need for informed decision-making. Civil service needs to be re-established as an important and exciting career for young men and women of the country. We are confident that the reforms, which are now on the anvil, will contribute significantly towards this end. It will empower the citizens of the country to access the facilities and services provided by public organisations without harassment and with ease. We hope to make dealing with government agencies much more enjoyable and productive than it is at present. We should also judge the efforts of governance from the point of view of how they impact on the citizen. The citizen has a right to expect value for money from the government and basic requirements for a healthy and fruitful life. It is the objective of the proposed reforms to make this possible.

P. CHIDAMBARAM
UNION FINANCE MINISTER

Growth that Carries Everyone Along

Empowerment means different things to different people. In the case of a first-generation learner, empowerment comes out of education. In the case of a landless peasant, empowerment comes from owning a parcel of land. In the case of a jobless youth, empowerment comes out of obtaining productive employment. In the case of people who are discriminated against on grounds of caste or religion, empowerment comes from being accepted as human beings and treated with dignity.

Empowerment, therefore, must be seen through the eyes of the disempowered.

There is of course one tide that will lift all boats. That is the tide of economic growth. Poverty is the biggest hurdle to empowerment. It is poverty that denies access to education; fails to create adequate number of job opportunities; forces a mother to give away her girl child in marriage. It is a matter of common knowledge that higher family income results in greater spending on education for the children; better food and clothing; search for better housing; more forceful assertion of rights and the willingness to seek legal remedies; and the capacity to influence, individually or collectively, decisions that affect large sections of the people.

It is in the countries with high per capita incomes that few people feel that they are powerless or disempowered. It is in poor countries that most people feel helpless and victimised.

I, therefore, believe that it is sustained economic growth—and the consequent reduction in levels of poverty—that will empower millions of people of India.

Sustained high economic growth is attainable.

India is often described as a poor country. I disagree.

It is a country where a large proportion of people are poor. There is no iron law which requires that the poor must remain poor forever or that a country with a low per capita income should remain so for all time.

Growth is a function of investment, and is a result of using vast human resources to exploit the abundant natural resources. On the one hand, there are millions of people who aspire to lift themselves out of poverty; on the other, vast opportunities which remain unexplored.

India has a long coastline of 7,600 km. From every point on the coastline, we can draw a straight line that is 200 km long, and all that water and all the wealth under that water belong to India. If we can find a way to exploit those resources through investment and enterprise, we can create millions of jobs and generate large incomes for millions of people. Besides, fishing would not be considered a degrading occupation; nor would it be demeaning to be called a fisherman.

We have coal reserves that are estimated to be able to support our fuel requirements for 200 to 300 years. Yet, these reserves remain largely unexploited. When we exploit, we do so inefficiently. If our coal reserves can be exploited efficiently through investment and enterprise, we would be able to create huge wealth that can be shared by millions of people.

Examples of this kind can be multiplied.

An empowered India is a nation where everyone in the working age group has work—a job or a business or a profession. Where everyone can aspire to aspects of life that go beyond work such as self-improvement, life-long education, entertainment and leisure. Where everyone can exercise his political and human rights without fear of discrimination or oppression.

I firmly believe that it is economic prosperity that will empower India. Sustained high growth is essential to establish the groundwork for this empowerment of every Indian in the working age group through gainful employment. The growth momentum observed in the last two and a half years is encouraging in this regard.

We need to not only consolidate but also accelerate this momentum. Through a combination of appropriate and timely policies and delivery mechanisms we need to enlarge the areas for, and enhance, investment; rapidly improve our infrastructure; and accelerate improvements in education and health of the people, particularly the vulnerable sections. That is the golden path to sustained, robust and inclusive growth. And the path to empowering India.

The world respects India. Some countries are in awe of India. India is respected not because it has acquired the capacity to launch rockets or satellites, or because of the size of its population, or because of its dominant presence in Asia . . . but because of its capacity to emerge as an economic powerhouse. The world recognises that when India emerges as an economic powerhouse, it will be unstoppable. When India is unstoppable, no one will feel disempowered.

SHEILA DIKSHIT
CHIEF MINISTER, DELHI

The Potential of Participatory Democracy

As a student, I often wondered: what is the true meaning of our democracy. What does democracy mean to the high-flying businessman, the trader or the daily wage earner? The scenes of festive enthusiasm in elections; the long queues of old men and women, escorted by the young, braving inclement weather, waiting to seal their destinies at the polling booth; the process of elections appeared to be a great leveller.

Whether you are rich or poor, whether you have come to the booth in a luxury car or on foot, whoever you are, whatever be your position in the society—you have but one vote. This in itself is an impressive sign of a healthy democracy.

Most of my adult life, I have observed this phenomenal feat of our democracy in absolute awe. Doubts on the maturity of an electorate often charged with low levels of literacy and high levels of expectations evaporate with every single election. The wisdom of the voters comes out so clearly in the results that one cannot but salute the foot soldiers of democracy.

I have been fortunate in working with Shri Rajiv Gandhi during those heady days when an entire country dared to dream. One of his major concerns was witnessing Indian democracy becoming a once-in-five-years photo opportunity for the awestruck media, with occasional reports of more exciting visuals from some corners of the country.

He aspired to raise the levels of involvement and responsibility of the people of the country beyond elections—in the process of governance, which touched their lives every day. He found the top-down approach of planning not only inefficacious but also arrogant. How could a bureaucrat, sitting in Delhi, plan the location of a check dam in a village in Geedam in the remote block of Bastar? He found it unbelievable.

The 73rd amendment to the Constitution was targeted at removing this feudal distance between the government and the governed. This initiative to revive local self-government was the most important step taken by any government in recent history, followed only by the RTI.

When I became the chief minister of Delhi, I decided to translate Rajivji's dream of 'participatory democracy' in the city by introducing a non-political initiative of involving, as a beginning, the resident welfare associations into the day-to-day governance of their area.

The bhagidari movement—as it is known—was a result of hectic consultations with various stakeholders of governance. People had doubts. The traditional power structure—both political and administrative—needed to be sensitively engaged and convinced that bhagidari essentially meant participation by the governed in the process of governance. bhagidari would complement the power structure, not in any manner undermine it.

The movement of 'interactive governance' is seven years old now. We have seen it grow into a sure-footed assertive entity by itself. Our bhagidars do not supplicate—they initiate discourse; they kick off debates; they protest; they wish to know. They empower us. It is with a sense of satisfaction that I can say that bhagidari has become a dynamic force that does not come in our way but often shows the way.

Peoples' movements owe their birth to a common cause. When they stray away from the underlying cause, their end cannot be far. Digression is a risk that such movements can ill-afford. Forces disinterested in the well-being of this movement have attempted to undermine it by treating it as a fertile, readymade grazing ground.

The bhagidars realise the importance of confining their involvement in governance to what is pertinent to their raison d'etre. They have so far ferociously guarded the movement from vested interests within and without. My faith in the apolitical robustness of the movement stems from this continued vigil against forces that may digress and confine the perspective of this peoples' movement into narrow confines of inter-party politics.

Armed with the twin powers of the right to know how they are being governed, and the right to tell the government how they wish to be governed, citizens of Delhi no longer wait for elections to interact with their governments. Both set targets for each other beyond the confines of election manifestoes and citizen charters.

To me, this is the empowered India of the 21st century—rising from its knees to its feet.

PRIYA DUTT
LOK SABHA MP, CONGRESS

Protect the Rights of Children

More than 60 per cent of the country's population resides in rural India, so the first thing to do is make the villages more liveable in order to control migration to the cities and empower India. This will take care of a lot of problems like crime and rampant unemployment. When a farmer who is unable to acquire a single morsel of food is assured at least a daily meal on the streets, he's tempted to take up the offer. Every day there are thousands who come to the cities, but stay with disappointment.

This wasn't always the case. There was a time when small-scale industries were encouraged in the rural sector and they flourished. We need to empower our rural artisans again by sanctioning fuss-free loans so that they don't fall into the trap of moneylenders.

In every sector, there are government schemes that gather dust. The social welfare department has provisions for women, the disabled, even sweepers. But nothing is implemented. Although these provisions are offered for free on paper, I don't agree with handing them out. People only appreciate something when they have to pay for it, be it a token amount of Rs 2.

I strongly believe that education empowers, and not the kind that's achieved just by going to school. I'm talking about all-round development. More than 50 per cent of the children in urban areas are educated in municipal schools, yet we don't feel the necessity to better the facilities offered there. Our society is consumed by building elite educational institutions that cater only to a certain section of people.

I also feel strongly about the rights of children. This country is fast becoming the paedophile capital of the world. The cases of abuse, be it mental or physical, go up every day. And the official figures are only half correct. What are these children going to contribute to society if we don't look after them in their formative years? We are contributing then in producing disturbed adults.

We're too obsessed with furthering India's economic growth and don't pause to think about society. It's great that the economy is booming, but a country's success is determined by how it treats its citizens.

One of the main problems is that people believe that as individuals their voice will be drowned. It can start with something as simple as casting your vote. During elections, excuses are abundant—I didn't know it was election day or it's a holiday or I don't want to go out. It needs to be understood that if we are going to blame politics for everything, citizens are also responsible for having allowed that person to come to power.

Whenever I go to a party, there are always heated discussions on the sorry state of the country. But at the end of it, it's party talk and won't amount to anything. We lack today a sense of nationalism. What I want to tell people is that it's important to exercise that one power which the Constitution allows us. I took up the responsibility of a young politician because it gives me a bigger platform to voice my concerns in parliament, principal among which is the issue of child rights.

GEORGE FERNANDES
NDA CONVENOR, FORMER DEFENCE MINISTER

Bharat and India as One Family

To me, India Empowered means a country where poverty has been eliminated and no one goes to bed without a meal. Where the old slogan of roji, roti aur makaan (job, food and house) is a reality and no more a slogan. Where the State looks after the citizens' health so that no one has to die at the hospital gates for want of medicine they cannot afford. A nation which is at peace with itself and with its neighbours with no power on earth daring to threaten it.

Where religion does not divide the people but binds them in love. Where man-woman equality is not a favour to women but a dogma. Where child mortality is a bad dream from the distant past. Where all children—from the prime minister's to the sweeper's—have the same opportunities to study and learn so that talent stands out and mediocrity is left behind.

When the casual way farmers are treated by the political establishment, the government and corrupt financial institutions is over and farmers are given the same respect which any other labouring class receives.

Where dynastic politics which breeds corruption, generation after generation, has no space.

Where truth reigns and lies are shown up for what they are, whether uttered by an individual or by a journalist or by a politician or within a family. Where justice is not on sale and the unjust get the punishment they deserve. Where the curse of the caste system has been ostracised and the whole nation works together to raise India to its heights in the spirit of Vasudaiva Kutumbakam (the whole world is one family).

If I am not mistaken, it was the then leader of farmers, Sharad Joshi, who divided India into two parts, Bharat and India. In this divide, India was the land of the haves and Bharat, the land of the poor. The rich landlords were a part of India along with industrialists, while the small farmers and workers were Bharat.

The 'reforms', whatever they may mean, have not bridged this divide. If anything, the 'reforms' have widened the divide, with the poor becoming poorer and the rich growing richer by the day at the expense of the poor. It is not that the reforming Indians were not aware what was waiting for the poor of Bharat. But it was not their concern. Their eyes were riveted the manna that was about to drop for them from heaven.

After all, it was Jesus who said, 'To those who have, more will be given, and those who have little, even whatever they have, will be taken away from them.'

It was under the leadership of the United States—whose white population believes that theirs is god's own land—that the 'reforms revolution' started. Indians, who benefited from the largesse they received from the US, joined its bandwagon. Thereafter, many natives joined in. To cut a long story short, Bharat is going down as India is shining.

When Charu Mazumdar started his revolution in Naxalbari in West Bengal in 1967, it was a few months after I had entered parliament after defeating S.K. Patil in south Mumbai constituency. Dr Ram Manohar Lohia called me over to his residence and asked me to proceed immediately to Bengal and meet Charu Mazumdar. The brief he gave me was to see if we could establish a political relationship with him.

Though Naxalbari had made a deep impression on me, the violence built into it was not something I could appreciate. I mentioned this to Dr Lohia. He told me to discuss it with Charu Mazumdar and his associates and said nothing remains static in politics, a version of which I had an occasion to hear from the British prime minister Harold Wilson: 'Seven days is a long time in politics.'

The Naxal movement began among the farm labour whose exploitation by the landlords was crying to the high heavens but the Congress government of the day had shut its ears to their cries, so rooted were their interests with the landlords. The tea labour in West Bengal's huge tea gardens was mostly indentured and included as many women as men, with the women's population often being more than that of men.

Working conditions in these tea estates were so miserable that more often than not, the sick were allowed to die rather than provided medication, a situation that prevails even now in the Assam tea gardens.

Whatever may be the state of the Naxal movement at the moment, it cannot be denied that it is only through their work among the most deprived among the country that they have established control over vast areas from the north to the south and the east to the west. All efforts of every government to deal with the Naxal movement have failed for the simple reason that no government could relate itself to the poor and the dispossessed.

The empowerment of India, that is Bharat in this case, must start from the lowest rung of the ladder of our society. If it does not, talk of empowerment is bound not to take us anywhere. India may have to go through what Latin American countries had to go through. To avoid this, India will finally have to extricate itself from the rigid grip of corrupt, vested interests and continuation of the British raj that goes on under different colours. All else will be mere tinkering.

GOPALKRISHNA GANDHI
GOVERNOR, WEST BENGAL

The Afflicted Have to Be Heard

I function out of a 200-year-old building, the Raj Bhavan in Kolkata, which has had fifty-one tenants, thirty-two in British times, nineteen since independence. The British governor-generals, viceroys, and governors living in it were uninterested in empowering Indians. They were fairly clear about what they were out to do in India.

Until, of course, it was time for them to leave. The last British governor of Bengal, Frederick Burrows, in genuine puzzlement asked Mahatma Gandhi in October 1946, 'What would you like me to do?' He got the reply 'Nothing, Your Excellency'.

What of the governors in India today? Does the Mahatma's advice to Governor Burrows apply to them as well? Constitutionally speaking, yes. It is the legislators and ministers who have to act in democratic India. Empowering the unempowered is the legislators' privilege and duty. Where do governors come in?

The oath which governors, upon entering office, subscribe to is instructive. It obliges them to 'preserve, protect and defend the Constitution and the law.' This means that governors must exercise their prerogatives and, equally, respect those of the elected government. But the oath also binds them over to 'the service and well-being of the people of the State.'

Gandhi could not, would not, have wished it to be otherwise. But Gandhi apart, what do the people expect the governors to be doing for them? How do governors perceive their engagement with the people? I can only see it in terms of furthering the empowerment of the disadvantaged—the women of India before anyone and all else.

State governments run the empowering engine. The Constitution positions the governor in the engine car, but not in the engine-driver's seat. It places them a little behind and above the driver, at a point of slight elevation, from where the driver's skills, reflexes and direction can be overseen, from where the governor can also see the track ahead and render timely warnings, encouragement and sometimes, blow the whistle, without any backseat driving!

That 'track' in our kind of democracy, with our kinds of developmental challenges, can only be in terms of empowering our people. For there can be no 'well-being of the people' without bringing them out of their chronic and multiple despondencies and bringing in them a sense of their self-esteem and self-worth.

In my limited experience I have found one method of empowerment, even if it is often transient, even momentary. And that is to platform people, real people—our most numerous reality. To listen to them and make those directly responsible to do the same. When a noun 'platform' becomes an active verb, a non-entity becomes an entity, a digit becomes a person, and a thought, a fear, an emotion finds its voice.

And when that voice, that true voice is heard there is no mistaking it. It is simply too powerful in content. Which is why in the several open discussions that we see on television (the best thing about our TV channels) it is some unknown face, some unheard voice, that invariably carries the show. In the numerous letters that I receive every day, it is from the simple postcard, the inland letter, written in the correspondent's own hand that I get my most interesting, important and serious mail. Likewise, in the course of my travel within West Bengal, it is the face lost in the crowd of welcomers, the hand raised above the occupiers of front seats, the persistent if hesitant gaze of a bystander that educates me and, in fact, empowers me.

It is from those that I receive the most valuable insights into life's taxes and dividends in Bengal. It is from them that I see life as it is lived—whether in a dilapidated rajbari where the impoverished family still looks after its terracotta temple, or in Kolkata's red-light district Sonagachi where many of the residents are minors and 9-10 per cent HIV positive but where their amazingly bright children attend school run by NGOs. In a Farakka bidi maker's hut where a thousand rolls must be made for something like Rs 35 but where a girl is reading, as part of her syllabus, the Preamble to the Constitution of India. In the villages adjoining the Bhagirathi, Padma and Ichhamati where those rivers' meandering fury obliterates homes and homesteads in a trice but where agriculturists return to the land, with a song on their lips, as soon as the crisis abates. All of them need empowering and all of them, by their response to timely action, empower society and government in turn.

More often than not, this 'true' voice is a woman's voice. It has spoken to me with the unmistakable ring of an urgent truth in the Sunderbans to ask for life-saving embankments in the tide-swept mangroves. I have heard it spoken in Darjeeling to describe the fear of drug abuse, in Murshidabad about the gross inadequacy of a khadi spinner's wage, in the 'Pagla ward' of a jail to ask for compassion.

When the afflicted feel they have been heard, they feel they count. When they know what they have said is being acted upon, they feel they matter. When they see change attributable to their intervention they feel they are participating. And that is when they share power. Empowerment is not a hand-me-down. It is a recognition of what, in a participative democracy, should exist but often does not and therefore has to be made available.

The first step towards that 'making available' has to be platforming people. Not tokenistically or symbolically but actually. For this, Commissions serving human rights, women, minorities, and heads of government department must be on the move, charaiveti! They must spend as much time 'out there' as at headquarters, organising jana sunwai sessions as a matter of course, undertaking field surveys in ways the Indian Statistical Survey can advise them on, with the respondents being leaders. Ashoka enjoined his amatya and mahamatra cadres to do as much. And he was an emperor.

Where do legislators fit into all this, one may ask. Are our assemblies and parliament not a form—a prime form—of jana sunwai in themselves? Of course they are, and so are our panchayat bodies. They are most certainly so in West Bengal.

Whenever I have seen women pradhanas and zilla sabhadhipatis in West Bengal, a few of them of tribal and minority backgrounds, I have felt a surge of hope. But can there be anything like enough or too much of contact and conversation between and with the people? We as part of 'the people' have never felt we have been heard enough, have we?

Our legislatures are meant to enact, our executive to act. But apart from acting and enacting, there is an interacting that is needed alongside. And a reacting. The conversation that gets drowned in our speeches, the understanding that is lost in our engagements, the rectification that is forgotten in our justifying—all these need to be redeemed. And when they are, they cannot but lead to empowerment.

India enfranchised is not enough. Ask the man and even more so, the woman, who did not vote. And ask why.

K.P.S. GILL
FORMER CHIEF, PUNJAB POLICE

Strengthen the Security Forces to Crush Terror

'Where the mind is without fear'. That, in a single phrase, is my ideal of an India empowered. This ideal is under constant threat, a brutal reminder of which we have seen in the attacks in Delhi. But the idea and spirit of India are not threatened only when Delhi or India's parliament are attacked. They are undermined when the most powerless and insignificant of our citizens in our farthest peripheries are terrorised by the lawlessness and violence that have become endemic to so much of the country.

We have a very poor memory for history, and an obsession with the moment, with the latest sensation. That is why we forget that India is one of the few countries in the world which confronted and defeated a virulent terrorist movement—in Punjab—which was externally supported for nearly a decade. It has been done before, and with clarity of mind and determination, it could be done again.

But fighting terrorism requires a clear mandate that will allow our forces to do what is necessary to crush—and I use the word advisedly, for there is no gentle way to defeat terrorism—this hydra-headed monster. I have said this repeatedly, and will reiterate: if they are suitably empowered—legally and technologically—there is not a single terrorist movement in India today that our security forces cannot control within a year.

But there are no easy options in the war against terrorism. I recall an Israeli scholar's comment: 'Terrorism is a war without beginning or end. Fighting terrorism, consequently, is a way of life.' This is profoundly significant. While our enemies dream of a 'war of a thousand years', the time-frames of our responses fail consistently to go beyond the weeks and the months. More importantly, though every Indian sees himself as threatened by this vicious war, he does not see it as a war in which he has any part—it is something that the 'government' has to confront, and the actual fighting is the business of the security forces.

These attitudes display enormous and, after all these years, unforgivable ignorance of the character of terrorism, and to expect these to produce people who will actually stand up to violence, resist or help apprehend perpetrators, give witness and help prosecute and punish murderers, is to expect the impossible. Nor can they produce leaders who will go beyond the current mindset that seeks to purchase peace by bribing terrorists and other perpetrators of violence.

At the height of terrorism in Punjab, most political parties in the state were embracing groups of terrorists, and this continues to be the case in theatres of terrorism across India. The tendency to make peace with terrorists and damn the people is rife among our 'leaders'. But negotiating a settlement with terrorists that brings them to the centrestage of political power is not peace; the absence or cessation of violence is not peace; peace is the absence of fear.

Terrorism and crime are not the only sources of fear. Indeed, almost everyone lives in a state of perpetual fear in India. Each individual who comes in contact with the petty bureaucracy or other instruments of the 'State' is totally terrified; only the rich and powerful escape this, confident that they can bribe their way out of everything. But they fear the poor and build high and guarded walls around their tiny islands of affluence.

The minorities live in fear; as do the majorities. In India, every community is a minority somewhere. And wherever any community is a majority, it has behaved atrociously towards local minorities. But the greatest and most pervasive is the fear of not knowing where the next meal will come from; the fear that the tenuous livelihood that puts food on the family's table may abruptly vanish.

Today, the whole nation is based on an edifice of counterfeit ideas, ideologies and political doctrines. We have counterfeit peace movements, counterfeit human rights, counterfeit secularism, counterfeit development, counterfeit philosophical and political approaches to terrorism—mere slogans intended not to find solutions or lasting remedies, but to secure personal projection and publicity on politically correct platforms.

Even our 'revolutionary' parties and doctrines are counterfeit, seeking power to become not the harbingers of a society without fear, but inheritors of petty tyrannies and the worst of despotisms. Our whole polity is today based on the inculcation of violence in society, polarising populations into hostile caste, communal and political groups, willing to commit murder, rape, arson and pillage, one against the other.

There can be no permanent restoration of national confidence and capacities unless we are able to restore the authority and prestige of lawful governance in every area within the country, and to provide unconditional security and complete freedom from fear to all who accept the rule of law.

I.K. GUJRAL
FORMER PRIME MINISTER

Do Away with Exclusivity

Empowerment is a philosophical and historical process. It began with the French Revolution and continued with many others, particularly the Russian Revolution. Its philosophy and progress took birth after the Industrial Revolution, which is perhaps the most significant revolution as it triggered many things, particularly the concept of empowerment for the depressed sections of society.

The most significant concept the Industrial Revolution gave us was the idea of educating workers, as it could not make workers productive without education. After all, it is only feudal societies which are content with non-empowered workers, and it reached its height with the concept of slave societies.

The phenomenon of empowering those segments of society which are essential for making societies more productive came with democracy. It is through the institutions of democracy that more people were brought into the stream of production.

It is a matter of some satisfaction that our republic, which is 58 years old, has acquired inner strength for introspection, and is in the process, through the media, parliament and social debate of re-examining the process of democracy to see if it is not just the right to vote but of inclusiveness too.

This process has many impediments—some are historical, cultural and importantly, gender, though the post-Industrial Revolution particularly felt the need to bring women into the productive circuit. A new impediment is the idea of exclusivity: those who have entered the empowered circle do not want more to come in.

Since growth and development in our societies is uneven, state-wise and in regions, we see more social experiments today than ever before. And the latest experiment is the concept of coalition governments, which have come to eradicate this unevenness in the country.

Coalition governments are an effort for inclusiveness so that those regions and segments of society whose presence in legislature is small get an opportunity to participate in governments. While many cynically point to the absurdity of two-member parties, I look at this trend positively as it is an attempt to eradicate this unevenness.

Therefore, to accelerate this process of inclusiveness, there are certain programmes and agendas which need urgent attention—reforms in judicial institutions, and of the electoral process. The twin process will also take care of the eradication of illiteracy as a part of the reform process, and I wholeheartedly support it.

Similarly, another extension is the right to information and the introduction of e-governance. This is crucial for land reform. I would also say at the same time that I have had the honour of introducing the Women's Reservation Bill in Parliament. I faced opposition from both sides of the House. This resistance continues to be an expression of a medieval outlook and, therefore, the Bill needs an urgent push.

It must be said that in this new phenomenon of re-alignments, the role of the middle-class, particularly the urban middle-class, has been positive because the urban middle class is a product of the Industrial Revolution and its march.

Democracy as an institution is meant to pursue the process of empowerment of those who are denied their rights, all the time. However, disempowerment in the name of history, culture, caste or gender is not confined to India alone, even countries in Europe and South America are still not giving its people the right to vote. In west Asia and the Islamic world, large populations still do not participate in the empowerment process.

In our case, the Indian parliament and legislatures make rules to identify those taboos and practices that impede participation in democracy and empowerment. In our context, the transfer of power is our empowerment, which was achieved through property rights. This is why the Indian freedom struggle had focused on land reforms. However, the process has only been partially implemented, which is why we see some states more democratic, and in those which have refused to reform, backwardness is very obvious.

Today we are discovering our faults in the process of empowerment. And those who are deprived come out louder and more assertive with every election.

In an ideal society, governments alone cannot accomplish this progress, it requires a re-education of society. Fortunately, the emphasis on the importance of a scientific temper is a concept which is entrenched in our society, from Buddha to Gandhi. It is also the reason why the concept of a scientific temper has found a place in our Constitution. Scientific temper basically means the courage to be self-critical. And that is why we need universal literacy and adult franchise because these would help us in understanding social stigmas and social realities.

I would, therefore, conclude by saying that in these 58 years, we have covered a good part of our journey for the empowerment process but much remains to be done.

WAJAHAT HABIBULLAH
CHIEF INFORMATION COMMISSIONER

When People Change Their Own Lives

What is the India of my dreams? India is so great, so rich in texture that such a vision cannot be encapsulated. For me India is no mere geographical entity but an idea in continuous evolution, a microcosm of the world.

In the 1960s when I began my career in public service in the Jammu and Kashmir cadre of the IAS, the wound of the Partition was still raw. The cost in terms of human suffering arising from the miscalculations that had resulted in the Partition, rending apart the entire cultural legacy of Punjab, was not easily forgotten. Gandhiji, known to all Indians as the Mahatma, had warned that independence with partition would be 'like eating wooden ladoos, if they eat they die of colic; if they don't, they starve'. By the 1960s the affliction Gandhiji foresaw was widespread. The pain of partition was unspoken but cut deep.

India to me is as Shakespeare's Cleopatra through the eyes of Enobarbus: 'Age cannot wither her, nor custom stale/ Her infinite variety'. Diversity is the soul of India and her greatness. It has deeply troubled me from my early youth as to why groups of fanatics from among Indians should want uniformity in a culture of so ineffable a beauty in the richness of its contrasts. To me this has been the surest means of trampling India's soul and has led to her blood being shed.

My own faith, Islam, had come to India as a maritime religion of merchants, and struck early roots in the deep south in that form, as it spread through Sri Lanka over much of southeast Asia. But its impact was felt as a fully developed imperial power in the north of India. Its ingress also almost coincided with the transformation of the first phase in the historical trajectory of Islam, from its early eclectic form that had reached out to the oppressed of all faiths, seeking knowledge from all sources, culminating in the coruscating civilisation of Andalusia.

This tradition had made the Abbasid Caliphate a bastion of learning and enlightenment to fill the hiatus created by the decline and fall of the Roman empire and all its intellectual accoutrements. This is the intellectual trend manifested in Alberuni's *Kitab-ul-Hind*. In 1017 AD, at the behest of the marauding Turkish adventurer Sultan Mahmud of Ghazni, Alberuni (aka Al-Biruni), mathematician and astronomer, travelled to India to learn about the Hindus, 'and to discuss with them questions of religion, science, and literature, and the very basis of their civilization'. He remained in India for 13 years, studying and exploring.

Alberuni's study on almost all aspects of Indian life is among the most perceptive of any foreign scholar's. In his notes, today's readers can find not only elaborate descriptions of travel tales, but also discussions of divinity, literature, and mathematical equations, always sympathetic and often admiring. Yet Alberuni was but an example, albeit indeed an outstanding one, of the Muslim mindset of the times.

The transformation and the collapse of the established order in Islam came with the general irruption of Chengiz Khan's hordes on the Islamic world from the east and Crusaders from the west in the 12th and 13th centuries. That is also the time that imperial Islam came to India in full force. But side-by-side the spiritual aspect of Islam gained a growing audience, which accounts for the resurgence of Islam after its political eclipse. The traditions of the Chishti order, established in north India in the 12th century, set the theme for a convergence of cultures in India.

In Kashmir, the Sufi tradition retains its vitality to this day with the Rishi silsillah, an offshoot of the Kabrawi order, having scaled unprecedented heights in its founder's quest for a union of faiths in Kashmir. Located in Harwan, close to the bank of the Dal lake, the living khanqah of the 20th century Sheikh Mirak Shah has remained a haven of peace in the suburbs of today's Srinagar even as violence has swirled about its neighbourhood.

This then has been the role of Islam in the history of India, with its ramifications for Kashmir, to which I repaired to commence my career. The faith developed a distinct identity—the Hindi Muslim world was deeply influenced by the ancient heritage of Hinduism. India saw a surge in the spiritual form of Islam in the various schools of Sufi thought which had preceded the invasions and went on to becoming the foundation of the vibrant form that Islam took in India. It struck a responsive chord in the Bhakti movement, among the sages of which it was often difficult to distinguish adherence to a particular faith.

India will always be empowered if she remains true to this inherent tradition of harmony. But what does this mean in practical terms? The answer surely lies in empowering our people to live their lives in the way that they find best suited to them which will inevitably mean by living according to that hallowed tradition.

Today, the nation is faced with dramatic change. Governance itself finds transition accelerated both in concept and form. From a means to perpetuate imperial rule, governance developed into a means of seeking equitable economic growth. The initial Indian political leadership was westernized, if not in its demeanour, certainly in its approach. The civil services were therefore an object of respect. Service, even though not legally so, was in practice close to being hereditary.

This civil service oversaw the running of a 'socialist' economy: the State was omnipresent. The welfare State was seen as a necessity, but time has shown that its achievements were hardly commensurate with expectations, or indeed with the investments made. Now the State finds itself in a period of transition across the board: social, economic, political.

What then are the future prospects? I see the bureaucrat of the future as a facilitator, and also because of wide field experience, a potentially effective motivator. But to become an agent for change, an action plan will be required for an effective and responsive administration.

In the 73rd and 74th Amendments of the Constitution, we can find the instruments for ushering in a new era with greater public participation in governance.

Much will depend on how the new institutions are used by the public and by the bureaucrats. But in a time of change and restructuring, bureaucracy, designed to maintain the status quo, is by its nature risk-averse and thus change-resistant. It instinctively withdraws from being responsive to new ideas.

With an increase in the range of demands on the government arising from decentralisation and outsourcing, there is actually likely to be an increase, not reduction in government size. The remedy lies in overhaul of the delivery mechanism.

There is a general consensus that good governance must be participatory, transparent and accountable. Thanks to the colonial tradition, the present system in India, however, is firmly grounded on mistrust. The reason for this can be found in the legacy of governance in India; stemming directly at the district level from the Mughal, adapted and extended with an archaic secretariat system of the colonial. An elitist structure informed both systems and continues to subsist.

The welfare state strongly influenced by the wartime licensing legacy for distributing shortages introduced India to independence. The economy therefore remained rooted in the concept of shortage. To make this governance participatory Mahatma Gandhi called for panchayati raj: 'Independence must begin at the bottom' he said. 'Thus, every village will be a republic or Panchayat having full powers. It follows, therefore, that every village has to be self-sustained and capable of managing its affairs even to the extent of defending itself against the whole world.'

On the other hand, the foremost constitutionalist of the time, Dr B.R. Ambedkar, was cautious of such a course. Introducing the draft constitution for a second reading, he asked, 'what is the village but a sink of localism, a den of ignorance, narrow mindedness and communalism?' So panchayati raj at the time found place only in the Directive Principles of State Policy.

Today the democracy that was born in those heady days has begun to flower, the envy of the world. Part IX of the Constitution, added through the skillfully crafted 73rd Amendment, seeks to ensure that every Indian, disempowered or disadvantaged, is given full responsibility and a share in governance, with the power to confront exploitation, discrimination or oppression of every kind.

The empowerment of women, Dalits and tribals in this manner bears a special significance. And because every village now has that right to self-governance, all of them have the power to overcome social tension and conflict. And the Right to Information Act of 2005 will guarantee the other essential elements of good governance: transparency and accountability.

So when every Indian realises the power that has been placed in his hands, and begins to exercise it with responsibility, India will grow into the world's most intense democracy, with her people responsible for living lives of their own choosing, in keeping with their own cultures and traditions of every hue.

The danger of majoritarianism will thus stand eliminated, together with domination by caste or creed, which proved to be the undoing of Europe in the 20th century. This is the instrument that can set an example to a globalising world by weaving together the wide variations in India's cultures and traditions into a tapestry of social accord.

And the fruition of this ideal will to my mind empower Indians, and by harnessing their latent strengths, the repository of thousands of years of human endeavour, empower India, with a power beyond anything that she has ever seen.

BHUPINDER SINGH HOODA
CHIEF MINISTER, HARYANA

Pre-empt Social Conflict

The only way to understand the present is to understand the past. The history of economic development shows that societies with political stability achieve a higher rate of economic growth. The era of belligerent economies, sustained by gun-boat diplomacy, developing at a faster rate is over.

We live in an era of enlightenment and democracy, enjoining on the operators of power to be liberal, fair-minded, educated with an international outlook, have utilitarian assumptions, and ensure the decentralisation of power and rule of law.

Social unrest, political instability, economic upheaval, exploitation, moral degradation and corruption weaken democracy and make the middle classes panicky, two fundamental requirements for the rise of fascist forces. Political stability and economic development need peace and avoidance of social conflicts. We must be prompt in addressing people's problems and redress their grievances before they seek manifestation in radicalism.

The strength of the chain lies in its weakest link. The face of the poorest is an indicator of the health of the economy of a nation. In a democracy, conducive conditions for people's participation in all economic activities, as stakeholders and recipients of the fruits of their participation should be created.

There were inequalities in the past but people were neither aware of them, nor were the inequalities so glaring. The pace of economic activities has to be accelerated to create new and more avenues of employment to absorb the unemployed youth who have become a burden on the precious resources of their families and a nuisance to society. Matrimony, as much as money or jobs, is a matter of great concern.

Our old education system has reached its nadir. Government schools are not turning out good quality students and there is mushrooming growth of private schools even in the countryside. A massive overhaul of this education system is the need of the hour. Before students are taught, the teachers require our immediate attention: we need to teach them to teach their students. A class should not have more than forty students and the teacher should be held responsible for the progress of his students.

To turn out skilled manpower to take up the challenges of the 21st century, the State should start more and more IT centres and provide them with tools to sharpen their skills and use them properly. The vision of the late prime minister, Rajiv Gandhi, should penetrate the new horizons of information technology.

Foreign trade works as an engine of economic growth. Colonial powers acquired secure markets in their colonies and trade with them boosted the economic development of the home country. Under the WTO, the world is the market and India must secure a place in it. For that, states should set up Special Economic Zones (SEZs) and each zone should specialise in different commodities for exports. China entered the world market at a much later stage. In a short time, it has captured all the world markets, leaving India and Japan behind. Outsourced call centres provide opportunities for employment and for crucial foreign exchange. The large English-speaking Indian manpower is an advantage which must be maintained. China has started a massive programme to teach 30 million Chinese the English language to siphon off outsourcing jobs from India to China.

Massive and rapid industrialisation is imperative to absorb the semi-skilled and skilled manpower now out of jobs. Our textile industry has become a thing of the past. Attractive and cheap textiles from South Korea and China have left our textile industry non-competitive. There is a need to revive this industry.

An international outlook and a propensity to grab opportunities are the need of the hour. For a fully developed economic superstructure, we have to pay attention to the creation of infrastructure. Power is a prime priority.

FDI is needed for creating infrastructure. For that, all avenues should be exploited. FDI investment in China is over $30 billion per annum, which is about ten times that of India's. No doubt overseas Chinese, out of patriotism, invest in China and that investment attracts more investment there. China has built a good infrastructure which attracts more FDI.

India should explore and motivate overseas Indians to invest in India.

Those who were a part of the huge brain drain from India should be made to see India from a different prism. The Indian economy flourishes on the prosperity of the agriculture sector which has, unfortunately, developed a tendency to stagnate. The era of Green Revolution and White Revolution is passe. We need a second revolution of that sort in view of the unchecked population growth. This demographic effect has reduced people's purchasing power and consumption.

We have to increase agriculture production and increase the purchasing power of the rural masses by providing them jobs so that the wheels of national economy remain on the fast track. The Rural Employment Scheme is a step in the right direction to provide them jobs and create infrastructure.

Democracy requires that the scales of social injustice are held in perfect equilibrium. For social justice, people's participation in democratic institutions and the creation of new leadership at the grass-root level, Rajiv Gandhi visualised the panchayati raj system. This is a new step in decentralisation of power. These institutions need government support and finance, so that elected representatives are responsible to the people.

India has entered a new era of coalition politics. Coalition-dharma demands adherence to the Common Minimum Programme. Past experience shows the tergiversation of the so-called secular outfits, in making private deals to remain in power, had eroded their credibility among people.

The success of ruling parties and coalitions lies in learning from the failure of their predecessors. We have to take care to see that no section of society feels alienated, especially the minorities and weaker sections. Peace and political stability are imperative for economic growth and to redeem our pledge given to the people at the time of elections.

NITISH KUMAR
CHIEF MINISTER, BIHAR

Regional Imbalance Damages the Whole

I believe India can be truly empowered only when every Indian is empowered, when every region is empowered. But today, whether it is per capita income or agricultural productivity or industrial growth or rate of investment, there is tremendous regional disparity in India.

It is particularly stark in the eastern region of the country. The eastern region, which was once the most developed region of India, is suffering on every front. At the time of independence, the eastern region was the seat of power—it had the highest agricultural production, natural wealth, educational opportunities. But today it is at the bottom of the scale.

Take the case of Bihar. In 1947, Bihar contributed as much as 25 per cent of the country's sugarcane production. Now it is reduced to a bare two to three per cent. In recent years, there has been some progress in West Bengal and Orissa, which have become self-sufficient in food. But that is not enough. We have the best agro-climatic conditions in the country. But no one is exploiting it.

The Green Revolution was confined to north India and its gains have reached saturation point. But Bihar has the potential to increase its current agricultural production by at least three times. It has fertile soil and the right climate. Foodgrains, pulses, fruits and vegetables grow naturally in abundance. But there is no systematic effort to harness the huge potential.

Bihar was the first state to officially abolish the zamindari system after independence. But land reforms came to a standstill. Fragmentation of land has been its bane. In order to realise its potential, Bihar needs massive investment in irrigation, agro-industries and related fields which has not been forthcoming. Those who say no improvement is possible are mistaken. The Milk Revolution in Bihar that came about when Dr V. Kurien's National Dairy Development Board (NDDB) took the initiative is a case in point. Similar revolutions are waiting to happen.

Besides agriculture, Bihar has untapped potential in every field—industry, education, human resources. Most people are unaware that Bihar has one of the highest rates of savings in the country. The people of Bihar save much of their earnings in bank deposits—partly because the standard of living is low and there is relatively little scope for consumption. But despite the huge savings, the credit deposit ratio is the lowest in India. This means that leave alone investment from outside, even the savings of the people of Bihar are not being invested for the development of the state.

We are very rich in human resources. There are over 18,000 Bihari students studying in various educational institutes in Pune alone. More students from Bihar sit for the UPSC examinations than from anywhere else in the country. There is great thirst for education in the state.

During the days of the freedom struggle, people took their own initiative to set up schools and colleges in various parts of the state. But despite this thirst, despite the innate talent in the region, there has been no systematic investment in the field of education for years together. There is no state initiative and private initiative has died out.

Instead of seeing our population as a burden, we must learn to see it as an asset that needs to be harnessed. If a person is unskilled and unemployed, he is a burden. Once he is endowed with the right education and skills, he becomes an asset.

It is time that the rest of India realised that we cannot prosper as a country, we cannot become an empowered nation unless we address the growing regional imbalances. It is not enough to have a 7-8 per cent national growth and 4 per cent agricultural growth if this growth is not spread evenly.

India cannot be empowered if that empowerment is confined only to a few western and southern states. The continued neglect of the eastern region, in fact, poses a great danger to India as a whole. If such regional imbalance persists, then the ensuing frustration and despair will turn the neglected regions into breeding grounds of extremism. Not just Naxalite extremism, but criminal gangs too will grow. And their impact too will not be confined to just one region. Its adverse effects will spread to other parts of the country.

That is why I think it is imperative that we focus on the development of the eastern region—not just for its own sake but for the sake of the country as a whole. The private and public sector must realise that it is in their own long-term interest to invest in this region and ensure that it does not decline further—and bring the rest of India down with it. India, I repeat, cannot achieve peace and prosperity and justice if its growth remains lopsided and uneven. How can India be empowered when the eastern region, despite its great potential, remains neglected and undeveloped?

MAYAWATI
PRESIDENT, BAHUJAN SAMAJ PARTY

Power to the Deprived Majority

I believe the time has come for true cooperation and coordination between the Centre and the states if the country wants real economic emancipation and political empowerment for its deprived and marginalised people. Since the Centre proposes and the state dispenses, it is important to keep in mind that all the economic policies pursued by political powers reach and benefit every section of society.

No section should remain hungry, poor, unemployed. Everyone must have at least two meals in their stomach, a roof over their head and clothes to cover themselves. I will be very happy when this happens as it will make 'Bharat Mahan'.

It is a pity that 58 years after independence, the Centre and states are entangled in problems, and that even today, 50 per cent of the population lives in abject poverty. If political powers had worked to uplift the plight of even 2 per cent of the poor people every year since independence, we would have had no one living in poverty today.

In this country, the weaker sections constitute the vast majority of 85 per cent of society—from SC/STs, OBCs, MBCs, religious minorities—yet, they are consistently and studiously ignored and neglected. The caste system continues to divide and split them at all levels. Therefore, it is imperative and urgent to unite them and transfer power into the hands of this majority. Bahujan Samaj means this—Bahu (majority), jan (people). Power belongs to this majority.

Yes, there are dozens of schemes launched in the name of the deprived people. But there is no action on the ground, it does not reach the target group. The reason why these schemes are never implemented is because of lack of vigilance and corruption.

I believe it is crucial that schemes are monitored closely and the government institute monitoring cells at the ground level. I've also seen that funds meant for SC/STs are constantly moved to other sectors, which further robs them of their due. I've seen this myself—as chief minister of Uttar Pradesh thrice, I was forced to keep a strict watch on all the schemes I had announced and would personally monitor the movement of funds to this sector.

I believe it is also crucial for state governments to ensure their people are not forced to leave their homes and seek greener pastures in other states. It is the Centre's responsibility to help and fund states to develop their economic might, so that people can seek employment in their home towns. Migration tears up families, breaks up homes and pulls the social fabric apart.

As a woman and a Dalit, I would like to tell the young women of this country to excel in every field and not lag behind men. It will have two beneficial effects—the children, the new generation, will be inspired by mothers; and, economic empowerment will ensure equality at home between husband and wife. This is good for the family and for the country.

Success is not difficult to achieve, but I must warn them that they will have to work hard, there will be all kinds of difficulties in their path, but they must not be afraid. They must have the courage and strength to go on. It is a lesson I learnt long ago.

U.S. MISRA
DIRECTOR, CENTRAL BUREAU OF INVESTIGATION

National Clean-up Begins with the Bureaucracy

For me, a corruption-free state is an irreducible pre-requisite for empowering India.

When I look back at my nearly three decades of experience in tackling corruption in public service, three salient archetypal examples come to mind. First, there was this corrupt civil servant who retired with all benefits. He also enjoyed a reputation for efficiency and honesty! He never faced a single vigilance inquiry throughout his fruitful career.

Second, there was this corrupt bureaucrat who faced a case of disproportionate assets (possessing assets beyond his known/declared sources of income). The case was investigated and chargesheeted in two years. The trial dragged on for nearly two decades. He retired from service and died before the end of trial. The fruits of his corruption accrued to his family.

Third, a very famous tycoon started his life as an ordinary dealer, but rose up through systematic serial bribery of public servants in almost every sector to become one of the most successful industrialists in about twenty years.

From these examples, you can draw the following conclusions about corruption:

- It's a low-risk, high-gain activity.
- It's not restricted to a single institution, region, area or country, it is a global pandemic.
- Corruption is as extensively prevalent in the private sector as in the public sector, although the latter is better known because there is

greater visibility and accountability there.

- Everyone rails against corruption, governments pass laws against corruption, but corruption neither fades nor dies; it remains, although it may change its forms and regions of infestation.
- Most people are actually opposed to corruption only so long as they do not stand to benefit by it.
- There's negligible social stigma attached to the archetypal upper world 'suite crimes' of corruption like 'contract-fixing', 'policy-fixing' 'legislation-fixing' etc. than to archetypal underworld 'street crimes' like 'contract-killing', 'theft' etc.
- The network of dishonest and corrupt public servants is more extensive and more formidable than that of the honest public servants.
- Efficiency is valued more than ethics; or, in other words, ends justify the means.
- There are no formulae or quick-fix solutions for curbing corruption, least of all the laws, and one may do well to bear in mind the experience of imperial Rome which had so many laws against corruption but was finally ruined only by corruption.
- It remains the sworn enemy of integrity, which is imperative for the survival of a country in the long term for as that grand patriarch of democracy, Edmund Burke, once wrote, 'In a state long corrupt, liberty cannot survive'.
- Investigating and prosecuting corruption is more difficult than being honest in public service.
- It is almost an ineradicable phenomenon that can best be controlled following a cumulative convergence of individual, social and political interests/inclinations.

For me, above all, corruption is the most insidious and dangerous enemy of empowerment because it is invisible. In India, corruption is a deeply entrenched phenomenon. Corruption is like diabetes: once it afflicts a country, there is no final cure, only enduring control thereafter. Corruption is one of the greatest challenges of today and is eating into the vitals of society making good governance almost impossible, thwarting economic progress and hurting the interests of the poor and the under-privileged.

Corruption impedes all aspects of development, disturbs economic decision making, deters investment and undermines competitiveness and economic growth. It also increases the gap between the rich and the poor. According to the Hon'ble Supreme Court of India: 'It is sad but a bitter reality that corruption is corroding, like cancerous lymph nodes, the vital veins of the body polity, social fabric of efficiency in the public service and demoralizing the honest officers. Efficiency in public service would improve only when the public servant devotes his sincere attention and does his duty diligently, truthfully, honestly and devotes himself assiduously to the performance of the duties of his post. The reputation of the corrupt would gather thick and unchaseable clouds around the conduct of the officer and gain notoriety much faster than the smoke.'

It may be said that the surplus legal power of the bureaucrat and the politician's deficit legal money, combined naturally with the surplus money power of the businessman, deficit of legal power, provides a formidable terra firma for corruption. This alliance is one of mutually assured benefits. Bribery benefits the giver as well as the receiver. To this cause may be added, the colossal indifference of the public over time, broken by the odd impulse-driven tactile interventions. Corruption is one of the oldest residents of private-sector origin in the public bureaucracy and it cannot be evicted in a day, but it can be quarantined.

To me, implicit in the empowerment of an Indian is his inalienable right to benefit from an instant, incessant and impartial implementation of law by the State. To Indians restoring cost-free rights (non-bribe-oriented invocation of law) is itself empowerment. Without power, rights are mere words, which with the passage of time (through misuse and disuse), lose their power to inspire and invoke confidence and respect from the general public and corresponding compliance from the State. This is the source of the cumulative discomfiture of the citizen with the State.

That is why, for me, real empowerment is to enable a citizen to feel comfortable in India. It is his country. He should feel it. It is possible only if the State does enable a citizen to realise his right to corruption-free governance (or in other words, cost-free delivery of public goods and services)—in short, what I call, bureaucratic hygiene.

I know several remote villages in the country where the poor people devote most of their entire daily earnings to get their next ration of food by paying 'speed money' to the Food and Civil Supplies Corporation officials. To this poor man, a clean government means empowerment because he can enjoy the fruits of his rights, that is, he gets more food for less money; he saves more money; he can afford to send his children to school; he can afford to hope to live and to learn; and, with knowledge, add more quality to his empowerment. If he can get some relief from the tyrannical trinity of government in rural areas—the revenue clerk, the police constable and the tout—he is empowered.

The late Rajiv Gandhi had lamented that only 15 paise out of every rupee spent by the government finally reached the targeted individual and the rest got lost on the way. To these poor folks, imparting the awareness of a complaints mechanism, vigilance department, CBI etc. would be a banal exercise.

Poverty has not only made them ignorant, it has rendered them immobile. They have neither the inclination nor the capacity to trek/travel all the way to the cities and file complaints. They hunger first for food and then for knowledge. The government is obliged to give them both. It can give the second only if it can give the first for, after all, one must be alive to learn. The government can give them both by providing a corruption-free public service in the food, health, welfare and education sectors. In other words, nutritional and health security lays the foundation for empowerment, while knowledge may add quality to the empowerment.

I have met persons from the private sector who have shared amusing anecdotes of being fleeced by public servants on some issue or the other. They say in private, 'What to do? One has to live with it'. Similarly, I have heard some public servants confess that they were once very honest but took to the path of dishonesty because 'Almost everyone is doing it, so why not I?' So, if everyone is involved in corruption in some way or the other, does it mean that there is no escape from corruption in India? Wrong.

These questions, when properly examined, actually reveal that most persons, public servants and private citizens are prisoners in a bad system. Not to say that some of them may be downright hypocritical but, by and large, most people live with corruption because they are unable to find or forge a coalition of the willing to limit or terminate corruption. This is a very dangerous predicament for a citizen.

He lives with corruption because he has no choice. He is deprived of his choice, which means his liberty, the power to choose. The citizen is effectively disempowered. This is part of why I say that central to the objective of empowerment is cleansing the bureaucracy. How does one go about empowering a disempowered citizenry? One must understand here that empowering a 'disempowered' citizenry is a more difficult task than empowering a hitherto enslaved citizenry, because while with the latter, it is usually only about education, with the former it is about prevailing over a crusty cynicism. There are numberless suggestions and recommendations that have been made over the years in several editorials from time to time in the country as also in the odd judgements passed by the constitutional courts. But, there are some that I feel may be of practical relevance and result-oriented applicability.

In my years in the CBI, I have realised that the investigation of corruption cases is basically a work of accelerated criminal audit. An

88 U.S. MISRA

anti-corruption officer is an auditor with some police powers of search, summons, seizure, arrest and prosecution. But at the core, the work is one of criminal audit—to ascertain whether there has been any deviation from the manual of office procedure; if so, whether the deviation may be one of benign and casual negligence or malign and motivated negligence; and if the latter then whether this has also resulted in any violations of any criminal laws and if yes, whether this was motivated by any extraneous considerations.

Proper auditing could have checked, detected, exposed and held the persons concerned to account and effected recoveries. Timely and effective auditing could have even prevented it in the first place. In India, the comptroller and auditor-general of India is a constitutional authority and he can use the prestige, powers and resources of his office to re-orient the role, scope and face of auditing of all central government funds allotted to state governments for the implementation of various schemes in concert with the CVC and the CBI. I feel, these joint ventures, when they detect fraud, must focus less on prosecution than the recovery and re-use of the illicit proceeds for the original public purpose.

Proactive and pre-emptive auditing, combined with surprise checks, laced with 'Special Drives' would go a long way in bringing the government to the underprivileged and thereby laying a terra firma for empowering a vast segment of our people.

Constitutional functionaries and bureaucrats with security of tenures can and must flex their bureaucratic muscles to make a difference. They must draw succour from developments like the recent enactment of the Right to Information Act and electoral reforms.

Further, the entire panoply of corrupt practices (nepotism, favouritism, periodic/ceremonial gifts, habitual concessions and commissions) has its origins and primary sway in the private sector. For empowering India through the cleansing of bureaucracy, it is not enough for the public sector alone to come forward; it is necessary even for the private sector to do so.

Reforms, like charity, begin at home. India expects its industrialists and business houses to implement their recipes on ending corruption in their organisations first, which includes, 'Thou shalt not offer any bribe to get your work done—anywhere'. The profiteering privateers have been able to put a lot of spin to their association with bribery by saying that they are its victims. They would not like to admit that they are its principal architects. In India, bribe giving is worse than bribe receiving because the receiver gets only what is given, whereas the giver gets what he wants. The ultimate loser, of course, is the State. It is trite that if every businessman follows the laws in India, particularly the tax laws, he would never become so disproportionately wealthy.

The media rails about corruption in the public sector, but only squibs about it in the private sector—the source and sustenance of the evil. Most importantly, the stigma of a corruption crime is not as much as that of a conventional crime such as theft. The society has hence to generate sustained measures for spreading awareness against corruption and for educating the people. There has to be an ideological attack on corruption in which the intellectuals and media can play a significant role. Let the corrupt officials be despised, ostracised—let them not handle important portfolios. Many beneficiaries of corruption, according to one estimate, are only about 5 per cent of the population. Hence, we can mobilise the might of the remaining 95 percent in this fight.

The Right to Information Act, already in place, must be put to effective use and NGOs must associate actively in anti-corruption efforts. Leadership is all about enriching the environment in which decisions are generated and resources managed. Its absence has been felt in some of the key areas of governance for a very long time. It is high time that someone did what everybody wants done—transform anti-corruption rhetoric to reality.

MEHBOOBA MUFTI
PRESIDENT, PDP

End the Secular Vs Communal Debate

Imagine an India where a billion people wake up to their rights and responsibilities in a thriving democracy. Indian democracy works at two levels—one during the election where the involvement of common masses is total; and post-elections, where people's participation is almost negligible.

Power given out by the masses through their vote becomes a prized possession shared by politicians and bureaucrats. Right from decision making, formation of policies and their implementation, everything is done in the name of the common people but they hardly enjoy any involvement in this process and lack a mechanism to seek accountability from the ruling elite.

How to make masses partners in the power structure? How to make them aware of their rights over the government that they have chosen? How to educate them to demand good governance as their right, seeking their welfare first and foremost in the shape of the right to protection of life, irrespective of religion, caste, creed and colour and basic amenities like access to education, health care, roads, water etc.?

It is astonishing that a country established on the tenets of secularism is still engrossed in the debate between secular and communal politics. Ever since Independence, politicians seem to be caught in the rhetoric of secular and non-secular, thus continuously avoiding the real issue of the ever-widening gap between the haves and have-nots, the educated and uneducated. What could be a more stark example of this divide than that of the continuous suicide of farmers in supposedly prosperous states?

Instead of dubbing each other 'pseudo-secular' and 'communal', 'nationalist' and 'anti-national', political parties, especially those which hold power, should start competing with each other in providing good governance. A large chunk of our population, be it minorities, backward classes, tribals and people below the poverty line, are still a deprived section of our society and thus at times become a breeding ground for crime and violence.

Although the Indian economy is growing with the sweat and toil of ordinary Indians, its fruits remain confined to a small section of society. No one questions this unjust system and it may be they are not even aware of it and have unconsciously become a part of this system. The majority of our population, be it Hindu, Muslim or any other section based on religion, region or caste, works very hard to make both ends meet and instead of addressing their problems, we just give them the pill of secularism versus communalism.

The time has come when this debate has to shift to governance and non-governance. Decentralisation of power by regional forces from the Centre to the state has been the first step in the right direction in the last 15 years to accommodate the regional aspirations and development of different states. But unfortunately this decentralisation too has consolidated its strength not on the basis of good governance but on the basis of the so called secular, communal, caste divides.

Imbalance in the representation at the Centre by states is the biggest hurdle in the way of achieving a fair decentralisation. In our present system, the more populated states get more representation in parliament, thus enjoying an indirect monopoly at the Centre which deprives the smaller and less populated states from being part of the national decision making process and the Central government.

Take the example of Jammu and Kashmir—we have six parliamentary seats, which is negligible when compared to states like UP and Bihar.

The control of more populated states over the parliament by sheer numbers needs to be changed. In fact, it is ironic that states which follow the population control policy vigorously are in a way punished because population is still the main criteria to form new Lok Sabha constituencies.

There is a need to look at this aspect of the highest institution of democracy urgently and take steps to make it fair like the United States, where people in smaller states like Wisconsin and New Hampshire get as much importance in the presidential elections as larger states like California. The American model might have its own shortcomings but the example can help us in the process of total and fair decentralisation and give a profound sense of belonging to smaller states.

Then, protection of life should be a matter of right as provided by the Constitution rather than a political favour given out to minorities or any other underprivileged section of society as part of electoral politics. India as a nation has to channelise its human and material resources in a manner that the feeling of being part of India, be it anyone, is there. Let people judge a party not on its political and emotional rhetoric but on the basis of its day-to-day performance in improving the lives of ordinary citizens. Let there be cooperation and competition between states above party lines so that they complement each other in becoming economically self-reliant for the collective benefit of the people.

India will be empowered when state governments, run by political parties with varied ideologies, compete with each other in providing good and fair governance, rather than emotional rhetoric based on divisive slogans of so-called nationalist and anti-national or regional, religious and caste loyalties.

In fact, the empowered sections of our society like politicians, bureaucrats and media can play an important role to change this senseless debate of secular versus communal, majority versus minority, nationalist versus anti-national, upper-caste versus lower-caste and replace them with much more profound and relevant issues like food, shelter, schools, hospitals, roads, water and electricity.

There also needs to be a general consensus among all parties, cutting across electoral politics, regarding very sensitive issues like the Kashmir problem which has been eating into the vitals of the country for decades.

The leadership at the Centre has to have the will and determination to find a lasting solution to this burning problem, while taking into account the aspirations of the people who have been suffering for so many years.

Empowerment of India also means ensuring that women's empowerment starts right from the family. Give women equal rights in love, care, confidence, education, property and decision making. This has to be echoed in policy making bodies like the parliament and assembly as well. Imagine an India where no one is above the common person. That is India empowered.

PRANAB MUKHERJEE
MINISTER, EXTERNAL AFFAIRS

Enable All: Institutions, Individuals and Family

Empowerment to me means internalisation and implementation of the normative values of democracy, freedom, equality, education and equitable socio-economic development, as enshrined in our Constitution, by the vast institutional network that subsumes the organs of both state and society. These comprise the legislature, the judiciary, the executive, and the media and are complemented by civil society and its institutions in the private sector with the individual family at the core.

Consequently, institutional rectitude and self-regulation by way of the conduct of one's duties and obligations are of paramount importance in how truly empowered India becomes in the years ahead. This is applicable across the board to all those who have either been elected or appointed to discharge certain functions as part of the democratic dispensation. The core integrity of purpose exuded by the individuals who comprise the institutional soul, where the larger common good transcends individual sectarian interests, will be the ultimate test of meaningful national empowerment.

Chanakya, in his many writings, refers to the centrality of yogakshema—or the 'well-being' of the people as the central purpose of state structures and related governance. History tells us that over the centuries, the security and prosperity of the individual are closely linked to the texture of governance and the manner in which it is perceived by the common man. Only credible systems, institutions and individuals can bring about a positive change in perceptions.

If one billion plus Indians feel adequately empowered and this is reflected in their improved quality of life, it follows that India as a nation would exude a quiet confidence in a holistic manner. This abiding pattern of equitable and sustainable empowerment in turn must be encouraged and nurtured in the entire region so that there is a sense of shared security and prosperity.

In the changing global system, security is indivisible and no single nation can island its sense of security and be oblivious to the region it is located in. The rash of recent global terrorist attacks indicates that distance no longer confers invulnerability.

I believe that in this context, empowerment has a critical role to play—for it is a combination of enabling the individual by way of skills and opportunities—as also instilling a degree of enlightenment that is in consonance with the collective ethic.

When globalisation of our prosperity and security has become inevitable, recognising what constitutes equitable empowerment at both the individual and institutional level is imperative. As a member of the political constituency, I also acknowledge that the elected representatives have to lead by example—by way of institutional rectitude—and this is an onerous responsibility.

However, there can be no single view on this and hence, public debate of this nature is welcome and should strike an empathetic chord with the 'argumentative' Indian.

K.R. NARAYANAN
FORMER PRESIDENT OF INDIA

The Suppressed Must Assert Their Rights

'I have finished writing my article but I want to go through it again. When do I have to send it to the *Indian Express*?' K.R. Narayanan asked his close aide and former press secretary S.N. Sahu on October 26. Told he had time, the former president, who had graciously agreed to contribute to the series, told Sahu: 'Leave it on my table. I want to have another look.' Three days later, Narayanan was in hospital. Hours after his death, Sahu called up the *Indian Express* to say that the article was on its way. In the piece, Kocheril Raman Narayanan captures the India that he wanted to see all his life. In his death, his own words, therefore, ring as the most eloquent tribute to his vision.

Empowerment has meaning and significance only when the dispossessed and the disinherited have access to the basic necessities of life and are given opportunities to play their rightful role as the citizens of our country.

The real empowerment of India began with the struggle for our independence, at the centre of which remained ordinary people. Mahatma Gandhi harnessed their power to fight against the mighty British empire. It was a remarkable example of empowerment of a disempowered people in a society riddled with social injustice and religious discrimination.

It is difficult to empower people unless we address the issues concerning equality and equality of opportunities for the vast masses of people who have to struggle for their daily existence. Empowerment thus means uplifting the unprivileged and making them partners and beneficiaries of nation-building activities.

Empowerment means improving the status of women and treating minorities with care and concern. Therefore, any attempt to empower people must begin from below. The heroic struggle of Mahatma Gandhi, Babasaheb Ambedkar and Jawaharlal Nehru brings to us the examples of landmark initiatives which aimed at empowering the people of India.

Harking back to the freedom struggle we find that people under foreign rule had no means of opposing their exploitation and demanding independence and democracy for their development. A completely subjugated and disempowered people suddenly found within themselves immense strength to confront the majesty and might of the British empire.

How did that happen? We all know that by removing fear from the minds of people and infusing among them moral strength and authority, Gandhiji transformed their outlook and wielded them as a powerful weapon in the non-violent struggle for independence. In that historical context, empowerment had a connotation which derived legitimacy from the moral ethos of our society.

After almost six decades of our independence, we have made tremendous material progress and consolidated our democracy. The whole of India and, in fact, large sections of the population are now empowered to take India forward. It has now been acknowledged by the world that India is fast emerging as a major economic power determining the course of human history in a manner which gives confidence that we will get back our rightful place in the comity of nations.

The talk of empowerment makes us feel confident about our future. But we feel disheartened to see the decline of standard of behaviour in our public life. Empowerment of India thus would mean restoring the moral dimension and values to our public life.

Without morality and values, the empowered India would be devoid of depth and content. Today, when the whole world exclaims about India's ability in diverse fields and hails its emergence as a major power in the economic and scientific arena, we need to introspect and ask ourselves if we have lived up to the ideals bequeathed to us by our freedom fighters and the founding fathers of our Constitution.

An empowered India bereft of respect for women, values of civilised existence and morality will collapse in the face of the disaffection and discontent of those who have suffered for centuries.

FALI S. NARIMAN
JURIST, MP

Just Formal Equality for Women Is Not Enough

I would like to see India empowered by the economic and social emancipation of its women (all 496 million of them)—not in theory, not by enacting laws, but in actual practice. How do we treat our women? In one word, badly. Our Constitution provides for equality between the sexes.

But the founding fathers—we always use that expression because out of 197 members in the Constituent Assembly, only ten were women!—realised that equality between the sexes was an aspiration, not a reality. So they empowered the State (that is parliament and state legislatures) to make 'any special provision for women.'

Now, after 56 years, despite all the special provisions made for women, the attitudes of men have not changed. The truth is that we are today still an overpoweringly male-dominated society. And you just cannot change chauvinist attitudes by making laws; it is possible only by promoting social consciousness and an enlightened understanding: in other words through meaningful education.

Which prompts me to recall a story about the Mahabharata—not the story of old, but a story of modern times, a true story. A few years ago, Kartikeya Sarabhai, son of the great scientist Vikram Sarabhai, witnessed in Avignon (in France) the performance of the great Indian epic Mahabharata, a production by Peter Brooks.

It depicts the entire tale of how Yudhishtra lost all his wealth in playing dice with Duryodhana and continued with the game even whilst continuously losing and ultimately offering his wife Draupadi as a wager. The tale is familiar—after he loses, Draupadi is fetched by force to the victor who starts removing her garments. And then a miracle occurs, fresh garments are seen to close her body, and good men praise god and weep.

After seeing the Mahabharata at Avignon, Kartikeya Sarabhai came back the same evening and wrote a poem representing the thoughts of Draupadi and offered it to his sister. The poem 'I Draupadi' is inspired—but it is also poignant and expressive of the reality of conditions of women in modern India.

In the poem Draupadi says:

'All rights belong to husbands, so says society,
But to be shared by five, a commodity in the market place?...
All this I accepted, became the wife of five—to each gave a son
I was the only wife of none.'

And then it goes on:

'Gambling they went, invited by Duryodhana
Lost all they had, losing even themselves
I unspared was dragged into the court of men
Which were these bonds of Dharma
That tied my husbands?
What kind of husbands these, that are tied by the Dharma of lies?'

And the poem ends with a condemnation of the male gender for forsaking equality in practice:

'Years went by, our lives we lived together
Started on our journey's end towards the snow-clad Himalayas
I fell first, no Pandava stretched a hand
Towards paradise they walked, no one stayed by my side.
Then, I realized heaven too must be only for men
Better then to rest in the warm embrace of this snow.'

The significance of the poem written with such spontaneity by an Indian male about Indian women highlights the difference between formal equality, hypocritically mouthed by us all, and the actual inequality which the fate of Draupadi has eternally symbolised: the inequality that women have had to bear, and continue to suffer, even in present day India.

KAMAL NATH
UNION MINISTER OF COMMERCE & INDUSTRY

Exports as Key to Employment

Despite its many diversities, India is one of the youngest nations to have attained an almost unparalleled status in its unique intellectual abilities. Its demography reveals an incredible transformation with over 400 million educated Indians between the age group of 20 to 40, and 60 per cent of the population below the age of 25. The beginning of the century saw the unveiling of the world's largest English-speaking work force, with technical skills. It also saw the empowerment of the individual to extract and enable his personal future, guided rather than dictated by the state.

Empowerment of India is, therefore, the empowerment of its youth, with the right to education and employment, the right to embrace new frontiers and unleash their true capabilities. Empowerment to me is synonymous with employment. To be empowered is not having to go without the basic necessities of life to which all our citizens are entitled. Gainful employment provides these necessities. There can be no economic freedom—indeed no freedom at all—without employment, and likewise, without employment there can be no empowerment.

While software, IT services and BPOs have grown tremendously, this is not enough for a country of India's size and the diverse composition of its youth. The biggest challenge that India faces today is to generate employment for its huge labour force of unskilled or low-skilled workers, whom the services revolution has not been able to absorb.

We need a 'manufacturing revolution' running in parallel with the 'services revolution' to be able to respond adequately to the massive challenge of employment generation and alleviation of poverty.

Exports represent the incremental production that is not absorbed in the domestic economy. To that extent it represents the potential for greater economic activity. Export growth leads to higher employment.

The experience of countries like China, Malaysia, Thailand and others is particularly relevant in this context. They have successfully built up export oriented manufacturing industries to create job opportunities on a massive scale.

Nearer home, there have been numerous individual instances of exports creating income and wealth. There is the instance of the sudden transformation in the lives of women in a remote village of Gujarat brought about by a huge export order procured online for ties with ethnic design. There is the interesting case of the Chanderi fabric and how a UNIDO-McKinsey marketing strategy for the fabric has changed the lives of 24,000 Chanderi weavers. Clearly, such instances can be multiplied manifold to demonstrate the positive impact of trade on job creation.

Given that India is still predominantly an agrarian economy with over 600 million people dependent on agriculture for their livelihood, agriculture has tremendous potential to bring prosperity to our people. It also has the largest potential for increasing employment in some of the poorest regions of our country. We are the largest producers of fruits, vegetables and milk in the world and yet 40 per cent of our agricultural produce rots. We more or less meet our domestic food needs, but the real boom can be had through exports. If we can tap the export potential of this crucial sector by developing cold chains, food processing and food packaging industries, we can literally provide tens of millions of jobs in the rural areas.

Indeed, no empowerment is possible in India without empowerment of the Indian farmer—in fact, the entire agricultural sector. The ministry of commerce and industry is pursuing the development and upholding of farmers' rights, at the national and international fora, to ensure that the Indian farmer takes his proper place in the country's national development, and in international trade. Focus is also on Agri Export Zones to ensure that the fruits of a buoyant economy accrue to the farmer, through local and foreign trade.

In divesting itself of powers, the State has ensured that at different levels of self-governance, people are able to manage their innate abilities and resources better with a fresh and generative understanding between the people and the administration. Even the non-agricultural, rural-based economy of the village artisan has received due attention. Bharat Nirman is an ambitious yet pragmatic effort towards this end. Handicrafts and other cottage industries are being reorganised to create an export strategy that would benefit the country's village craftsmen. Our cottage industries in backward and rural regions will not only become self-sufficient but they have an enormous potential to become one of the country's leading export sectors, with their exquisite workmanship, which fascinates the western and eastern mind.

The ministry of commerce and industry commissioned a study on employment-oriented export strategy. The report submitted by RIS (Research & Information System for developing countries) in June 2005 showed that the 26 per cent increase in exports in 2004-05 (from 63 billion dollars to 80 billion dollars) created 1 million additional jobs.

This pioneering report highlights the vast opportunities for expanding exports as well as employment that remain untapped. When we achieve the US $150 billion target for exports (set for 2010, but which I hope we can reach earlier) we will have created 10 million new jobs in manufacturing and ancillary areas such as transportation, accounting and trading.

India empowered is the empowerment of the individual in all its core sectors. It is the power that comes from the nation's youth with its unquenchable thirst for knowledge, energy for success and the will to achieve. India empowered is the strengthening of each sector that our economy and health as a nation, depends upon.

In conclusion, I need to reiterate that India as a fast developing economy is harnessing its potentialities and empowering its multitudes through education, employment and economic growth of its agricultural and rural sectors, by a planned and judicious disempowerment of the State and the empowerment of India. As we make India an international trading and manufacturing hub, we can trade our way out of poverty as some of our Asian neighbours have successfully done. And as this metamorphosis reaches its acme, the country will have collectively responded to the call for the restoration of the nation's pride of place in the world hierarchy.

R.K. PACHAURI
DG, THE ENERGY AND RESOURCES INSTITUTE (TERI),
CHAIRMAN, INTERGOVERNMENTAL PANEL ON CLIMATE CHANGE

Climate Change and Resource Regeneration

India empowered to me means a country that has succeeded in reviving and restoring its badly depleted ecological and natural wealth. India's record of managing its natural resources leaves a dismal trail of serious degradation and damage which affects the livelihoods and economic well-being of all its people. All our rivers have been polluted to a level that does not even permit washing of clothes.

It was not too long ago that one could drink water flowing in a river without any threat of serious disease or toxic effects. Today, we have a large industry that produces bottled water, the value of which counts as part of our GDP. Indeed, it is sad that we carry out a number of economic activities, all of which are accounted for in the measurement of our economic output, while imposing a huge social cost on our natural resources.

Restoring India's natural wealth is not the wide-eyed dream of environmental idealists. It is an economic imperative. Nature provides us with a flow of services on which all economic activities depend critically. TERI carried out a major project, which was completed in 1997 on the eve of the celebration of 50 years of independence, in which a rigorous estimation of the damage and degradation of India's natural resources in the first 50 years of independence was attempted.

In economic terms, this amounted to over 10 per cent loss of the country's GDP, including high levels of sickness from air and water pollution. Air pollution, for instance, results in high levels of sickness, which leads to absenteeism and loss of productivity, which can be estimated. To these can be added the cost of medical treatment and health care resulting from the effects of air pollution.

Unfortunately, in this country there are very few organisations which carry out detailed natural resource accounting. If this was to become a regular feature of our assessment of economic activity, we would find that in actual fact, because of the negative impacts of the production and consumption of some goods and services, we are actually limiting economic progress and welfare. A major question that arises in this context is related to the equity effects of production and consumption in an economic system.

The depletion and degradation of natural resources impose the worst impacts on the poorest sections of society. One estimate indicates that about one-third of the goods and services used by poor people come directly from services provided by natural resources. These would include food, fodder, fuel, drinking water and material for construction of dwellings and shelters, as is the case typically within tribal societies. Economic policy should target as much the reduction of our natural debt as it does the national debt.

Quite apart from the anomalies in accounting at the macro level, today we are also ignoring serious environmental challenges at the household level. Good quality fuelwood traditionally used for cooking is just not available for poor households not only in rural areas but also in urban slums. The result is that women and children, in particular, spend hours inhaling harmful pollutants in front of cookstoves burning inferior twigs and leaves and even rubber tyres.

A detailed exercise carried out by TERI estimated that around 2.5 million people in India die prematurely each year as a result of air pollution, the bulk of which is the result of indoor air pollution. Yet, we still have no solution that can provide a clean affordable fuel for the poorest people in this country. Subsidies on kerosene only serve those who are engaged in adulteration of other petroleum products. If the same total subsidy was provided to photovoltaic devices, our rural households could within five years get one light bulb each, without smoke and recurring fuel costs.

To some of these down to earth problems affecting human society, we can add the growing threat of climate change, which results from an increase in the concentration of greenhouse gases in the earth's atmosphere, the most important of which is carbon dioxide produced since industrialisation began through burning of increasing quantities of fossil fuels.

Climate change is likely to have serious impacts on India through altered precipitation patterns, higher temperatures and heat waves, melting of the Himalayan glaciers, adverse effects on health as a result of the greater spread of vector-borne diseases and the threat of sea level rise for our islands and coastal areas. The mitigation of climate change requires major efforts at the global level under the UN Framework Convention on Climate Change and its derivative, the Kyoto Protocol, but as yet the action taken on the ground by the world collectively is decidedly weak.

One aspect of climate change is the inertia in the system, which will result in impacts of climate change continuing for decades, if not centuries. A country like India, therefore, has no choice but to adapt to climate change. This means that with increasing water scarcity, a more responsive and responsible system of management of this precious resource is required. Our agriculture will also require development of new species and strains that are drought-resistant and salt-tolerant to ensure that agricultural yields do not go down.

The threat from climate change to agriculture is a worldwide problem. Lester Brown has written that China, which is consuming more and more grain for producing animal protein despite a decline in agricultural production, would place heavy demands on world foodgrain stocks. All of this could adversely affect food security for the entire human race in future. Climate change can only exacerbate this trend. But let us in this country, at least, restore the natural resources that we have destroyed, or else a heavy price will be paid not only by this generation but also those yet to come.

M.K. PANDHE
PRESIDENT, CENTRE OF INDIAN TRADE UNIONS (CITU)

Empower Wealth Creators, Not Accumulators

My experience in life teaches me that in the present social system the empowerment of an individual is decided by the wealth one owns. Even with ill-gotten wealth or money power, one is in a position to influence others, achieve one's objectives. The vast masses, the creators of wealth who do not own it are totally powerless. They find it difficult to meet the needs of human existence.

Empowerment of India, according to me, cannot be achieved without the common man getting an adequate opportunity to be part of human development. Any talk of human development is meaningless unless every human being is provided shelter, nutrition, education, right to a healthy life, medical facilities, access to cultural activities and a peaceful retired life. According to a UNDP study, India ranks 127 among the 175 countries in the Human Development Index. It speaks volumes about the low level of empowerment in India.

With huge unemployment prevalent, I do not think that we are making meaningful progress in the empowerment of India. Attractive balance sheets of the corporate sector, showing high profits, do not create a good impression when there are daily press reports of the suicide of some breadwinner because he was unable to feed his family. It saddens me when I see tribals starve to death. I always feel that the accumulators of wealth are the cause of poverty and destitution of our teeming millions.

India claims to have no money to generate more jobs but there is no dearth of money when it comes to vulgar displays of wealth at the marriages of the rich. Despite election rules, there is no shortage of funds for some political parties. Crores in public funds are pilfered by bureaucrats and corrupt politicians. Money laundering by the top strata of society is yet another instance of the drain of national resources. If these are used to improve the quality of life of the common people, the country can advance in the correct direction.

Democracy cannot really benefit the people unless the power of money and muscle is forcibly broken by a popular movement. The social backwardness of the poor is allowing this inhuman exploitation. Conscious elements in the society must come forward and develop the social consciousness of the powerless. Real awakening among them will generate a powerful force to make India empowered.

Today those who own the means of production are the empowered strata of society while those who toil to produce goods and services do not enjoy any power. The empowered strata are in a position to corrupt the bureaucracy to their advantage and strengthen their empowerment. They at the same time add to the poverty of the common people and adversely affect human development.

Communal forces preach hatred against other religions and divide people. Without combating these forces effectively, India's march towards empowerment will become ineffective. Casteist elements also play a divisive role and damage the cause of national interest. They have to be countered.

As long as women face gender discrimination, the empowerment of the country will only be a mirage. Sexual harassment of women at the workplace continues to increase despite Supreme Court rulings. Dowry deaths, torture, child marriage etc. underline the need for stringent action against perpetrators of such crimes.

Social oppression of Dalits and tribals continues unabated. Unless they are organised and there's a determined struggle against social oppression, this downtrodden strata will not see the light of empowerment.

India continues to engage the largest child labour force in the world. This shame cannot be eradicated unless their parents are given wages above the poverty line, allowing them to send their children to school instead of making them work in unhygienic conditions.

The toiling masses of India can open the vista of their empowerment only by organising themselves and fighting the prevalent social injustice. Only through a determined struggle can they overthrow the yoke of money power and become masters of their own destiny.

Trade unions and other mass organisations play an important role in this historic struggle. However, one cannot ignore the fact that vested interests can carry out nefarious activities through political parties. To fight the political empowerment enjoyed by these parties, the toiling masses of India must have their political party without which they cannot fight the money power and the mafia.

I do not agree with the advocates of partyless democracy. They deny the right to have a political weapon to politically fight the policies of tycoons who are bottlenecks in the struggle for empowerment of the common people. I am convinced that it is only the people of India who, with their struggle against the usurpers of power, can empower themselves and India.

PRAFUL PATEL
UNION MINISTER FOR CIVIL AVIATION

Decisive Action for the Nation to Take Off

Ladies and gentlemen, India One is boarding for take off. We want you to be incisive, decisive and responsive. This will take us to our destination. Our land of plenty and opportunities will be truly empowered only if we heed the announcement to be truly incisive, responsive and decisive.

While being realistic we must accept that we have come a long way in the past six decades. We have continuously battled with an inner struggle—should we or should we not? And in our quest for striking the right balance we have ended up losing many opportunities for our country and our people.

What was good for us from the 1950s to the 1980s cannot hold true today. In the rapidly changing global scenario, we have to find our rightful place in the community of nations. The stark reality is that we cannot be insensitive to our multiple issues of poverty, illiteracy, sanitation, health, huge unemployment, regional imbalances to name a few.

Simply copying any successful model elsewhere would be utterly foolish. Just as we cannot ignore the aspirations of the young restless Indians who by virtue of the internet, mobile telephony, TV and enhanced education have brought in a new dimension to the way we think, decide and govern. And let me tell you, negotiating between the two opposite dimensions is no mean task, especially in a democratic system where no interest can be ignored.

I went to the United States for the first time in 1974 and came back in awe, completely bewildered. The following year, I went to Thailand, Malaysia and Singapore and heaved a sigh of relief. At least we were ahead of them. Only 20 years later, I discover, and it is for all of us to acknowledge with admiration, the giant leap taken by them. And three years ago, when I went to China, it left me thinking. It is true that China or Thailand may have showcased only a part of themselves for the world to marvel at, but one cannot be cynical about this. At least a beginning had been made.

And how do we move quickly forward? My view is that we will have to decide on six to eight key parameters which require equal emphasis. I say equal because while health, education and irrigation are very important, electricity, roads, communication, shipping and aviation are no less important.

Unfortunately, we generalise in many areas and spread our resources very thin. Consequently we end up with every sector struggling to realise its full potential. I feel we need to expand and enlarge the pie to allow both public and private sectors to grow and contribute. Remember the long wait list for gas connections, telephone connections, etc.? And on the flip side, the IT and communication revolution has given us millions of high-end jobs and actually brought the country and the world closer. Not to talk about our supremacy in this sector which the world reluctantly acknowledges.

Just a case study in aviation, since I happen to be there: a few logical steps, not radical, and it's a wake up call! More airlines, more flights, more choice, competitive fares, new aspirations, many jobs, tourism— both domestic and international—and enhanced economic activity. Besides of course, the great support to exports and agriculture.

A farmer near Nashik or Amritsar feels he needs an airport near him as only then can he realise his fullest potential. Or the agriculture minister of Jammu and Kashmir asks me to get his harvest of cherries airlifted to Mumbai or Delhi so that his farmers get good returns. Or a working-class person, who travels once a year with his family on holiday, being able to fly. These are just a few examples!

Who would have thought that aviation can, in this decade, be amongst the highest investment sectors and the highest employment sectors, besides bringing the country closer? Remember it's still easier and cheaper to fly from Delhi to London or Singapore than it is to Kerala.

To add to that, our country lost out on connectivity and other countries became hubs for India. Do you know of any international traveller who connects elsewhere out of any Indian airport, or uses our airlines to travel beyond our shores? Further when we enlarge the pie in power, roads, ports, railways, education, healthcare, irrigation, water, sanitation, we could have a heady cocktail!

Nonetheless we must give a better future to the millions of Indians who need it as of yesterday. We must think big. Remember the Victoria Terminus Station in Mumbai or the Brooklyn Bridge in New York was made more than 100 years ago. What we make or do today must be good for at least the next 50 years, if not another 100.

I am many a time amused when we plan infrastructure depending on present-day needs as even now we are only four-laning the existing highways or only expanding existing terminals at airports. And what about our execution? A few mistakes may occur but it cannot deter a nation. That is why we need to be incisive, responsive and decisive. At least we will have taken off!

NAVEEN PATNAIK
CHIEF MINISTER, ORISSA

The Weakest and the Poorest Must Empower the Nation

India prides herself on being the world's largest democracy. Democracy means the rule of the free. But too many Indians are not yet free. Poverty and illiteracy have kept too many Indians enslaved, exploited by the powerful and the corrupt. When not exploited, they are often patronised. We even use a constitutional term, originally coined to ensure economic and social equality, by calling a huge mass of our population 'backward' to justify our condescension. But do we really know what we mean when we use the word 'backward' so freely?

In my state, considered among the poorest in India, a quarter of the population is from the tribal communities, considered the most backward and certainly the most exploited in Indian society. Yet, in October 2005, two Oriya tribal girls represented the whole of India at an international forum on children's development in Beijing.

The 12 year old daughter of a daily wage earner and the 10 year old daughter of a village school teacher, are both child reporters of a local monthly journal. In Beijing, they presented papers covering gender and children's issues, tribal culture and the economic development in their areas. 'I want to be a journalist. I really enjoy my work as a reporter under the programme. It also increases my sense of responsibility towards my community,' the younger girl told a press conference.

I recently met a group of tribal students of Malkangiri, one of India's most deprived areas. They belong to the Bonda tribe, a tribe not only considered backward, but also primitive. They were the first children from their community to have completed high school. Each student shared the same ambition, to return to Malkangiri as a teacher and empower other children.

Then we have the tenacious Tulsi Munda, a tribal woman who has released hundreds of tribal children from a future as exploited daily labourers by setting up a school in Orissa's mining area. As a girl, Tulsi Munda had herself worked in these mines as a labourer. It is an interesting fact that when tribal children go to their schools, they are out-performing many children attending general schools in the rest of the state. If only the others could be as forward as such 'backwards'.

Padmashri Tulsi Munda pioneered what is today in Orissa a phenomenon, the growing strength of women. As an administration, we thought it would be a slow and painful process to get our poor and reticent women to join self-help groups. But Orissa's women proved us wrong. They seized the opportunity and in only five years and with an initial investment from the government of only Rs 1 crore, Orissa has self-help groups of more than two million women, who have banked over Rs 100 crore.

The women of these groups have gone from breaking stones by the roadside to becoming masons and plumbers and electricians. They hold their own assets and are passionate about educating their children. They often head pani panchayats that have been set up all over Orissa to give villagers control over their own water resources. And free of the spectre of destitution, they are changing the social fabric of the state.

As one group told me, there is a big difference between a single woman going with a grievance to a police station and a thousand women going with her. These women are no longer afraid of the powerful, whether they be policemen, bureaucrats, politicians or even their in-laws. If only everyone were as fearless as these women have become.

Among many different groups of people in Orissa, I have begun to see evidence of what V.S. Naipaul calls a 'million mutinies', the small rebellions against entrenched injustice which can change society. But I have also seen that unless the cancer of corruption is eliminated, ordinary Indians will continue to fear the powerful.

Corruption corrodes every vital part of the machinery of justice— economic, social and political. Where corruption is rampant, citizens are reduced to election fodder, forced to watch the money they pay to the State in taxes disappearing into the pockets of those who are supposed to be their guardians. And social justice becomes the law of the jungle in which only the fittest, or should I say 'the fattest', survive.

Above all, in governance, corruption generates and feeds inefficiency so that no matter how much money is spent, children are not taught, patients are not treated, jobs are not created. We have tried to fight exploitation: from small but vital steps such as banning school-children from lining sun-scorched streets awaiting the motorcade of a passing VIP to that vast and prolonged task of bringing transparency and probity in governance, not sparing even the privileged and the powerful.

I believe India will become empowered only when corruption ceases to be tolerated, freeing those who are its greatest victims from corruption's many forms of intimidation. And then, the people themselves, be they ever so 'backward', are more than capable of empowering India.

SHARAD PAWAR
MINISTER, AGRICULTURE & CONSUMER AFFAIRS,
FOOD & PUBLIC DISTRIBUTION

A Paradigm Shift in Agriculture

People living in rural areas, irrespective of whether they own land or not, are my deepest concern. Agriculture impacts and gets impacted by the entire spectrum of activities that one can visualise in the rural space. Agriculture not only meets the basic needs of India's growing population, its direct linkages with industry are on the increase owing to the increased demand for processed agricultural commodities and goods by consumers.

For many rural areas, the rural non-farm sector has little capacity to generate growth on its own. Agricultural well-being is the engine of growth for this sector too. The key to a farmer's prosperity—and the prosperity of the entire nation—is in transforming and rejuvenating Indian agriculture.

Not only is it a major segment of our economy, contributing almost a quarter of our GDP, it is, more significantly, also the provider of gainful employment and incomes to the maximum number of people. Overall, an enormous potential exists for the rapid growth of the rural economy on the basis of this country being endowed with abundant arable land, favourable seasonal conditions and shifting consumption pattern—driven by increasing income levels.

The impact of agricultural growth on farmer employment is apparent. It has been estimated that one incremental percentage growth in agriculture leads to an additional income generation of Rs 10,000 crore in the hands of the farmers, thereby increasing their disposable income and ultimately their purchasing power.

Owing to diverse and favourable agro-climatic conditions, India has a significant comparative advantage in agricultural production and the potential to be globally competitive by producing a wide variety of high-quality produce.

These advantages, if leveraged optimally, can translate into India becoming a leading food supplier to the world. Further, with a population of more than one billion, growing at about 1.6 per cent per annum and with favourable demographics, India is a large consumption hub for food products.

In empowered India, which is overall an empowered rural sector, we will be able to obliterate poverty if farm produce is better connected to markets. The persistence of poverty is a moral indictment of our achievements.

Participation and inclusion are central to our approach to poverty reduction. Co-operatives are an ideal instrument in such a strategy, and the country has long drawn on the strength of the movement. Meeting the challenges of globalisation requires strong local communities, strong local leadership and strong local solutions.

Co-operatives have proved to be a key organisational form in building new models to combat social exclusion and poverty, for example, through local development initiatives. Co-operative members learn from each other, innovate together, and by increasing control over livelihoods, build up the sense of dignity that the experience of poverty destroys.

To reduce rural poverty, we have to address the entire rural space— all of rural society and both the farm and non-farm aspects of the economy. While past approaches have identified most pieces of the puzzle, we now have to put them together in a way that attains this objective.

In addition to enhancing agricultural productivity, competitiveness, sustainability and fostering non-farm economic activity, the government's development priorities are now geared to accelerating poverty reduction in rural areas by improving social well-being and managing and mitigating risk and vulnerability of rural people.

Agriculture is facing a fundamental change. Human population growth, improved incomes and shifting patterns are increasing the demand for food and other agricultural products. At the same time, however, the natural resource base underpinning agricultural production is under threat, with growing threats to genetic diversity and the degradation of land and water resources.

Revolutionary advances in biological and information sciences offer great potential to address these resource constraints. However, making their benefits available to small-scale farmers is a major challenge. Urban consumers, both domestic and international, are increasingly driving the transformation process by demanding diversified, high-quality and safe foods.

International trade is increasing rapidly in response to these demands, bringing with it a set of global governance treaties and regulator frameworks whose implementation requires local capacity. How to lever these shifts so that small and impoverished farmers reap the benefits is a major challenge.

The government has put agricultural growth back on top of the development agenda. But 'business as usual' will not suffice. The dynamic changes now influencing agricultural production, diversification and competitiveness require a thorough re-analysis to develop better ways to support tomorrow's agriculture.

Most high-potential agricultural areas of our country have now reached the limits of land and water resources that can be exploited. The closing of that land frontier—not to mention the acute water scarcity in many areas, diminishing returns and negative environmental effects from high levels of external inputs—means that future growth in these areas will largely depend on the substitution of inputs with knowledge.

This means that future agricultural growth in these areas will be increasingly knowledge based and the growth in total factor productivity will now need to be the major source of growth in the coming decades.

While the Tenth Plan assumed that agricultural production would grow at the rate of 4.0 per cent, in the first three years of the plan, the achievement is just 1.5 per cent of growth.

It is to reverse this situation that the government of India has laid its priority to give a 'New Deal to Rural India'. This envisages reversing the declining trend in investment in agriculture, stepping up credit flow to farmers; increasing public investment in irrigation and wasteland development; increasing funds for agricultural research and extension; creating a 'single market' for agricultural produce; investing in rural electrification; investing in rural roads; setting up future commodities markets and insuring against risks which are inevitable in an increasingly commercialised agrarian economy.

A comprehensive programme for rural infrastructure development has been initiated under the umbrella of 'Bharat Nirman'. This is a programme for time-bound investment in rural housing, rural roads, rural water supply, rural electrification and rural connectivity.

In the area of agricultural diversification, a National Horticulture Mission has been launched which will ensure an end-to-end approach having backward and forward linkages covering research, production, post-harvest management processing and marketing, under one umbrella, in an integrated manner.

In terms of post-harvest technology, programmes have been approved for strengthening marketing infrastructure like cold chains and godowns. A new Seeds Bill is under consideration in parliament. Seed production also happens to be a weak link in the chain of increasing production.

An 'Integrated Food Law' is being formulated to bring convergence in the laws dealing with food, to promote the food processing industry in the country. The Essential Commodities Act has been liberalised in order to remove all restrictions on the movement, storage and marketing of agricultural commodities.

The Forward Contract (Regulation) Act has been amended to allow future trading in important agricultural commodities. However, there are still several barriers in the transport, taxation and retail trade sectors which need to be removed to achieve a single common market for the country.

Expansion of warehousing services in rural areas and the stepping up of marketing credit to farmers have been identified as other important areas of reform in the agriculture sector. Legislation is now being formulated for the introduction of a negotiable warehouse receipt system in the country which will result in large benefits from increased liquidity in rural areas, lower costs of financing, shorter and more efficient supply chains and enhanced rewards for grading the quality of commodities, development of other productivity–enhancing agricultural services and better price risk management.

It will also improve and standardise existing warehousing facilities for the agriculture commodities in the country and will also enable the banks to improve the quality of their lending services to the agricultural sector. All these developments will in turn result in higher returns to the farmers and better services to the consumers.

With these developments, commodity exchanges could be effectively linked to rural godowns and markets as an alternative marketing structure for discovery of futures prices and to cover price risk.

E-linking of spot markets with commodity exchanges will go a long way towards bringing single-window solutions for the farmers comprising warehousing, credit, insurance and marketing based on the dissemination of price signals to the farmers at the time of sowing itself. These initiatives would achieve a nation-wide integration of agricultural markets and enhance the competitiveness of farmers in national and global markets.

The government is committed to reforms in agriculture which will facilitate large-scale private investment in every step of the value chain. The belief is that both the market and the State have an important role to play in agriculture.

Bringing in the private sector—both as a competitor and as complementary to the public sector—adds greater strength and value for money. Both must work complementarily to benefit the farmers and their families and at the same time, make business sense.

We have a two-pronged agenda—pushing through the specific enabling reforms in agriculture, and working with state governments to convince them to implement relevant reforms at the earliest. Several states stand convinced and are well on the path of doing so, while others too will have to follow suit.

The Indian agriculture sector has the potential to transform India into the leading agro economy of the world. However, a holistic and integrated approach is required to achieve a sustainable development of the sector. A paradigm shift is required in the outlook to agriculture production, to marketing orientation, and from a quantity to quality focus.

A scientific and innovative agricultural approach to agriculture will enable us to compete globally in cost and quality with respect to global benchmarking and our core competitive strengths in various agriculture products.

SACHIN PILOT
CONGRESS MP, LOK SABHA

Every Region, Every Religion Has a Stake

The largest democracy, land of spirituality, one-sixth of humanity, cricket crazy, IT superpower: India is described in many different ways. The challenge lies not in describing India but in understanding it.

For those of us who believe that this country will reach greater heights and join the league of top nations, we must also understand the inherent contradictions we possess and the many challenges that lie ahead.

As India turns 58, we can take pride in how we have embraced and preserved our democratic values but at the same time also be aware that we can't afford to abuse our liberty and freedom. We have become self-sufficient and self-reliant in many areas but we need to match global standards if we are to take on a leadership role.

We have flourishing metros and millions in our middle class but we need to bridge the rich-poor, urban-rural divide. We have more mobile phones than landline connections but there are millions that are yet to make their first phone call. We are one of the world's oldest civilisations with one of the world's youngest populations. We have twenty official languages and yet a third of the country cannot read or write. Six Indian women have won Miss Universe/Miss World titles in the last 10 years and yet female infanticide is endemic. We consume a fifth of the world's total gold output and our share of world trade is less than 1 per cent.

However, India can leapfrog to the league of developed nations. That is possible because we have the workforce, we have the technology, we have the potential, we have a fantastic knowledge base and a talent pool, and most importantly, we have the spirit.

I also believe that when we talk of growth, development, prosperity and progress, we need to take every single Indian along with us. Make every section of our society, every region and every religion a stakeholder in our collective future. Empowerment has to be both economic and social.

We still have in our country people who live in constant fear of almost everything; the need is to be able to break the shackles around our fellow citizens. In a new India, we ought to have a more tolerant society. A social set-up that respects every race, culture, religion and community. We cannot afford to deviate from the path of secularism and pluralism. Not because it's stated in our Constitution or because our elders have mandated it, but because it is the need of the nation.

No country can have economic progress if there is social unrest and communal tension. We cannot have sustained growth if we are plagued by communal rioting. Religious or racial superiority has to take a backseat to economic prosperity. And this can be achieved only if we accept social equality and religious harmony as imperatives for our nation-building.

The political leadership of a country, to a large extent, is responsible for the direction a country is headed. India is almost as passionate about politics as it is about cricket!

And as much as we may deny it, the fact is that politics and politicians find themselves as topics of discussion in the sitting rooms of our cities, at the tea stalls of our towns and on the verandahs of our villages. Therefore, as politicians, we have a great responsibility to discharge and our endeavours ought to be in making the system more transparent, more accountable and more delivery-oriented.

VASUNDHARA RAJE
CHIEF MINISTER, RAJASTHAN

Bridge the Inequities, Leverage Our Strengths

American statesman Robert Green Ingersoll said, 'There is something wrong in a government where they who do the most have the least. There is something wrong when honesty wears a rag and rascality a robe; when the loving, the tender, eat a crust, while the infamous sit at banquets.' Strong words, but true, more so in the Indian context. India empowered to me is an India which is free from hunger, an India where gender is not a burden, an India where there are sustainable livelihoods for all. In short, India empowered is a prosperous India.

Prosperity, to the average man, indicates a better quality of life. Better than others, better than yesterday. This can be ensured by allowing better access to resources and opportunities. These resources and opportunities include access to basic amenities like safe drinking water, proper education, healthcare and a social security net. India is still infamous for its pathetic primary education system vis-a-vis the IIMs and the IITs. It is gaps like these that have to be bridged to ensure prosperity.

Henry George, in 1879 in his seminal work *Progress and Poverty*, said, 'So long as all the increased wealth which modern progress brings goes but to build up great fortunes, to increase luxury and make sharper the contrast between the House of Have and the House of Want, progress is not real and cannot be permanent'.

To bridge these inequities, it is important we leverage our strengths and garner our resources and use them optimally. Sustainable use of resources calls for perceptive planning. It is also essential that political parties and various pressure groups rise above petty differences and agree on priorities in sustainable development. Irrespective of affiliation and ideology, I believe there can be a commonality in development goals.

Sustainability of a development initiative is determined by the carrying capacity of the resource base. Be it a forest, a road, a school, it is vital that the pressure on the resource is not allowed to cross the critical threshold. This can be possible only by diverting the increasing demand onto alternatives. So we will need new schools, more roads and need to plant more trees. In case of natural resources, the off-take has to be in sync with the input into the base. It makes good business sense not to eat into the capital.

The next important issue in prosperity is diversification of income sources and tapping the inherent capabilities of 'groups'. Indeed, from a purely agrarian economy, India has transformed, thanks to the manufacturing and services sectors. Yet, there exists a sharp rural-urban divide. This stems from the differences in opportunities for various social strata. At the village, town and community level, it is important that diversity of opportunity be created and people be organised in 'groups'. It is the lack of equality which makes it imperative that the disadvantaged work in groups. This allows smarter utilisation of scarce resources. These groups may be self help groups, water users' committees, forest protection and management committees or any other. It is also a welcome sign that often these groups act as 'watchdogs' and perform admirably in the role of 'social conscience'.

In recent times, empowerment of grassroot institutions including the panchayati raj institutions has been much talked about. On paper, transfer of funds, functions and functionaries sounds good. Yet, such empowerment is of little use unless capacity building and extension precede it. There are too many micro-level social inequalities which need to be addressed, before these institutions become truly 'peoples' institutions.

Transfer of technology to the disadvantaged is an essential task in the quest for prosperity. Technology today permits optimum usage of resources. This is why the 'Village Knowledge Centres' are important. This is exactly why we want to popularise drips and sprinklers in Rajasthan. Every empowered country knows that water is a fundamental necessity and finds ways of providing it.

Worldwide, the adage 'user pays' is the 'in' thing. The common man is supposed to pay for water, for roads, for conservancy and even policing. Yet, more often than not, political compulsions prevent us from instituting user charges. All over the country, electricity companies are in the red, urban bodies are bankrupt. Are these symptoms of prosperity?

On the other hand, it is time the citizen is not made to pay for inefficiency. The citizen pays tax. He has the right to see his money used properly and not in profligacy or to line the pockets of the dishonest. Our citizens are what make India a successful democracy. They have the right to proper governance. The citizen has the right to know how he is being governed, how 'his money' is being spent. It is imperative that the common man walks into the collectorate, the police station, the municipal office or the bank for his legitimate needs and grievance, without trepidation.

One of the more redeeming features of the country's progress is the enhanced levels of private initiative in development. Today the country is full of examples of successful private-public partnerships. Corporate social responsibility is taken seriously. This is something that requires more institutionalised support. Similarly, non-governmental or voluntary initiatives in development management are also something to be supported. The voluntary sector is an important limb of governance. Good initiatives of theirs need to be replicated. With their support, an active social capital of communities can be developed. This is the primary step in empowering communities.

India is a federation of states. Maximum resource mobilisation is by the Centre while service delivery is through the states. There is a pressing need to cater to requirements and performance. Terrain, demography and climate will have to be factored in while deciding allocations. Provisions will have to be made in scheme guidelines keeping in mind micro-conditions. The floods of Assam and the drought in Rajasthan will have to be catered to individually. Area development, resource base management and developing the human capital are of equal importance on the path to prosperity.

While it is fashionable to wax eloquent about India's 'Unity in Diversity', we usually tend not to discuss the vast inequality in resource distribution. A lot of the country's inequalities have their roots in this resource variation. Every year, eastern India reels under the fury of floods while we in Rajasthan stare at cloudless skies. To our north are neighbours gifted with perennial rivers while we are at the mercy of their whims and fancies. No, India is not equal. The India of tomorrow cannot afford this inequality, such partisan approaches to development.

Our food stocks are high and we lead the world in cutting edge IT. Rich in mineral resources, a mega-biodiversity, human resources, we have it all. Yet we are part of the third world. We as a nation are unable to attain our true potential because poverty levels are still very high, in spite of substantial investments in poverty-alleviation schemes. Social inequities are still commonplace and the quality of basic health care and education leaves much to be desired. As long as we do not attend to the basic malaise, i.e. quality healthcare and proper education for all, development in this country will be restricted to a few urban centres.

Without substantial improvement in the status of education and health care and removal of poverty, the growth of the country cannot be ensured. At the same time, for growth, it is essential that a minimum infrastructure be in place. Being bashful while talking about China will not help. We too need to identify 'nodes' and focus infrastructure and radially connect these nodes. This is not an easy task. This is not, however an impossible task either. As it is said, if we have the will, we will find a way.

In recent times 'growth mediated' development has been a buzz-word in development management. Indeed, economic growth allows resource generation. These resources permit increased public spending in social services. Yet, it would be incorrect to expect automatic removal of deprivation and impoverishment just because of economic growth. Increased income to the poor is only a part of the exercise. It is even more important to attend to those 'unfreedoms'—a term used by Professor Amartya Sen while pointing out that preventable diseases are prevalent, illiteracy is unceasing, needless hunger and premature mortality does exist, as does social exclusion, and economic insecurity.

Professor Sen has opined, '. . . the ability of the poor to participate in economic growth depends on a variety of enabling social conditions. It is hard to participate in the expansionary process of the market mechanism (especially in a world of globalised trade) if one is illiterate and unschooled, or if one is bothered by under-nourishment and ill health, or if social barriers (such as discrimination related to race or gender) excludes substantial parts of humanity from fair economic participation. Similarly, if one has no capital (not even a tiny plot of land in the absence of land reform), and no access to micro-credit (without the security of collateral ownership), it is not easy for a person to show much economic enterprise in the market economy.'

How do we empower ourselves if we do not factor in these basics? India is what the states make it. If states do poorly, so does the country. Except for islands like Kerala and Tamil Nadu, the rest of India needs to do a lot more in achieving proper levels in terms of human development indices. Indeed, the development agenda of India is much larger and complex than say the Millennium Development Goals (MDGs). India, like any other country has to follow its own development agenda most suited for its peoples' aspirations and its resources. However, no party or group would argue that the MDGs are unachievable or untouchable.

Just as the nation needs its own development agenda, the states too have their own requirements. Rajasthan with 10 per cent of the country's landmass is the largest of states. In many ways, Rajasthan typifies all that is lacking in empowering the people in its truest sense. A part of this is its historical burden. The rest is due to apathy in policy making in the recent past. In a struggle as epic as its timeless history, Rajasthan is struggling to get out of poverty, malnutrition and severe gender inequity. Rajasthan is struggling to empower its masses.

Quite often the state's development efforts face a roadblock in the form of acute recurrent drought. Drought is a calamity which is not dramatic like a cyclone, an earthquake or a tsunami. Yet it eats into the very vitals of a states' economy. The government has little option but to divert scarce resources meant for development to provide relief. Would it be that illogical to ask for a bit more concern about the states' requirements—from the Centre and from neighbours? I was in Bangalore in February 2005 and at the behest of Dr Kasturirangan, saw for myself the activities of the 'Akshay Patra Trust'. What I saw was a modern clean and hygienic kitchen where a nourishing hot meal is cooked for thousands of school children from poor families and served to them at their schools. I visited a few of the schools. I saw healthy, intelligent and smart children who did not hesitate to quiz me in English on the largest bird in the world and what 'STF' stood for. These children were from the poorest strata of the city.

On my request, the 'Akshay Patra' has started operations in Jaipur city. They are feeding 25,000 children in Jaipur. Not only this, they have also started decentralised kitchens in Baran, a backward district where a primitive tribe called Sahariya reside. There they are feeding over 5,000 children and mothers in thirty-six villages. Not only this, there are a number of corporate social initiatives like the one by Havells India who are using their factory kitchen to cook and supply meals to 2,000 children in schools near the industrial area. This is what 'hope' is all about.

The challenge is big. We have thirty-two districts and over a crore of children. We are looking for ways and means to involve donors, business houses and self-help groups to take over this programme totally and deliver a mid-day meal in all schools in the way it should be done. A healthy child is an attentive child. Similarly, it is essential that the pre-school child (age group 3-6 years) too gets the benefit of a hot cooked meal. A proper mid-may meal goes a long way in ensuring 'nutrition security' and not just food security.

In tribal areas, where populations are always susceptible to the vagaries of climate, the food security issue crops up again and again. In the 21st century, residents of Kalahandi, Purulia and Baran should be as secure as residents of Jaipur and Bangalore. We have emulated Madhya Pradesh and are distributing a kilogram of iodised salt each month to all tribal families. A small intervention like this can counter iodine deficiency and its fallout rather easily.

Benjamin Disraeli had correctly observed that 'the health of the people is really the foundation upon which all happiness and all their powers as a state depend'. In matters of health care, issues that frequently crop up include shortage of resources and manpower and regional inequities in access and outreach. As urbanisation progresses, curative services favour the non-poor.

It has long been debated as to why public health programmes have low levels of efficiency, effectiveness and accountability. In my opinion, firstly it is because of the lack of evolution in the skill-sets of healthcare managers. Secondly, there is a lack of ownership of public health programmes by communities. The third reason is the lack of synergy. In government systems, most people like to function in isolation. This typically leads to limited synergy between sanitation, hygiene, nutrition and drinking water issues. The entire problem is compounded by stark bureaucratic insensitivity. Yet, in a welfare state, it remains the responsibility of governments to extend a minimum level of healthcare at affordable prices. It is a fact that in rural India, a poor family is debt-ridden for life if a family member is hospitalised for a life-threatening ailment. Hospital expenses alone ensure families stay below the poverty line.

Health insurance goes a long way in providing security to a poor family. Dr Devi Shetty's Yashashwani scheme paved the way for rural health insurance. We in Rajasthan are in the process of insuring the families of 2.5 lakh dairy co-operative members as a pilot project. A debilitating disease should not be allowed to reduce a poor family to penury.

An evolved society is typified by gender justice. Gender justice is about ameliorating conditions regarding position of men and women in society—where there are differences in opportunities, roles and situations between women and men, particularly differences in access to power and control as well as economic issues. These differences are influenced by factors like unequal access to and control over resources and property, inequity in education and training, employment, decision-making; unequal access to and control over benefits that are generated from resources or development interventions; gender division of labour within families and communities.

Historically, under the garb of socio-cultural and religious strictures, women have not been treated fairly, leave aside equally. Human rights are a matter of equality. Women and men are equal; therefore, they have equal human rights. These rights include the right of choice and security in marriage; the right to land, property and inheritance; reproductive rights; the right to education and employment; the right to their individual identities; and the right to freedom from violence. The social and economic structures and conditions that disqualify women from getting the same treatment, advantages or privileges as men, even though they have equal rights to these, are issues of equity. These issues require urgent attention.

As a citizen of 21st century India, the India of Sania Mirza, Kalpana Chawla and Kiran Mazumdar Shaw, I hang my head in shame when I hear about conscious female foeticide. Is the girl child still so unwelcome? The Rajya Sabha has just passed an amendment to the Hindu Succession Act ending decades of discrimination between men and women in matters of inheritance. Women will now become equal shareholders in family property. But the task is far from done. There is a need to revisit the gender discriminatory provisions in the various personal laws of communities in this country. After 58 years of independence, a group of clerics issue a 'fatwa' that women of a particular community are not to participate in a democratic process! True empowerment is still far away.

Not many of us spare a thought to the niche requirements of the fairer sex. Lack of toilets and drinking water in schools is a major reason as to why girls drop out more than boys. Some of our initiatives are directed at these necessities. We are providing proper drinking water and toilet facilities in schools as this has a direct correlation with retention of the girl child. The tribal girl often has to travel long distances to school. We decided to give all school-going tribal girls of classes IX to XII bicycles to enable them easier access to education.

In a welfare state, development cannot be directed by market forces alone. Ours is a pluralistic society and allowances and provisions have to be made for the disadvantaged. We need to have clear policies for empowerment of women. Organising women to be economically productive citizens is both a challenge and a fulfillment. There are unique reproductive and child health requirements without attending to which emancipation of women shall remain a dream. I have already talked about the retention of the girl child in school. Similarly, the adolescent girl has special nutritional requirements as has the pregnant woman and the lactating mother. This is why we are appointing over 25,000 extra workers called 'SAHIYOGINIs' in anganwadi centres so that doorstep services can be provided. The departments of health and woman and child development are co-operating to have, on a fixed day, a mother and child health and nutrition day at each anganwadi centre; to help in post-natal care and immunisation. Indeed, these are small steps, but with a potential that defies computation when it comes to empowerment.

To reduce the gaps between the 'haves' and the 'have nots', positive discrimination in favour of vulnerable segments is important in order to create a level playing field. The girl child and the tribal boy both need to be supported so that they can compete as equals with the urban sophisticate. This might not make good business sense, but it does make better social and, if I may add, good political sense.

There are no short-cuts to success. Success is a journey we need to traverse together. It is essential that formally or informally a national agenda for development is decided upon. The country cannot afford quarrels in development. The requirements are real and the goal of prosperity is common. With limited immediate resources, prioritising interventions is vital. In the road to development, every partner has to live up to its share—both duties and responsibilities. It is important to realise that programme quality has a greater bearing on outcomes and not the pace.

To sum up, good governance is a must. My India of tomorrow is where there is equality of opportunity for all. Where performance is rewarded and the disadvantaged are cared for. In my India, one's caste, creed, sex or religion will not put him or her at a disadvantage. My India of tomorrow is where men and women are really equal. In an empowered India, the states are stronger—leading to a stronger, better India. My vision for an empowered India is real. I am confident of the future. All it needs is to start believing.

N. RAM
EDITOR-IN-CHIEF, THE *HINDU*

The Power of the Fourth Estate

If you asked professional journalists in most countries what the purpose of journalism was, the most likely answer would be: to empower citizens with the information, analysis, and insights necessary to be 'free and self-governing' (as a soul-searching exercise by a Committee of Concerned Journalists in the United States discovered a few years ago, to no one's particular surprise).

This, at any rate, is journalism's 'high ground' stance. Unfortunately, in many developed countries, 'mature media markets', the public doesn't buy this. In the United States, for example, the public perception of media power and its use in recent decades has been largely negative, as evidenced by the findings of a series of public opinion surveys. There have been many efforts to overcome the institutional deficits, including, most recently, the Journalism Credibility Project of the American Society of Newspaper Editors.

Fortunately, in India, the public's perception of media power and its use seems to be a lot less negative, although this statement is based on an insider's impressions and is not backed up by any survey data. There are two major media traditions in India, the older tradition of a diverse, pluralistic, and relatively independent press; and the younger tradition of the manipulated and misused broadcast media, state-controlled radio and television. However, it can be seen that the two established media traditions are no longer what they were widely recognised to be for most of the 20th century.

The Indian press is still widely recognised as the most pluralistic, the least inhibited and the most assertive and independent in all the less-developed world. In terms of number of newspapers and circulation, India is among the top four performers in the world. In fact, the world newspaper survey, '2005 World Press Trends,' unveiled by the World Association of Newspapers at its Seoul Congress in May 2005, spotlights India, at 78.80 million copies daily, as the country with the world's second-ranking daily newspaper circulation (after China, and ahead of Japan, the United States and Germany).

According to the National Readership Survey (NRS 2005), there are an estimated 170 million readers of daily newspapers and an estimated 200 million readers of all publications across India. A heartening feature of the media landscape is the rising profile of 'rural' readers who constitute 48 per cent of all daily newspaper readers.

This is in striking contrast to the situation of two decades ago. However, women and, unsurprisingly, the most oppressed sections of society continue to be severely under-represented in the ranks of daily newspaper readers in the country. There are about 500 million adults who do not read any daily newspaper. Interestingly, about 314 million literate, or neo-literate adults are not newspaper readers at this stage of social development, which suggests there is plenty of space for print media growth in the near term.

Despite its late start, television has taken off and how. It has emerged as the premier mass medium and is well placed to widen the dispersion gap between itself and the other media and also to close the gap with the press with respect to advertising revenue and financial clout. Terrestrial television is exclusively Doordarshan; satellite television, on the other hand, is largely non-Doordarshan.

NRS 2005 estimated the reach of television across India to be 108 million homes and 453 million viewers; within this, cable and satellite television had an impressive reach of 61 million homes and 206 million viewers. The survey also underlined what has been known for some time: television is way ahead and the principal source of information and entertainment for the millions exposed to mass media.

Satellite television has certainly changed the nature of the media ball game in south Asia. According to the findings of a study by David Page and William Crawley, it has made 'a huge difference to the choice of viewing available even in small towns, tremendously increased viewing options, opening windows to worlds which were inaccessible before except to the well-to-do, and provoking a lively and often heated debate about the implications for nations, communities and cultures.'

However, most critical observers would qualify this by saying that while cable and satellite have tremendously increased viewing options, they have, with certain splendid exceptions, failed to offer a better and richer choice of television content. They have promoted increasing fragmentation of the television audience. They have raised serious concerns about purpose, orientation, taste, and decency.

While offering some worthwhile and occasionally excellent news, feature, sports, educational, and entertainment programming, they contribute to the 'dumbing down' that television, when it goes for the least common denominator, is adept at doing. A negative development on the media scene is the apparent decline of radio, once considered the mass medium with the greatest potential to reach every section of the population at an unmatchable cost advantage.

According to NRS 2005, radio reaches only 23.10 per cent of the adult population (the proportion is the same for rural and urban India) compared with a much better population coverage in the 1980s. The good news is that the following for FM radio seems impressively on the rise, with the 96.8 million FM listeners representing a 100 per cent increase over 2002.

There can be no doubt that web-based or online media—defined as 'digital, interactive, multimedia'—have made a qualitative difference to the Indian media landscape, and especially to the practice of journalism. In 2005, virtually all Indian newspapers and broadcast organisations of significance had an online presence. However, for a complexity of reasons, the 'new media' in India have not become truly mass.

NRS 2005 has estimated that the country has 11 million internet users (compared with six million in 2002). Even assuming that the NRS findings on internet use are underestimates and industry estimates are more realistic, the current ballpark figure cannot be higher than 20 million, which is hardly significant in relation to the country's population base. In my view, which may reflect an insider's professional bias to an extent, India's broadcast and web-based media have a long way to go before they can come on the same page as the press—with respect to empowering India.

Even in the pre-Independence era, the press learned to act very much like a player in the major league political and socio-economic arena, despite its well-known limitations in terms of reach in society, financial viability, professional training, and entrepreneurial and management capabilities.

The First Press Commission noted that in 1953, the circulation of dailies per 1,000 in the population (the internationally accepted indicator of social diffusion of the press in various nation states or languages) was 5.4 against the backdrop of an all-India literacy level of 16.4 per cent.

Yet, at least for the whole history of the nationalist press (which can be said to have begun with the founding of the *Amrita Bazaar Patrika* in 1868) and possibly for longer than that, print journalism has been contributing to the empowerment of India in some significant measure.

From a statistically insignificant pre-Independence base, India's daily newspaper circulation climbed to 3.15 million in 1957 and 5.11 million in 1962. It would take the press three decades after the transfer of power to cross the 10 million mark. It would take 32 years of independence for the total circulation of Hindi daily newspapers to finally overtake the total circulation of English language dailies in India.

From the early 1980s, the upswing in circulation and readership has been quite spectacular (despite certain recessionary phases). Yet, while the absolute numbers are enormous, the social reach of the Indian press must be characterised as underdeveloped—about 60 copies of daily newspapers per 1,000 in the population, which compares very poorly with the social diffusion of the press in all developed, and also many developing, countries.

There is also the phenomenon of uneven development. This means, among other things, vastly uneven dispersion among regions and states, between urban and rural India, between men and women and among social classes.

That the strengths of the press in contemporary India are primarily the strengths of history is beyond serious dispute.

These advantages have largely been shaped by historical experience and, in particular, by the association of newspapers with the freedom struggle as well as with movements for social emancipation, reform, and amelioration.

The long struggle for national emancipation; controversies and battles over ideas, social reform, radical and revolutionary aspirations and movements; compromising as well as fighting tendencies; and the long-term competition between self-serving and public service visions of journalism—have all found reflection in the character and performance of the Indian press over the long term.

However, there are plenty of indications that while the press, television, and radio have become very big players in the political, socio-economic, and cultural arenas, the core values of journalism in all the media streams have come under pressure and even threat from various sides.

Confusion reigns over the functions and roles of journalism and the media vis-a-vis the market and society. Increasing concentration of ownership in some sectors of the Indian media; higher levels of manipulation of news, analysis and public affairs information to suit the owners' financial and political interests; unmistakable tendencies of tabloidization and dumbing down; the downgrading and devaluing of editorial functions and content in some leading newspapers and broadcast organisations; the growing professional willingness to tailor news and the editorial product to subserve advertising and marketing goals set by owners and senior management personnel; Murdoch-style price wars and aggressive practices in the home bases of competitors raising fears about media monopoly and rampant corruption are deeply worrying tendencies.

Journalism in India seems to be on the cusp of a transformation that is hard to comprehend by those caught up in it. The key question that needs asking now more than ever before is: do our news media contribute, in substantial measure, to empowering India—or are they interested mainly in empowering and enriching themselves? Prime Minister Manmohan Singh implied this question in his Ramnath Goenka birth centenary address when he asked: 'What kind of media does India need and deserve? Should the market define the media or the media define the larger market of ideas, values, goals, and information needs both for the classes and the masses? ...What should our agenda be? . . . Have we no larger mission in hand?'

These questions challenging the purpose, functions, and roles of journalism were raised in the context of a 'new awakening in this vast, plural society of over a billion people,' an awakening heralded by 'restlessness and ferment at the grassroots.' (We need not concern ourselves here with the question of whether Dr Singh's government has pursued, in any way distinguishable from previous regimes, a mission and an agenda of 'nation building, caring for the underprivileged, seeking better governance, making ourselves a more humane, prosperous, creative, free and liberal society,' as the prime minister implied in that lofty speech of August 2004.)

To figure out whether India's news media—or at least a critical mass within every stream—can contribute soundly and progressively to empowering India, a debate focusing on the functions or roles of the news media as well as the guiding principles of journalism, becomes a professional and intellectual priority.

ANBUMANI RAMADOSS
UNION MINISTER FOR HEALTH AND FAMILY WELFARE

Good Health for All

India has lived in its past glory for long, now is the time to look towards the future. Endowed with ancient glory, rich history and a vibrant culture, India need not be dependent on the west for its day-to-day activity in terms of innovation and inventions.

It is time we stop talking about mythology and talk about technology.

India made a tryst with destiny in 1947 to usher in a prosperous and peaceful nation. We made a solemn pledge to empower India politically, economically, socially and culturally so that we could banish the traditional ills.

Politically, we have empowered Indians with voting and fundamental rights by ensuring 'one person one vote'. Today, India has emerged as the largest and most populous democracy in the world with a democratic parliamentary system. The three pillars of democracy, namely legislature, executive and judiciary, have been adequately empowered to ensure national security, national integration, social harmony, secular fabric and integrated development to promote people's welfare.

But India still has a long way to go to be empowered. India can be empowered only when its average woman is empowered. Until 75 years ago, she was not allowed to vote, until 50 years ago she was not allowed to go to school, until 25 years ago she was not allowed to work. Now it is all changing. Today women have started competing with men but still have a lot of catching upto do. India will be empowered only when all women are educated and employed.

On the economic front, India has now matured into one of the fastest growing economies in the world. But for me, the country can safely be divided into two Indias—the rich and poor India. While the rich comprise just 10 per cent, 90 per cent are poor and the gap is widening.

We seemed to have created islands of wealth in an ocean of poverty, generated employment in the midst of a globalised development framework. Dualism—prosperity in one sector and pauperism in other sectors—has become the order of empowerment. In the midst of a burgeoning population, India has created a scenario of writing on the sands and having it constantly washed away by the waters.

India's progress in science and technology has been phenomenal as India is the third largest reservoir of scientific and technical manpower in the world. The IT explosion, the surge in biotechnology, pharmaceuticals and the agricultural revolution has put India on the global map.

While the health status of the nation has improved, we are yet to reach our cherished goal of health for all. While on the one hand, India has become a medical destination and there is reverse brain drain in the health sector, human development indices are still below acceptable marks—especially infant and maternal mortality. Indian has been ranked 127th out of 180 countries in Human Development Indices for three consecutive years by UNDP. The country has also not shown expected results as far as population stabilisation is concerned.

The country can again be divided into two Indias if we consider the development indicators in the north and south. If south India had been an independent country, it would have been a developed country way back. It is not that I am trying to differentiate or discriminate between the two parts, but the poor development indicators in north India are a crude reality, in spite of the fact that maximum policy makers were from the north. Indicators in north-east are even worse.

Gandhi has said that India lives in its villages. Over 73 per cent of India's population still lives in the rural areas and they have access to only 25 per cent of the health care facilities. The 25 per cent who live in towns and cities have 75 per cent health care access.

To rectify the deficiency, the government has launched the National Rural Health Mission for the entire country focussing on eighteen states in the north and north-east. The aim is to bring down infant mortality, maternal mortality and stabilise population, provide nutrition, sanitation and drinking water, and ensure quality health care for even the last person living in the last village. This Rural Health Mission is the biggest programme in the health sector post-Independence and the results will be visible in the next three years.

Another factor which is worrying is that the process of empowerment has not yet become meaningful to people who are craving for empowerment. A major chunk of Indians from scheduled castes, scheduled tribes, other backward classes and minorities still remain marginalised. This neglect is unfortunate.

The growing economy can bear fruits only if it is able to pull up the development indices. The UPA government is trying to improve these indicators with focus on social policies. The government's priority areas are health, education and agriculture. All these years, people in Delhi have been thinking that India lives 60 km around Delhi. Now because of coalition politics and regional participation, policies and performances are being distributed equally.

I feel India can be empowered only when it provides education, employment, housing, food, health care, clean drinking water and sanitation for all its citizens. Providing these basic facilities to a sixth of the world's population living on 2.4 per cent of the world's land is a highly challenging task. A government, tries its best to fulfill these basic demands.

I feel the basis of all problems in the country, whether it is education, health sector, infrastructure, agriculture etc. is the population explosion.

On a visit to South Korea, I found that the country can compete with Europe and America as far as its development is concerned. Forty years ago, people in the country were standing in a queue for one square meal and today the situation has been totally reversed. The change has been brought about because of the concept of ownership about the country among the people and not the individual. There, people would talk about 'our country', where as we in India are still talking about 'I', not 'us'.

I feel India has a long way to go to be empowered but it is on the right path. India can be empowered when there is participation by the community, when there is ownership that it is 'my country' rather than 'I', when people do not depend on the government for everything, when people abide by all laws and there is no problem in enforcing them, when policy makers and the public work towards building a modern and self-reliant India.

SYED KALBE SADIQ
VICE-CHAIRMAN, ALL INDIA MUSLIM PERSONAL LAW BOARD

Not Muslim Indians But Indian Muslims

By sheer strength of their numbers, Muslims constitute the second largest segment of the country's population. But even after 58 years of independence, they have remained one of the most educationally backward communities. And for this, I don't blame anyone else. The fault lies within. It is the Muslim leadership which is responsible for the plight of their brethren.

Islam is a hundred per cent rational religion but over the years it has become a hundred per cent emotional religion and the change is due to lack of education. Getting emotional on the slightest pretext is no solution to problems which have bedeviled the community, we have to adopt a rational approach.

'*Kisi qaum ko doosri qaumein pada-likha nahin sakti*' (no community can be educated by other communities). The Muslims will have to open schools and colleges for the empowerment of the underprivileged amongst them. The country cannot progress with the Muslims remaining educationally backward—hundred per cent education is needed.

I am not in favour of job reservations for the Muslims, but yes, I want reservation for them in the academic field, free education up to a certain level and quality education. In Meerut, I happened to interact with a Jain leader who informed me that there was total literacy among the Jains which was due to the fact that the Jain community had its own schools and colleges. The Jain leader told me that educational empowerment was possible only because there were no pandits in the institutions. Unfortunately, the reverse is the case with the Muslims; while we have mullahs aplenty, schools and colleges are missing.

A lot has been said about madarsa education and the modernisation of curriculum. But it is indeed regrettable that knowledgeable persons are talking about baseless issues. Here too, the problem lies within. True, children have benefitted from madarsa education but installing a couple of computers in madarsas is not going to serve the purpose. There is no way out. Science and technology have to be accorded top priority for infusing change. While schools and colleges impart a scientific temper, madarsas teach students to become good human beings which, I must confess, is very difficult. Three qualities are imbued in Islam—intellect, knowledge/education and spiritualism.

The curriculum system in the madarsas should allow freedom of thought to students who would then be able to gain knowledge of religion and the world so that once they graduate from madarsas, they should become role models for Indians in spiritualism and humanity.

Having said that, I want Muslims to be given their rights as Indian citizens. They are not Muslim Indians but Indian Muslims. I was in Gujarat when violence broke out in February 2002. I was taken safely to the airport by a Hindu whom I did not know. Since good always emerges from evil, Gujarat has been been an eye-opener in several respects. True, Muslims bore the brunt of the violence but Gujarat has also weakened divisive forces, which manifested in the NDA losing power at the Centre. Indeed, had the Delhi bomb blasts occurred 10 years ago, Muslims would have been massacred. That there was no backlash was solely on account of the majority community becoming mature. Not only should we thank Allah, Muslims should join the mainstream. India cannot move ahead without the Muslims. They should understand that India is a boat and they are in it.

I am not aware how communal violence broke out in Mau as I was away in Africa. But in my address to the annual conference of Jamaat-i-Islami Hind in Azamgarh, I emphasised that those who were killed in Mau were human beings and efforts should be made to ensure there's no repetition of such brutality.

Nations have become big and communities have progressed because they have the luxury of complete freedom of thought, speech, religion and preaching, but no freedom of violence. Here, I would like to mention the US, notwithstanding the fact that I was deported from that country last year. I don't know why it happened. Contrary to what has been said about the US reaction in the aftermath of 9/11, when I reached America I was informed by Islamic centres that immediately after the terror attack, they received calls from the police telling them that they were US citizens and were not responsible for the tragedy. I was told that the churches came forward to offer church buildings to the Islamic centres if they were having difficulty in preaching. Instead of hounding Muslims, the American authorities tried to understand Islam and Islamic philosophy.

P.A. SANGMA
FORMER LOK SABHA SPEAKER

Youthful Promise of the North-east

I consider quality education as the greatest implement that can empower an individual as well as a society.

There are three basic areas that need to be strengthened. The first is social empowerment—quality education for all is a must. Millions of children are still deprived of the very access to basic education. We have not been able to create schools for them within their localities. Instead, we have created two types of education, one for the rich and one for the poor. How can we dream of achieving an empowered India with this kind of disparity in the most important input that shapes lives and builds character?

Next comes economic empowerment. We have not been able to come out of our slogan of poverty eradication. Poverty has crippled us. We must find ways to end this. And for that we need to go for a massive political empowerment programme. Women, for instance, are still struggling to get their share of the cake. We are still debating quota for women. Why not talk of equal share for women and men?

Political empowerment of women and weaker sections is a must. By this I do not mean reserved seats and quotas. Getting some people elected to parliament or state assemblies does not empower a society. They should have equal share in the business of governance.

Participation is the basic ingredient of a healthy democracy. People will have to participate in a big way. India will march forward in the right direction only when each and every citizen is socially and politically empowered. It is time we empower our entire population and motivate them towards a realisation of our president's vision of making India a developed nation by 2020. But for that, we will have to develop a sense of patriotism in every heart.

Today all of us say India belongs to us. But very few of us actually say that we also belong to this great country and give her our best. When I give India my best, I also give myself my best. For that we need to draw a clear roadmap, where strengthening our entire system, including our institutions, has to be the top priority.

I sometimes fear our system is fast eroding. There has been a decline in politics, governance, bureaucracy, intelligentsia everywhere. This trend has to be immediately arrested. Why are the best boys selected by UPSC opting out of IFS and IAS? Why do lesser number of boys want to become army officers? Why is the man on the street complaining that good people are not coming to politics? It is time we put the right people in the right places, be it the village primary school or the leader's post in the political party.

I would not say the people are bad. The people of our country have immense inner strength. I do not agree with those who say population is a big problem. Population is our asset which can be converted into strength. We must channelise human resources according to the inner potential of every individual. There is no lack of talent. The only tragedy is that we have failed to identify them.

And then, we have the best democracy in the world. Parliamentary democracy has been our biggest achievement since independence. Very few nations in the world have been able to successfully carry forward the flame of parliamentary democracy as we have done. In this respect, political parties have a major role to play.

Every political party, particularly the national parties, will have to take full responsibility of empowering the people. Good people will have to be attracted into politics. Every political party must incorporate a system of grooming future leaders. Every political party must practise inner-party democracy.

Being from the north-east, I must say a few words about my region too. There has been a two-way problem. While people in the rest of India have not tried to understand the north-east, the people in the region too have developed concepts based on past blunders.

The north-east will have to go all out to compete. Quotas and sops will not take the region anywhere. I am glad the younger generation understands this. The 'Look East' policy can change the very concept of development in the north-east. But before that, the people have to be empowered. The people of the north-east are also equally talented. But they must be given the right opportunity and a level playing field.

JYOTIRADITYA M. SCINDIA
CONGRESS MP, LOK SABHA

An Uncompromising Focus on Literacy

India would be truly empowered if all Indians acquire the ability to shape their own lives and also that of their nation. The Constitution of India does seek to empower all Indians by providing for equality of rights and opportunities. But this is only the first step, as the promise of the Constitution needs to be implemented and achieved collectively.

Over the last 50 years of our nation's brief history, we have travelled some distance towards ensuring equality of rights and opportunity to all our citizens. The one key achievement in this arduous journey has been the strengthening of democratic institutions in our country comprising the legislature, judiciary and the media. These now ensure the right to vote and free expression to all Indians. Over the years, the democratic process has percolated to the lower tier of our system, the panchayats.

However, the dream of a truly empowered India remains unfulfilled as discrimination remains. While we are blessed with a strong and autonomous Election Commission, there are parts of the country where criminalisation of politics continues to interfere with the right to vote and free expression. This is a challenge that we must confront with all our might and commitment and we must continue to strengthen democracy as it provides the basis for equal opportunity.

Political empowerment acquires true meaning only when accompanied by economic empowerment. Despite our numerous economic achievements, India remains home to the world's largest number of poor, numbering around 250 million. Rapid economic growth would have to be accompanied by targeted inventions such as Indira Gandhi's 'garibi hatao' and the latest Rural Employment Guarantee Scheme.

These have to be supplemented by an uncompromising focus on

ensuring that all Indians acquire literacy and the skills to partake of the benefits spread by economic growth and have access to affordable health facilities.

Even as governments at the Centre and states devise schemes to tackle poverty, employment, health, literacy etc., their implementation would remain tardy unless people become partners in their design and implementation.

India is a vast country and the needs of our people vary across regions and even across villages. Therefore, in each panchayat, participation of beneficiaries in the decision-making processes of development programmes is key to transparent and non-discriminatory implementation. This was the vision with which Rajiv Gandhi launched his model of panchayati raj. The result is that today in many villages, democratically elected bodies are deciding how education, drinking water supply, roads and health centres, water for irrigation should be managed and delivered to serve their communities.

This democratisation of development needs to be spread to all the 6,00,000 villages and thousands of cities of India. The roadmap is clear. Democracy is not good enough, nor is growth and development that does not include all. Democratisation of development is the only route to India's empowerment. This will enable all Indians to shape their own destinies and India would unleash our entire people's power to achieve the vision outlined by the founders of our republic.

P. SHANKAR
CENTRAL VIGILANCE COMMISSIONER

Make Corruption a Thing of the Past

India Corruption Study 2005, commissioned by Transparency International India, has brought out the sad and alarming fact that the common citizens of the country are being forced to pay a sum of Rs 20,168 crore annually to avail themselves of one or more of eleven selected public services in a year. And to think that we tend to dismiss this as petty corruption!

In the compilation of worldwide Corruption Perception Index by Transparency International, India again ranks in the low 80s. Every citizen of the country should feel ashamed of this as it hurts his sense of national pride and dignity as a citizen of a great country.

An empowered India to me, and to each one of us, is where the common citizen is able to get what he is entitled to without having to pay any bribe and without having to supplicate before an indifferent and corrupt bureaucracy. Without achieving this through a tangible and perceptible improvement in the quality of governance, all talk of an India occupying a high position in the comity of nations, as a strong economic power cannot but ring empty and hollow.

I do believe the situation is not beyond redemption or hope. The Central Vigilance Commission over the years has identified and suggested a number of simple measures which could achieve dramatic improvement in the current state of affairs. I am listing a few of the important measures below:

- Since the common man comes into contact mostly with public service organisations at the panchayat and state level, there is a need for making the state vigilance set-up independent and powerful. The guidelines set out by the Supreme Court in the Vineet Narain judgement need to be extended and made applicable to the states. This would include ensuring autonomy and independence of the state Anti-Corruption Bureau.

- Delay is the root cause of corruption. It is necessary to discourage delays on the part of officials in dealing with cases of public importance. The electronic file tracking system and regular publication of information on the processing of cases in departments and the time taken at various levels including the highest, will discourage such delays and make the public servants really responsible and accountable.

- Exercise of discretionary powers by public servants is another area to be checked. Discretion should be minimised, if not eliminated. All exercise of discretionary powers along with the public interest served by such exercise should be regularly put on the website of the organisations for all to see. This would deter arbitrary exercise of such power.

- Elimination of personal contact of the common citizens with bureaucracy has been found to be a simple and effective measure to improve the quality of service and eliminate harassment. E-governance is now recognized and accepted by governments at all levels. This should be extended to cover all areas of public service in a time-bound manner.

- Citizen's charters are invaluable in making public servants accountable but there is need for all citizen charters in existence to be redrafted with sharper focus on deliverables and also making them more customer-centric.

- Redressal of grievance is an area crying for improvement. There is need for appointment of empowered ombudsmen in all departments and organisations with significant public contact.

- The right to information is perhaps the most potent tool to eliminate corruption and improve governance. However, in order that the use of this right is not confined to matters of personal concern, there is need for NGOs to study each major government department and come up with guidelines for effective use of RTI in the larger public interest.

- Public procurement is perhaps the single largest source of corruption and leakage of public revenues. Procedures for purchases by government departments and public sector enterprises should be made more transparent and time-bound. Apart from publication of all tenders on the website along with downloading of tender forms, the tender results should also be made public within a reasonable period, say four weeks of the concluding day. Delays in deciding tenders should, without fail, attract vigilance investigation.

- Ministerial/departmental interference in the day-to-day functioning of the public sector enterprises needs to be checked. The recommendations of the study group headed by Arjun Sengupta require to be acted upon immediately. The PSUs should be totally left to the boards of directors for management and control. Such boards should be filled with competent professionals with expertise and men of integrity and credibility. Any talk of freeing the PSUs and banks from the purview of CAG or the CVC without such empowerment of the boards will only further stoke corruption and not achieve anything else.

- Action against public servants identified by the vigilance as responsible for specific misconduct needs to be severe and swift. Delays in taking action in vigilance matters should attract stringent penalties. The advice of the CVC in such matters should be binding on the disciplinary authority concerned and non-compliance should meet with the same kind of penalties as specified in the RTI Act.

- NGOs have a great role to play in making institutions like the CVC or the Information Commission really useful and effective in tackling the problems faced by the common man. In fact, they should serve as bridges between the citizens and public service institutions and replace the widely prevalent intermediaries.

I have confined myself to corruption in officialdom and deliberately omitted political corruption or corruption in the judiciary. It is true that the empowerment which we talk of cannot come about without corresponding improvements in these areas but I believe the electoral reforms proposed by the Central Election Commission and vigorously championed by NGOs like the Lok Satta will sooner or later bring about the required improvements. The 2004 elections certainly strengthened one's feeling of optimism.

The judiciary at the highest level has also shown its mind in dealing with the problem of corruption in the judicial services. Several state high courts have already started the exercise by showing the door to hundreds of corrupt judicial officials. My appeal to my erstwhile colleagues in the bureaucracy is, therefore, to do what we can to improve governance at our level and not plead helplessness and offer the excuse of corruption in the system as a whole.

Over the nearly 40 years of my public service, I have been fortunate to witness and be inspired by hundreds of dedicated colleagues who in their own humble way played according to the rules of the game and resisted all pressure from both within and outside the bureaucracy. I am sure there are still hundreds, if not thousands, of such public servants who along with the dedicated band of public-spirited NGOs will achieve the goal or dream of an India where standards of governance will be as high as anywhere in the world and where the common citizen gets value for the taxes he pays.

RAKESH SHARMA
THE FIRST INDIAN IN SPACE

Saare Jahan Se Achcha

Back in 1984, when I borrowed Allama Iqbal's immortal words 'Saare jahan se achcha' to describe how our beautiful country appears from space, Khushwant Singh wrote in his column, 'Perhaps, from those heights, he is unable to see Punjab burning'. Even though I am as Punjabi as he is, I did not join issue with him at that time but my response then would have been quite the same as it is today—a country is what we cause it to become.

If we are in the mess we are, it is not the country but we ourselves who are at fault. Our generations have a lot to answer for—both his and mine. However, at that point, while talking to the then prime minister, Indira Gandhi, I was truly proud of being the representative of one of the oldest and most diverse cultures on planet earth. I hold that opinion to this day.

The reason I am proud to be an Indian is pretty evident. There is no other country that has nurtured so many great minds. If we ascribe the Indian pantheon of gods to mythology, we still have to explain what it is about this country that provides the space for so many philosophies to co-exist and, indeed, influence the way we Indians live. We live our philosophies. The Buddha, Swami Vivekananda, Shirdi Sai Baba, Mahavir, Jiddu Krishnamurti, Mahatma Gandhi, Ramana Maharshi, Sathya Sai Baba . . . the list goes on; even Mother Teresa chose to stay on and weave her magic in our blessed land. What is with our country? We are special. Period.

We have given so much to the world. For the most part, the world has helped itself from our overfull coffers. They have taken untold wealth and, in recent times, our intellectual property. The developed world has made full use of our 'brain drain' in the mid-70s. It can be argued that Indian minds flourished and realised their potential in the entrepreneurial climate that was created by the west. The fact remains that Indian mind power did not generate wealth for India. And now that competition has increased, the west wants to work the same model but pay bottom rupee instead of top dollar to our—and I hate the expression—cyber coolies. They are moving their operations over here.

Whenever we sign mega deals nowadays, there are offsets which get bundled into the deal. We pay them huge amounts to get what we need but, in turn, they are required to give us more business so we can earn some of that expenditure back! Smart model. But what of the intellectual property that we paid out when our bright minds made all those technological gizmos for the developed world? Sure, their time was bought and they were monetarily compensated but, I believe, we need to put a bigger price on the sale of our intellect. We ought to have an offset in terms of a stake—a royalty if you will. Something that gets attached to the sale of knowledge and intellect that creates marketable value for the developed world.

Given our numbers and the volume of work we are doing in the knowledge domain, this arrangement will generate the kind of wealth that will stabilise the revenue streams for our people. So, why should anybody change the rules—it is, after all, a free market and if we do not work as per the existing model, someone else in Brazil or China might. They might and, therefore, it is necessary for Indian venture capitalists settled abroad as well as Indian corporate houses to support this model.

Philosophical pursuit has flourished only when there is a relative freedom from want. If we can get compensated for our intellectual input, we will be the richest nation on this earth. I am keen we get there because my vision for India is that our country can be the rallying point for a new world order. I believe that only we shall be able to discharge this role effectively because of who we are.

Our background, our rich and diverse culture is inclusive, not acquisitive. We need to go down this route because it needs to be ensured that humanity's common origin becomes its common destiny.

We, the inhabitants of planet earth, need to dissolve our national identities and become world citizens instead.

From space, boundaries and lines of actual control cannot be seen. Yet, we are busy dividing ourselves into narrower verticals of caste, creed, language and culture when, instead, we need to develop a global viewpoint. From my vantage point during the eight-day near earth orbit mission, I observed that spaceship earth is suspended in space with no evidence of life around—as far as the eye could see. Reason enough to get our act together and pull in a direction that ensures sustainable development and peace on earth. Further, I might add that it is not at all necessary to go up into space to come by this feeling.

So, does thinking along these lines mean I am willing to give up my Indian identity? Does it make me less proud of being an Indian? On the contrary, I celebrate the fact that my Indian upbringing and values has given me the outlook I have shared above. And now, I hope that you, the reader, is beginning to understand why I had said that our country is Saare jahan se achcha.

KAPIL SIBAL
MINISTER, SCIENCE & TECHNOLOGY, OCEAN DEVELOPMENT

Technology to the Rescue

Empowerment to me means the use of science and technology to resolve issues of everyday life. Recent natural phenomena should shake us out of our complacency. The tsunami on December 26, 2004, with the havoc caused in its wake; and the human tragedy witnessed in Pakistan and parts of Jammu and Kashmir on 8 October 2005 when a 7.4 Richter scale earthquake shook the foundations of weak and dilapidated structures, signalled the necessity for civil society to be armed with information to protect itself.

The tsunami caught us unawares. With technology in place, we could have saved the thousands of innocent people consumed by its wrath. While we upgrade our skills, find solutions through technology for becoming market leaders in the service and manufacturing sectors, we desperately need solutions through technology for improving the lives of ordinary people.

Water, without which we cannot survive, is becoming a scarce resource. The availability of clean drinking water for all is an urgent need. Remote sensing allows us to scan aquifers and water-management technologies can help us store water. We can, through technology, convert sea water to drinking water at low cost. A 10 million litre conversion plant will allow us to sell water at a cost of 2-5 paise per litre. Our solutions must be both accessible and affordable to the poor. We have simple accessible technologies for converting tap water into drinking water by eliminating all bacteria and viruses. Such solutions, though available, have not reached our people.

We have technologies for low-cost structures in India, affordable for the poor. Bamboo structures, with the tensile strength of steel, have the capacity to withstand floods. A 200 sq. ft structure with sanitation and other facilities can last up to 30 years at a cost of Rs 36,000. Such technologies are not yet accessible to ordinary folk.

Low cost vaccines for treatment of malaria, hepatitis-B, tuberculosis, and HIV and AIDS are not a far cry, if we put our minds to it. Some of these vaccines are already available and others are in the pipeline. We cannot afford high cost technologies for a population in which 500 million people earn less than 2 dollars a day. We need to come up with homegrown technologies which are both green and cost effective.

Our most scarce resource in the years to come will be energy. We need to use solar energy for our requirements. We have the luxury of an endless supply of energy in India where the sun shines 300 days in a year. Our transportation desperately needs new solutions to reduce the emission of noxious substances, which not only pollute the environment but shorten our lives. Gas hydrates in the ocean have trapped millions of cubic meters of pure methane gas. We need technology for its recovery and optimum use.

No one source of energy will meet the needs of a burgeoning middle class and the rural poor. A mix of technologies with simple low-cost solutions is the way forward. We need to empower our farmers, again through technology, by providing them genetically engineered seeds, which are resistant to both biotic and abiotic stresses and have higher nutritional value. We need farmers to apply best practices with seeds which are not spurious.

We need information technology to empower our farmers to sell their produce when market conditions are favourable. We must empower our farmers with agricultural produce with enhanced shelf-life. To benefit from such technologies, we need to develop cold chains from the field to the supermarket.

The condition precedent for empowerment is access to information. Availability and use of information is an empowering process. We need to inform ordinary citizens as to what kind of structures they should build when the next earthquake shakes their foundations. We need to inform ordinary people as to what precautions they must take if such an event occurs.

Solutions can and will be provided by technology. We need to inform all those living in our coastal areas how to protect themselves from the fury of a tsunami. It is through technology that we can reach them in real time or warn them in advance.

Science and technology alone allows us to put systems in place to predict the wrath of nature. Scientists must empower themselves to find solutions through technology. The people of India must empower themselves by having access to those systems. Empowerment is a process of partnership between government and civil society. In that partnership, technology must play a key role.

Technology is nothing more than the application of science for resolving issues confronting man. It is time to be friends with science and technology. For unless every aspect of human activity is rationalised by the use of science and every problem confronting man is resolved through technology, society can never be truly empowered. Embracing that mindset alone can empower our people.

AMARINDER SINGH
CHIEF MINISTER, PUNJAB

Agriculture Can Make the Future

These days we do get the impression that our country is progressing very fast. Our economy is strong enough to meet the challenges of the changing world economic order. It has also shown the strength to absorb severe shocks such as the tsunami and earthquakes. The country has maintained a steady growth rate even after meeting unforeseen financial requirements without external help or dependence.

The good news is that our foreign exchange reserves are rising; our growth rate is gradually improving; foreign direct investment is picking up in the most vital sectors of our economy; the need for better and quality infrastructure is largely realised and there is greater stress on that; the quality of the manufacturing sector is improving, and the services sector has expanded vastly, giving greater hope for a decent living.

But it's unfortunate that despite the all-round euphoria and hope, the agriculture sector is not showing signs of great revival. The growth rate in the agriculture sector has been 1.1 per cent as against the anticipated rate of 4 per cent. Even new investment in the agriculture sector does not seem to be picking up, giving little hope, if any, of its rejuvenation.

The need to develop modern marketing structures, and promote agro-processing units, diversification of crops and agricultural research and development does not seem to have attracted the desired attention of our policy planners to prepare our agriculturists for the challenges of global expectations in the WTO regime.

In Punjab, we can ill-afford to ignore our agriculture sector. It is a fact that the incomes of Punjabi farmers have declined over the years. The farmers get pre-determined prices for most of their produce through MSP which has got saturated. As per available information, during the last decade, the price that Punjabi farmers received for their agricultural produce increased by about 51 per cent as against the increase of 127 per cent in input costs. Not only this, leaving aside the compulsive value addition to paddy, no value addition is happening to existing crops for the benefit of the farmers.

The state has no major agro processing units other than rice milling plants. As a result, growth of the agriculture sector has stagnated at around 1.5 per cent in Punjab. Does the country have any plan for increasing the farmers' remuneration, people who brought it out from the disgrace of hunger, poverty and the food deficit? Today, we do not need PL-480. Nor are we dependent on any country to provide sufficient food for our population, primarily because of the Green Revolution in Punjab. The Punjabi farmers continue to do their bit even now to ensure the country's self-sufficiency in food. But not many of us realise that the same farmers who produce enough food for us are grossly indebted, suffering from multiple incurable diseases and staring at the severe problem of unemployment of wards and dependents. With the increase in population, their land holdings have fragmented to sub-optimal levels and have thus become uneconomical.

Most of the present generation of Punjabi farmers are compelled to move out of villages in search of jobs. This has not only resulted in lower economic and living standards but also poor social upbringing—many end up as drug addicts or in other social evils. We need to remedy this situation very fast, arrest the deteriorating condition of our farmers and the rural poor through some honest and credible action. It is only then that we can say that the country is getting empowered.

I accepted this as a challenge on assuming the office of chief minister. We promised to weed out corruption in public life and started a campaign in this direction. However, it did not take us long to realise that we had grossly underestimated the magnitude and dimensions of the crisis bequeathed to us by our predecessor government. Nevertheless, in pursuance of our promise of providing the Punjabis freedom from corruption and financial bankruptcy, we are following the path of good governance and transparent administration. We have ensured probity in public life and recruited people on merit, without any corruption and after dismissing those who entered the state civil services on the strength of money.

We all know that there are comparatively lesser incidents of corruption and nepotism in the west because public officers consider themselves more as referees than market participants, and power and responsibility are exercised as a trust for public good and not as an opportunity for private gain. We need to have a similar approach and address the issue of corruption in a non-partisan manner as a larger societal issue. Here again, the need to ensure credible action and a transparent system cannot be ignored.

During the last three years, we have taken many steps to improve the economic condition of our farmers and the rural poor as also to protect their rights. Our action to protect the water rights of Punjab is one such example. The other major credible action is to provide full power-input subsidy to all farmers of the state. Many economists questioned this decision. Perhaps they need to verify the facts more carefully: input costs of farmers are rising with grossly inadequate increase in output prices.

The debt burden of the farmers is increasing with no major relief in interest payable on agricultural loans. Capital formation and capital investment in the agriculture sector have been far too low when compared with its contribution to the nation's economy. What could have one done in such a scenario? Power-input subsidy was the only thing in our domain and we did that without any hesitation.

Some of our political opponents questioned our decision stating that we had wrongly withdrawn it earlier. We had promised free power in our manifesto. We had to withdraw this facility because of the financial bankruptcy that we inherited. Not only that, there was no money to make additional investments in the agriculture and power sectors, there was no money to provide for recurring costs of power supply. There were problems in even paying the salaries of government employees.

During the last three and a half years, we purchased power worth Rs 3 crore per day to ensure adequate supply of quality power to sustain and increase agriculture production. It is only because of this, and the resultant assured irrigation, that agriculture production increased from 22 million MTs to 30 million MTs in the last three years.

Diversification of crops is picking up gradually with increased cultivation of fruits, vegetables and other cash crops. Our major achievement has been the revival of the cotton crop with the introduction of BT cotton. Cotton production reached 23 lakh bales in 2005 after touching a low of 5.79 lakh bales in 1998.

We have also taken credible action to ensure better opportunities for people moving out from rural to urban areas by giving thrust to the promotion and development of industries in the state. The new industrial policy evolved and adopted by our government has started showing results—investors seem to be realising that there are no more bottlenecks for investment in Punjab.

During the last one and a half years, mega industrial projects of

Rs 20,000 crore have been sanctioned. Hopefully, results of this investment will be visible soon with greater employment for our youth. We also hope to achieve major gains for our traders and businessmen with the opening of trade with Pakistan via the Wagah border. A humble beginning in this regard has already been made.

Our commitment to help and ensure development of the rural poor and the underprivileged, particularly those belonging to the scheduled castes, is total. We have overcome initial financial constraints and set up a dedicated social security fund of Rs 450 crore for the social security and welfare of these segments of our population.

Today, village panchayats in Punjab are disbursing monthly pensions of Rs 23 crore to the rural poor, widows, destitute and the aged. They are also empowered to implement seventeen schemes of six major rural social sector development departments.

To be honest, I admit that the issue of rural indebtedness, the spread of incurable diseases in rural areas and unemployment are some of the major problems which bother me more than anything else, though the importance and urgency of developing quality infrastructure, including roads, bridges, power generation plants and social infrastructure, i.e. government schools and hospitals, cannot be undermined in any way.

I am determined to find and take all possible administrative and legal measures to tackle these issues. It will be sooner than expected that credible action in this regard is visible. Because the poor and sick living in rural areas without basic civic amenities will not make the country empowered. We need to take them out of their misery to ensure a richer and prosperous Punjab.

JASWANT SINGH
LEADER OF THE BJP IN RAJYA SABHA

Freedom from the Tyranny of Corruption

How do you empower over a billion humans, nearly 80 per cent of whom live in our villages? As Raja Rao movingly says 'there is no village in India . . . that has not Sthalpurana, a legendary history, of its own . . . In this way . . . past mingles with the present . . . The gods mingle with men . . .'

That is why the 'soul of India' lives in our villages as in no other land. It is this 'soul' which now needs nourishment: that would be the first empowerment; though I am not sure that we even reflect upon that void needing to be filled.

How to imbue an ancient land and an ancient society (the cellular core of our nationhood) with a conviction of belonging; how to imbue that 'spirit of India' with the conviction that it truly is a synonym of 'India that is Bharat' that is 'Hindustan.' And as 'Hindustan' is hamara, then it just cannot be that India is also the sole proprietary concern of just one family. That empowerment of the spirit of our land is yet to be attained, that first freedom from bondage we have yet to achieve. We submit too easily, readily in fact, to videshi vilayats. This is not a political, it is a spiritual point. If our spirit be not free and if the 'soul of India' remains in bondage then what possibly can just external 'empowerments' do? In substance they amount to nothing—also not of much use then all this wealth of India, real or potential.

I do not then know how familiar we are with that old vernacular saying: *uttam kheti, madhyam baan, adham chaakri, bheek nidaan.* Freely translated it counsels that cultivating the land is the best occupation, commerce is a middling option, to accept servitude (*chaakri* is almost impossible to translate) is condemnable, and begging of course, is forbidden.

We have, in practice, turned this sage counsel on its head.

Most of our citizens now want sarkari naukri and readily beg the State for any and everything that has to be done. In consequence, we have now become a political system riven with the arzi-navees (perpetual supplicants), required to beg, and that too, always in duplicate, in triplicate, in quintuplicate!

Free our land of this bondage; there is no empowerment without this freedom.

Fear stalks our land, fear of disorder, fear of the 'lawlessness of our law', fear of the petty, daily tyranny of our systems; the millions and millions of the minions of the system that proliferate, like insects during monsoon, whose only function is to bite the citizen, to extract blood, to tyrannise, to dis-empower India.

Can you instead dis-empower the million minions please? No, not through yet more politically exploitative legislation. A certain will, a mindset is needed. That will surely lead us to empowerment.

Empower India then by ridding India of corruption of all hues, of all kinds, but above all this 'corruption of our spirit'. It is this empowerment alone which can rid us of the crippling disempowerment of an ever spreading, constantly proliferating 'money corruption'.

I am paralysed with shame when I look around and see how widespread it is now, how without exception, how blatant and unchecked, how totally uniform in its spread—all political parties, all instruments of governance, private and non-government too, in fact, everywhere, at the Centre and in the states alike.

How can you empower India when you start by shackling all our citizens in this life-long bondage? India will be empowered only when we rid its fertile soil (spirit) of all polluting chemicals (corruption), when we water its soil with a sense of plenitude (Hindustan Hamara!). Only then will roots sink deep, a healthy plant then grow to be a young sapling (our young); to them provide the sustenance of health, nutrition and true learning, true education, and for all (not please on competitive political lines). Witness then the sap of life flow in an India empowered.

K. NATWAR SINGH
FORMER MINISTER, EXTERNAL AFFAIRS

A New Perception of India

In a globally integrated, instantly connected world, foreign policy cannot be separated from domestic policy. The empowerment of India in international relations is only a reflection of the empowerment of India at home. Every sinew of our internal strength is noticed by the world, every blemish is subject to instant scrutiny.

As our capacity to deal with our challenges at home increases, India walks with greater confidence abroad. As one more Indian child receives education, one more Indian village gets electricity and drinking water, one more far-flung Indian district is looped into a world-class highway, the image of India that is seen by the world improves, incrementally but irreversibly. It is a good time to be foreign minister.

For me, the empowerment of India has meant the transformation of this image over the years. The snake charmer has yielded place to the computer. What was once seen as a chaotic country is now seen as a vibrant, thriving democracy. The population that was once seen as a debilitating burden is now an enviable asset. The Indian immigrant, once considered an economic refugee, is welcomed now in an increasing number of countries.

India is no longer a country seen as home to countless impoverished millions in need of food aid, education and relief. It is seen as a country with a critical role in the twenty-first century, an economy that is both a very viable investment destination as well as a hub of growth, a polity that is a model for a functioning multi-ethnic, multi-lingual, multi-religious democracy. Today, it is no longer possible to ignore India's voice; without her, no calculus of the 21st century is complete.

What are the factors that have contributed to this sea-change in our standing abroad? To my mind, the most critical factor is the way we have nurtured our spirit of freedom and enabled it to enliven all our democratic institutions. The world today marvels at how we have managed to transform possible faultlines—be they of religion, region or language— into bonds that unite.

Our election process, peaceful transfers of power, flexible federalism, independent judiciary, freedom of debate—in parliament or in the press— has set standards by which the resilience of societies to handle political challenges is measured. Our billion-strong democratic experiment is unique and is seen as such. It empowers every Indian, at home and abroad.

The growing strength of the Indian economy is another crucial element in the process of our empowerment. Wide-ranging reforms, a determined bid towards global integration keeping in mind our own specific circumstances and a commitment to bring the benefits of development to every strata of our society have set the stage for phenomenal growth. The world is paying attention though much more needs to be done to attract the level of investment that we seek. But the effects of economic change have already empowered an increasing number of Indians.

The third factor that empowers us today is the quality of our education. This has transformed our population burden into a bank of talent. It has created and nourished our cutting edge IT industry. It has enabled India to become a nuclear power, a confident explorer of space frontiers, a leader in biotechnology—in fact, a giant of the knowledge industry.

When one is abroad, the true value of Indian education and scientific temper, often taken for granted at home, stands out as a major factor of our empowerment. Our efforts have to be aimed at extending this education of excellence to every Indian; the impact on India's empowerment will be manifold.

And one last point: India is empowered in the world today because of the philosophical underpinning of our foreign policy, the principles that we have held dear, the ideals that we have cherished. The relentless pursuit of peace, the willingness to engage, the enormous contributions to multilateral institutions and, above all, the independence of our decision-making have earned respect and admiration for our foreign policy.

Today we continue these traditions in our dialogue with our neighbours and in our energetic engagement with every major power and region in the world. Our consistent efforts to achieve close and friendly political relations, mutually beneficial economic linkages and increased people-to-people contacts are resulting in tangible empowerment for every Indian.

In the eyes of the world, an empowered India is no longer a matter of doubt; it is already a matter of fact.

RAGHUVANSH PRASAD SINGH
MINISTER, RURAL DEVELOPMENT

Bulb, Tap and Toilet in Every Rural Home

India empowered to me is a nation in which employment is guaranteed to every hand, a nation where food security is assured, where everyone has a place of shelter, every household has access to a safe source of drinking water and possesses a clean toilet, a nation whose agricultural fields have assured sources of irrigation, a nation whose villages have basic infrastructure such as road connectivity, electricity, telecommunication connectivity, proper health and education services, a nation with facilities for easy access to and freedom for exchange of knowledge and information and a nation with widespread and deep-seated grassroot democratic institutions.

India is empowered with a population resource of over 100 crores which constitutes 16 per cent of the world's population but has only 2.5 per cent of the world's area as its territory. The incidence of poverty is as high as 27.09 per cent in our rural areas and 23.62 per cent in urban areas. The population below the poverty line is living with income levels below Rs 327.56 per capita per month.

This section of the society needs empowerment in terms of right to work and we, therefore, need to develop policies which provide guaranteed job opportunities to job seekers. The National Rural Employment Guarantee Programme is an initiative in this direction but the test lies in its proper implementation which could be facilitated by a mature local self-government in the form of empowered panchayati raj institutions assisted by development functionaries, sensitive to needs.

Mahatma Gandhi said that 'poverty is the worst form of violence'. The condition of assetlessness, which is the root cause of poverty in the country, manifests in various forms: increase in stratification, class struggle, the Naxal movement, caste tensions and social disorder.

Our policies require focused provisions for the welfare of vulnerable sections and equitable distribution of assets. Those sections of society which have lagged behind because of lack of opportunities, economic reasons and social stratification are required to be given a proper environment. This will ensure they also feel they are respected citizens of the country, committed and proud of their nation.

Mother Teresa once said that 'we think sometimes that poverty is only being hungry, naked and homeless. The poverty of being unwanted, unloved and uncared for is the greatest poverty. We must start with our own houses to remedy this kind of poverty.' The entire environment needs to be sensitised towards togetherness of fellow citizens. There are no two opinions about the fact that prosperity is the outcome of hard work and timely exploration of opportunities but it is also a fact that a vast chunk of the Indian poor do not have opportunities. The social order should, therefore, be sensitive enough.

In a country where poverty permeates one-third of the rural poor, where untouchability continues despite stringent laws and public rage against its practice, where opportunities continue to be unequal, imagining an empowered society would be somewhat unrealistic. Empowerment requires economic egalitarianism and focus on the implementation of developmental programmes.

Economic programmes require to be structured so as to provide expanding space for vulnerable sections of society, i.e. scheduled castes/scheduled tribes, women, minorities and other weaker sections with suitable preferential treatment. Economic programmes should have more social and participatory content to facilitate more and more people involvement. Wage employment and self-employment programmes are examples of such micro-developmental structures and their expansion will lead to permeation of micro industries at the grassroot level.

The planning machinery responsible for the implementation of these programmes is required to provide technology and skill support so as to improve productivity. Given the decentralised nature and involvement of these programmes, there will be a need for very close monitoring and follow-up so that the fruits are not taken away by ineligible elements.

Our nation has shown remarkable improvement in various socio-economic development parameters in the last fifty years, but the rich-poor divide is widening. We need to have a system that is totally transparent and poor-friendly as well as completely fair procedures. The roots of backwardness also lie in the poor level of awareness in society.

Therefore, the country really needs to put in a lot of effort to make society aware and responsive.

A country whose economy is predominantly based on agriculture cannot be termed empowered unless the backbone of the economy, i.e. farmers, get due remunerative prices for farm products. Over a period of time, the cost of inputs has seen a rising trend whereas the prices of the product, which the farmers get, have been broadly constant. The rising trend, if any, is very marginal in terms of benefits to farmers and it largely benefits the middlemen.

While trading is part of economic opportunity, the same should not amount to exploitation. Since production has to precede trade, preferential treatment for profit opportunities to the producer is essential even for the trader to sustain his trade. The role of the regulator is, therefore, paramount.

The status of rural electrification manifests the divide in society. Vast areas in villages still do not have electricity and supply of reliable energy at affordable costs.

In our country, we still have about 1.5 crore families without proper shelter. The condition of slum-dwellers is still more miserable. The government has taken initiatives to construct houses on a large scale but the problem is multiplying because of unchecked growth in population and the division of joint families into smaller families, almost at the same rate at which new houses are getting added.

In our country, about 5,000 villages still have no source of safe drinking water and some 50,000 villages have insufficient supply of water. 2.16 lakh habitations are affected by water-quality problems. India empowered must envisage a safe and assured source of drinking water to every household.

Sanitation coverage in the country was 22 per cent in 2001, which has now gone up to 33 per cent. The problem of people defecating in the open is still very high, more prevalent in areas ridden with chronic poverty. The Millennium Development Goal stated by the United Nations envisages total sanitation coverage by 2015. India empowered must have individual sanitation coverage to each and every household. This is essential for the dignity of our women.

In order to improve living conditions in rural areas, the rural-urban migration must be checked and linkages from field to market must be ensured, every village must have provisions of all-weather road connectivity, telecommunication connectivity, electricity, satisfactory standards of health and education and other social services.

Empowered India ought to have world-class infrastructure to compete with the world community. To achieve these goals, a high level of knowledge base in citizens is required to ensure that the funds being passed on to implementing agencies are utilised properly.

In a vast country like India, natural calamities such as droughts, floods, tsunamis, earthquakes, etc., have played havoc. In all these calamities, from the viewpoint of an independent observer, it appears that the country has accepted them as acts of nature. For an empowered mind, nature is a teacher. Co-existence of man with nature is an age-old practice.

In a fast-changing technological era, we are required to be ready to withstand, absorb, endure and meet eventualities caused by these natural calamities effectively so that their effect on society is minimised.

For example, floods in north Bihar are a perennial problem. Every year, twenty-two districts get flooded, causing huge loss of property, lives, farmlands and infrastructure. A disaster management system equipped with data, technology and resources can meet the ravages of cyclic natural disasters.

For empowerment in the Indian context means economic strength with cultural diversity. Empowered India will be a country where every hand has access to employment and every face smiles at the end of the day, in contentment.

V.P. SINGH
FORMER PRIME MINISTER

Let the Disempowered Also Decide

If we look at empowerment, the idea has to address itself to the stomach, heart and mind. In that sense, we must also see how people have been disempowered in a particular set-up. By stomach, I mean hunger and livelihood; by heart, I mean freedom from fear and striving for a humane, social environment; by mind, I mean intellect and knowledge.

I would say the stomach is the most important because one who is hungry and poor is not only disempowered in terms of education, he is also denied dignity and respect.

What has been the situation in our society, so far? South Asian societies are hierarchical in order, where hierarchies mean monopolies. To that extent, whether it is social, economic or political hierarchies, they are all anti-democratic. So, if you need to empower people, the principle of democracy has to prevail at all these levels. This means the right to a reasonable livelihood, education and social security, and the latter can only come through social harmony.

If you look at the caste system, where a person's economic, political and social status are all determined by birth, then a vast majority of people have been disempowered for ages. But here too, the issue of social dignity arises once again. If you deprive a person of his dignity, you de-humanise him, and he becomes a machine. That was what was done to almost 80 per cent of the people of this country. The Dalits and backward castes were de-humanised to become machines, to produce. They had no share in anything—of the wealth, power and knowledge created by society. These privileges were assigned to the other castes: the brahmins owned knowledge; the kshatriyas wielded power and the vaishyas created wealth.

So, if we have to consider empowerment of Indian society, it has to be seen and dealt with in the Indian context. Empowerment does not merely come by writing about it in books, or even in the Constitution, we must have empowerment through practice, it must go beyond the legal context. This process of empowerment has to start by addressing itself to the historical process of the disempowerment of people in this country.

I must say, in the last century, we have seen many social and reform movements without aiming for power, which have triggered the empowerment process—with Jyotiba Phule, Gandhi, Periyar and others. They have worked to do away with social practices endorsed by society, ranging from sati to untouchability.

For me, empowerment means participation in the decision making process. For true empowerment, we must go beyond the state structure of benefits like education and jobs, and draw the disempowered to participate in the decision-making process of their society.

But we are still at the first stage in this struggle—we have to fight hunger, unemployment and social hatred. Until this war is won, empowerment will continue to be under constant threat. I think we have progressed on many fronts—some more, some less—but the poorer sections have not got their share as such.

Finally, do we all, as a country, participate in the same dream? For, countries do not live by statistics alone. Yes, statistics may be essential, but these are not sufficient. A country lives by a hope and a dream we all share, it is its biggest strength and character. Gandhiji gave us a dream of India and as young people, we lived this dream. It was not just about the British leaving India, but about social, economic and political dreams for the future. Those dreams have withered away today.

What we need to do is to once again dream for an India together. The dream will be to fight hunger, disease, poverty, injustice and give back to the people their dignity and respect. Death only kills once, but humiliation kills a thousand times.

SUSHMA SWARAJ
DY LEADER OF THE BJP IN RAJYA SABHA, PARTY SPOKESPERSON

Women's Voices for Change

How would I define empowerment? Empowerment per se means when people are not dependent on others, when they are self-sufficient. There was a time when as children we wrote essays on India's food problem. There was food shortage at that time. But then came a revolutionary programme and we are now self-sufficient in food and are in fact actually exporting food. You could perhaps call this empowerment.

We are at a stage when it seems that the 21st century will belong to India and India becomes, for all purposes, a superpower.

But, in my opinion, I will not think there has been empowerment till half the population of India, that is, women, are empowered. This is despite our self-sufficiency in food and our ability to defend our borders. We might be saying we are empowering women politically and economically. The truth is that there is a question mark over their very existence.

I am referring to female foeticide. Against 1,000 boys born, there are states where only 720 infant girls are born. It isn't that god has changed his attitude. It's just that people use science to determine the sex of a foetus and kill it if it is a girl. There used to be doctors who had posters over the operation table saying, 'Spend Rs 500 and save Rs 5 lakh'. Laws have been enacted to stop female foeticide. The Supreme Court is also seized of the matter. Yet, female foeticide continues.

Similarly, take the case of rape. In Delhi, not a day passes when a rape is not reported in the media. If you take into account all the crimes against women, the crime graph is high. In rape cases, the statistics are alarming.

That is why I always say that unless women are politically empowered

WOMEN'S VOICES FOR CHANGE 169

and are part of the decision-making process, all this talk of empowerment will come to naught. That is because it is authority that works.

Let me explain. My surmise is that a woman peon of a woman police officer is more empowered at home than a woman software engineer or a lady doctor. That's because in the case of a woman peon, her authority comes from the police officer she works with.

We have that in politics too. Women workers who are with us feel secure because they know that they can knock on our door at any time and we will stand by them. I'll give you an instance. There is a woman worker who works with me. She lives in the slums. One day she came to invite me for her daughter's wedding. She told me, 'It's all right if you don't come for my son's wedding, but you must come for my daughter's wedding.' I asked her why. The woman worker explained: 'Because her in-laws will see that there are powerful people behind my daughter.' This is empowerment.

We are fighting for 33 per cent reservation for women in the Lok Sabha and state assemblies. I truly believe that even if we have 33 per cent women taking part in the decision-making process, real empowerment will come. And once women are empowered, the whole country will be empowered. As we say, when a girl is educated, she actually goes on to educate two families. Women's reservation will also make gender issues more focused, and women in some areas will be more empowered.

It is a coincidence that I am writing this on the first day of Navratra. We will all see that on the eighth day, on Durgashtami, in Punjab and Haryana we will invite girls from the neighbourhood, worship them and wash their feet. But, a mere fifteen days later, if a daughter-in-law has a baby girl in her womb, we will ask her to abort the child. What kind of empowerment are we talking about? Does a girl have no right to be born and to live?

Even though the government is working consistently to empower women, the empowerment process will not be complete until we empower women completely.

B.B. TANDON
CHIEF ELECTION COMMISSIONER

Free Elections Are the Hallmark of Democracy

Empowerment to me is free and fair polls. A good election translates into good governance as it reflects the true will of the people and, therefore, the empowerment of India.

An election without any fear, without coercion of the electorate or forcible manipulation, that expresses the true sentiments of the people, will enable Indians to elect a government that can deliver on their aspirations. Empowerment of India begins when the political process is free of all malpractices, including criminalisation; that is, people who are involved in heinous and other serious offences and against whom courts have framed charges are not allowed to contest elections so that law-breakers do not become law-makers.

However, the Election Commission has its own constraints as it has to conduct elections according to the laws enacted by parliament. Within the given framework of law, the Commission has made an effort in this direction by asking the prospective candidates to file affidavits, as directed by the Supreme Court, about their assets and past criminal record, if any, before nomination.

These affidavits are posted on the Commission's website and also made available to the public free of cost. The Commission also encourages NGOs to disseminate the information contained in these affidavits to the electors before elections so that they can make an informed choice.

Recently, the Commission issued directions that if a non-bailable warrant is pending against any person for more than six months, action should be taken to delete his name from the electoral roll after following the due procedure prescribed under the law, as the presumption would be that such a person is not 'ordinarily resident' at the given address where his name has been enrolled as an elector. This measure would either make a person surrender before the law or else he will not be entitled to vote or contest an election.

The issue of criminalisation of politics needs to be given serious consideration at the level of political parties and there should be a national debate to provide adequate legal framework to check the growing trend of criminalisation in politics. I would expect that political parties, in the meantime, should follow a self-evolved code to deny tickets for elections to people with a criminal background.

Integral to criminalisation of politics is the role of muscle power and anti-social elements during elections. The growing trend of electoral violence has become a cause of concern. This has necessitated the ever-increasing requirement of police and paramilitary forces for ensuring peaceful conduct of polls. If people, political parties and the governments are sensitive to the fact that criminals and musclemen should be kept out of the electoral process, then this is empowerment in earnest.

India cannot be empowered if women electorate, weaker sections like scheduled castes, scheduled tribes and minorities, are denied equal opportunity of free participation in the electoral process through manipulation or force. The Commission takes special steps in sensitive and violence-prone areas in order to ensure that electors belonging to these sections are neither coerced to vote in favour of any particular party or candidate nor forced to abstain from the electoral process. Strict action is taken if misuse of government machinery to favour any particular group is noticed.

The Commission has made identification of voters compulsory through electors photo identity cards or other prescribed documents, at the time of polling, to curb the evil of impersonation. Now, the effort of the Commission is to have electoral rolls with photographs. Such rolls have already been published for the state of Kerala and the Union Territory of Pondicherry. This measure will build new confidence amongst the electors belonging to weaker sections to come forward and vote, as no other person will be able to impersonate and vote in their place. The Commission sets up special polling booths for their convenience. It is the empowerment of electors from the weaker sections that is uppermost in the mind of the Election Commission.

The issue of gender representation has so far eluded a consensus amongst the political parties. Statistics of several previous general elections reveal an abysmally low representation of women members in the Lok Sabha and the state legislatures. Pending legislation on the subject, I am all for political parties unilaterally ensuring that at least one-third of their candidates are women. Sure enough women representation should not be restricted to reserved seats only. I would like the political parties to be proactive and consider this suggestion rather than wait for the legislation providing reservation for women to be passed by parliament.

Another area of serious concern is the role of money power and the associated subversion of the democratic process on account of unchecked flow of funds for political campaigns and elections. Despite monetary ceilings that have been prescribed for the expenditure that can be incurred by any candidate during elections, use of money can only be described as very excessive and lavish. Certain loopholes still exist in our laws, particularly as there is no ceiling on the expenditure that can be incurred by political parties. This issue along with that of state funding of elections also needs to be considered and debated for a satisfactory solution to minimise the role of money power in elections. Money power in elections can disturb the level playing field and, therefore, can become an obstacle to true empowerment.

The Election Commission has been able to meet all challenges through its neutrality, transparency, rational decision-making, unbiased approach, credibility and apolitical image. I expect all public servants associated with elections to follow these principles while discharging their duties to empower the Commission and thereby empower people and the country.

Basically, I am for empowerment of all the stakeholders in the electoral process but this can only happen if there is a level playing field for all political parties. If political parties strictly follow the model code of conduct—neither finding ways to circumvent it, nor trying to unduly influence the voters—curb the evil influence of money in the electoral process and help in bringing transparency into the electoral system, then the day is not far when India gets truly empowered as. Its people will then make the right choice in electing their representatives who would, in turn, provide better governance and thus improve the quality of life for all citizens.

MULAYAM SINGH YADAV
CHIEF MINISTER, UTTAR PRADESH

The Elite Must Quit the Ivory Tower

It has been around six decades since India emerged as a sovereign nation and a beacon of hope for the cause of the marginalised nations and communities around the globe.

The most pertinent development has been the emergence of internal colonialism, wherein brown sahibs replaced white sahibs, anglicised sections of India took over reins of the State and embarked upon an ambitious but lopsided programme of state building, leaving a vast section of the society marginalised, under-represented and suppressed.

The Indian State emerged omnipotent and the bureaucracy carried out diktats of the elite, which was still under the spell of the west. The common people voiced their disagreement for the first time in a very vibrant and organised manner after the Congress party's tyrannical emergency rule marked by imprisonment of innocent opposition leaders for a period of over 19 months. Even elected members of the Congress party like Mr Chandra Shekhar, member of the Congress Working Committee, and Mr Ram Dhan, secretary, Congress Parliamentary Party, were not spared in this witch-hunting exercise.

Today we can claim with a sense of pride that there has been a 'Silent Revolution' in India's political spectrum with political monopolies being broken and commendable changes taking place in the socio-economic sphere. The subordination of the rural agrarian sector to urban industrial society has been done away with with the rise of the leadership of backward classes who succeeded in placing the contribution of rural peasantry in the collective consciousness of the nation.

This has been marked by corresponding changes in the breakdown of the Congress party's patron-client system, wherein the marginalised got a chance to cast their ballot but hardly got a chance to be elected. Empowerment has been made meaningful with the democratisation in the villages with redistribution of land, fair representation of all the sections of society and strong measures against any form of oppression.

But we have a long way to go and strive hard to realise the unfinished goals of our leaders. We can't afford to see only a minuscule section of society benefiting and cornering the fruits of development. India empowered to me is when Gandhiji's dream of swaraj is realised, when roti, kapda, bijli, sadak, paani, shiksha is for one and all.

We should ensure that our daughters are not discriminated against vis-à-vis the boys and are accorded equal dignity and space for individual growth and contribution to society. In Uttar Pradesh, we have tried to end discriminatory practices against women through the programme of Kanyadhan, where the state provides adequate grants for their higher education and marriage. I see the empowerment of women as a necessary precondition for the overall empowerment of society and the nation.

We have come through a phase when cataclysmic changes are taking place around the globe. Information technology and finance capital have shrunk the world into a global village and barriers of distance and knowledge have been eroded. Yet there are some movements which are regressive, feudal and discriminatory in nature.

There have been attempts by the armchair anglicised elite to berate the significant socio-political changes that have taken place in the last three decades. They refuse to come out of their ivory towers and continue to pontificate about the system through educational institutions, bureaucracy and mass media.

To me, India should shine for each of its citizens and not just for a select few. So empowerment should mean that any citizen of this nation has an equal right to don the mantle of prime ministership and not just any one particular class, that too in succession on the lines of the medieval notion of the divine rights of the king.

India empowered to me is when there is politics of tolerance, grace and dignity and not one of arrogance and senseless hatred.

SITARAM YECHURY
MEMBER, CPI(M) POLITBURO AND MP

Strengthen the Bonds of Our Commonality

To my generation, born after 'we, the people' gave ourselves this secular, democratic, republican Constitution of independent India, the visions of an empowered India would naturally be distinct, though not necessarily different or disconnected from the visions of the earlier generations that shaped the contours of modern independent India.

Born into a Telugu-speaking family, but born in Chennai, the capital of Tamil Nadu, educated in Hyderabad with a strong flavour of Islamic culture, married to an offspring of an Islamic Sufi and a Mysorian Rajput family, living and participating in political activities mainly in the Hindi belt for over three decades and being elected to parliament from West Bengal, I not merely recognise India's diversity but am its product.

India empowered means the celebration of this diversity, not the bemoaning of it. By the time my generation was born, Pakistan was a reality. We had barely passed school when Bangladesh became a reality. The vivisection of the Indian subcontinent, admirably aided by the British while they were leaving, has come down to us as a reality. This is not to suggest that history is either irrelevant or unimportant.

We draw our inspiration, our experiences and the psychology of our commonality from our history. More importantly, we learn of our mistakes from our history. We must learn them in order not to repeat them either in the present or in the future. India empowered means the strengthening of the bonds of commonality amongst our rich diversity, not the imposing of a uniformity upon this diversity.

Unfortunately, however, most of those who fall prey to various forms of chauvinism also belong to this generation, or even younger.

Communalism, casteism, regionalism, linguistic parochialism, or even militancy continue to recruit thousands of youth. Much of this is happening because of the nurturing of pernicious inward-looking consciousness. However, much of this is also taking place because the hopes and aspirations that accompanied India's political independence appear farther away from realisation than in the early decades of independence.

India empowered means the elimination of tendencies which feed such divisive trends. This means the need to address seriously the hopes and aspirations of the people and to make sincere efforts to accomplish them. India empowered means the uplift of our political independence into the true economic independence of our people. Once there are jobs for all, education for all and health for all, much of the material circumstances that feed such disastrous divisiveness will simply cease to exist.

It needs also to be kept in mind that the inability to improve the situation only constantly feeds the degenerative elements of our socio-political order such as corruption and nepotism. The dangerous implication of this is the unfortunately growing consciousness that only through corruption or connections in high places can anything be done in India. Such degeneration of political morality can only be arrested when the basic needs and aspirations of the people are met, or at least when it appears that serious efforts are being made to meet them.

But, can the political independence of our country be elevated to the true economic emancipation and independence for all our people? Surely, it can. It will take time, but unmistakably it can be achieved. India has tremendous wealth of material and mineral resources. Even with an education system that is fast reducing education to a privilege of the rich rather than as a right for all, India produces more skilled intellectual manpower every year than the whole of the European Union put together.

Our population, mistakenly often seen as a liability, is, in fact, our biggest asset. 54 per cent of India, today, is below the age of 25. We are one of the youngest nations in the world. If this asset is properly fed, nurtured, educated and healthy, then India will surely take on the world.

But then do we have the resources to feed educate and provide health facilities for all our people? Surely, we do. India today is a country with an alarmingly high level of economic inequalities. Yet, our central tax to GDP ratio is about 8, having declined from about 11 in the last decade and a half. In some of the Scandinavian countries this ratio is as high as 55. Many European countries have a ratio in the 30s. Even the Asian tigers of the past have ratios in the 20s. Surely, India needs to think hard as to how to enlarge the tax net, not necessarily to raise individual tax rates.

The concrete finer details of resource mobilisation to meet the needs of the people can and should be discussed in right earnest. But the fact remains that, yes, India over a period can meet the requirements of its people and turn that into a mighty human resource asset for our country's future.

India empowered, thus, means the true economic emancipation and empowerment of all its people. To achieve this, we require a system—politico-legal, socio-economic, cultural-linguistic—which actually makes people the masters of the country's resources and hence of the country's future. India empowered, thus, means a country where there shall be no exploitation of man by man. This is no wild dream of an idealist. This vision is perfectly tangible both in today's world and today's India. India empowered means the socialist republic of India.

ACTIVISTS, ACADEMICS, THINKERS

MEGHNAD DESAI
ECONOMIST

Respect for Individual Dignity

There is much to be celebrated. India is a leading democracy in the world and the only one in the Third World of any consequence. This is so despite all the fears and obstacles foreseen by critics such as Winston Churchill at the advent of its free existence.

A western model of democracy has flourished in India precisely because the ballot box has been used by the masses to empower themselves. The lower depths of Indian society—the untouchables and backward castes, the tribals, the rural poor, women in their deprived millions—have all gone to the polling booth time after time and exercised their power to dismiss or elect governments. Through it all, parties have emerged nearer to the identities the people value—of religion, of region, of caste, of tribe. No one designed this; few foresaw this. It is a miracle people have made for themselves.

The economy has also overcome its age-old inferiority complex. Indians no longer need recall the muslin of Dhaka or the textiles of Gujarat of old. India can now hold its own in global competition. For centuries, Indians did better by going abroad than staying at home. Now they can make it at home as well as anywhere in the world.

This miraculous turnaround happened when in 1991 a shy, retiring academic, my friend, Dr Manmohan Singh, got hold of the economy and began its reform. Now, after 14 years, he has resumed his command. But the old loser mentality of the Left which kept the economy in shackles for four decades is flexing its muscles again. The Left cares only about those who work in public sector enterprises—the aristocracy or shall we say the brahmins of the working class.

Between Nehru's death and the 1991 foreign exchange crisis, precious capital was frittered away in building an economy which generated very few jobs, neglected the rural areas and shackled the economy to a low 'Hindu rate of growth.' Whatever the rhetoric, going back to the old ways will condemn India to the slow lane again.

During the First World War, it was said that the British soldiers were 'lions led by donkeys'. This has happened in India after Nehru, Patel, Azad and Shastri did their work of laying the foundations of a clean and honest government. Since then, corruption has become sanctioned from the top and has spread to every corner of Indian life, not just among politicians but also in the civil service, army, police and even the judiciary.

The corruption is moral as well as financial. It shows itself in the failure to provide justice for victims of violence in communal riots as well as of upper caste violence against Dalits, for women subjected to rape and domestic violence and for habitual murders committed by politicians and their relatives. Even the prime minister is helpless against this tide of injustice.

India can be among the best and the most prosperous. But for this it needs to clean up its politics, to shed its feudal mores and become as democratic in its daily life, as respectful of individual dignity as it is inside the polling booth at election time.

NANAJI DESHMUKH
RSS VETERAN, SOCIAL WORKER

A Working, Partyless System of Democracy

After the installation of the Morarji Desai government in 1977, I began to realise that the kind of politics we practise in India and the party system we follow will never allow India to prosper. And by the time of the defeat of the Janata government in 1979, I was totally disgusted with politics. I was looking for an alternative system and drew inspiration from Jayaprakash Narayan's concept of Total Revolution. JP believed that that the future of India lay in a partyless system of governance.

I experimented with this concept first in Gonda in 1977, but it was in Chitrakoot in the 1980s that I became optimistic of the enormous possibilities of a Total Revolution. Chitrakoot was particularly symbolic for me since it was the meeting place of Bharat and Lord Rama, after he insisted on going into exile. Unlike today's politicians, neither of these two great giants of the past hankered for power.

My Deendayal Research Institution (DRI) has tried to make a difference in some eighty villages around Chitrakoot through the principles of integral humanism, Gandhism, socialism and Sarvodayavad. We keep reinforcing the point that an individual or an industrialist's prosperity should not be based on the exploitation of the common people. Instead we try and foster cooperation and empathy among people. The villagers have unanimously decided that nobody should work for his personal prosperity but work for the prosperity of the entire village so that no one in the village remains without the benefits of development.

For instance, the epidemic of litigation is rampant in rural India. Harmonious life has become impossible anywhere in the villages. Party politics also spreads divisiveness in society for electoral gains. Noncooperation and enmity among the villagers is the root cause for the misery of rural people. The villagers swayed by the arguments of the DRI started withdrawing their cases from the courts and settling their disputes amongst themselves.

I believe the costly allopathic system of medicine is not really relevant to the vast majority of our rural population, specially as it is not even accessible to them. At Arogyadham, the health care centre of DRI in Chitrakoot, we are evolving a system for gaining long life and health through the use of ayurveda, yoga and naturopathy. For improving rural health, Arogyadham has prepared a kit of thirty-three herbal medicines made from locally available herbs.

Our educational goal is to ensure that the new generation does not become self-centred. The real education of human beings is to endow them with human insight. Only then will the new generation think in terms of social welfare as a whole and not narrow selfish ends. This essential aspect is not possible by confining the students to only classroom education.

Mankind may live in either rural or urban areas; agricultural or industrial countries, but we are all totally dependent on natural resources. Along with agriculture, all sorts of cottage industries based on available natural resources can be developed in the villages. Through this process, both unemployment and poverty can be eradicated. DRI has practised this concept of total revolution successfully in eighty villages of Chitrakoot area. By 2010, it will cover 500 villages around Chitrakoot. It has arranged for the self-employment training for men and women of these villages in Chitrakoot through the Udyamita Vidyapeeth.

Several thousand villages of our country, including in the Chitrakoot area, are suffering from a shortage of drinking water. DRI convinced the villagers that as far as the problem of water was concerned, they would have to help themselves. If they depended on the government, they would never get water. The villagers understood this reality, as it was their experience of more than 50 years of independent India. The collective efforts of the villagers harnessed rainwater into well-designed ponds prepared by themselves.

In this way, not only was the problem of drinking water solved, irrigation of agricultural land was made possible. Earlier, in this area only one kharif crop was possible because of the vagaries of the rains. Today, farmers have created irrigation facilities for themselves and harvest a rabi crop as well. As a result, the annual income of every farmer has doubled. Poverty has been uprooted from these eighty villages with the villagers comprehending that working together is the only key to achieving prosperity for all.

In our country, where 80 per cent of the farmers have uneconomic land holdings, rural people are overburdened with debts. Even after 58 years of independence, no government has tried to solve this major problem of our rural population. The result is many farmers in different parts of our country are compelled to commit suicide. The DRI has successfully carried out experiments converting uneconomic land holdings into economic ones in the poor farmers' small holdings in the Majhgawan area of Satna district. Farmers who possess only 2 to 2.5 acres of land can live happily as they are able to save at least Rs 5,000-6,000 annually after meeting all their family expenses.

My vision of empowerment for India is that the experiment of Chitrakoot be replicated all over the country. I am particularly happy to have had the opportunity to express my views on a subject about which I feel very strongly, in a publication by the *Indian Express*. The founder of this newspaper, Ramnath Goenka, along with Ramdhari Dinkar, were the only two men who were really convinced by JP's dreams. No politician, except Chandra Shekhar to some extent, genuinely believed that JP's philosophy could be translated into practice.

MAHASVETA DEVI
WRITER AND ACTIVIST

Infrastructure for Our Tribals

Empowerment to me means the empowering of the people I have been fighting for for the last many years. Have they been empowered?

My activism started in the 1980s against the bonded labour system. Palamau was the place where I first encountered this abominable practice of making victims out of both tribals and non-tribals living in that area. I believe they are still made victims by the labour contractors, who recruit the rural poor from their homesteads and take them to all corners of India.

The main focus of my work has always been the tribals of India and the so-called de-notified tribes. In 1871, the British notified the nomadic tribes such as forest dwellers, salt cultivators, street acrobats and travelling salesmen as criminal tribes and the Criminal Tribe Act came into effect. Subsequently, these people were victimised and killed by the police and neighbouring societies. In West Bengal, there are the Lodhas of Midnapur, the Kheria Sabars of Purulia and Bankura and the Dhikaros of Birbhum.

When Budhon Sabar was brutally killed some time ago we went to court. While the case was on, I went to Vadodara to deliver a lecture organised by Bhasha, where I said it is not enough to work for tribals alone, we have to fight for the de-notified tribes as well. But I'm sorry to say that tribals as well as de-notified tribes have not received justice until now. In 1952, the government of India declared that there are no more notified criminal tribes. That is where it ended. More than two crore people are still totally denied basic human rights. Tribal land alienation is rampant all over India. Only the other day, forest officials forcibly evicted members of the Korku tribes in Karnataka. In Orissa's Kashipur, the tribals were forced out of their land since it is rich in bauxite and asbestos.

It is a tragedy that all over India, tribal lands are rich in forest and minerals. This wealth goes to make others rich while the tribals face eviction. An old government legislation disallows buying of tribal land by non-tribals, but that is a rule that is maintained only in spirit. I have information that even recently in North 24-Parganas in West Bengal, many tribals have lost their land. Tribal land rights should be rigidly enforced by the government.

I want to see an India where the tribals and de-notified tribes are assured of minimum human rights like land, education, electricity, roads and health facilities. Recently, I read that the West Bengal government is building roads in the tribal habitats of the state. If a road is built, both tribals and non-tribals benefit from it. It is also true for schools and health centres among others. Let India be truly empowered so that even de-notified tribals can feel they are independent, a feeling that they lack today.

As yet, it is only the rich and the educated who have largely benefited from India's independence. Such benefits have not passed over to that section of society that has been the most deprived, irrespective of caste, colour and religion. It is also true that in parliament, it is only the vocal, educated members who manage to get the maximum benefits and not those who come from backward areas and are not as educated.

For example, a person like Phoolan Devi was in parliament for a long time but she was not allowed to speak even for a single day. Recently, there has been talk about lowering the marriageable age of men from 21 to 18. This is absurd. If men are allowed to marry at 18, then should the marriageable age of women be brought down to 14?

Women can only progress as a group in India if there are enough women elected representatives. Even today, most women who enter parliament come from the educated class. Women's empowerment can only happen when each woman finds space to express her opinion independently. My vision of a progressive India is that of a country where there are no class divisions, where water for drinking and irrigation is assured, where there are enough employment opportunities and where there is food for all. All sections of people should equally share the wealth of the country.

It also pains me to see how Rabindranath Tagore's Santiniketan is being totally ruined by promoters and land sharks. We went to the Supreme Court on this, but flouting the Supreme Court's directive, unauthorised construction is going on. We no longer have the right to link Santiniketan with the name of Tagore, who had once asked Mahatma Gandhi to see to it that Santiniketan survives. If this is empowerment, it is tragic. Ultimately, if everyone working in the country justifies his or her salary with productive work, many of the grievances in India will be wiped away.

DHANANJAY DUBEY
STUDENT, BHU; BROTHER OF SATYENDRA DUBEY

Honesty without Fear

India, the world's biggest democracy, is not just a nation of over a hundred crore people but also an embodiment of their identity, their rich cultural heritage, unfailing endeavours, ever-increasing technical prowess, impeccable determination and strengthened infrastructure and economy. India today is empowered.

Our nation is no more the one it was a hundred years ago, ruled by the British. We have an admirable constitutional set-up—legislature, executive, judiciary—to take decisions and look after the welfare of the nation, the welfare of all Indians.

Now, the question arises: when we, as a nation, are empowered to take decisions, when we have the legal authority to decide for ourselves and for our people, why is there so much anarchy all around?

The country seems to have been dumped into the hell of corruption. We hear of scams, the indispensable bribe at each stage in the government machinery, the lawlessness, the nexus between politicians and criminals, the corrupt bureaucracy, the distortion of the level-playing field, the triumph of mediocrity over excellence . . . the list is endless. Why? It's high time we start introspecting.

Introspect and you will realise the high ideals we set for ourselves 58 years ago. A virtuous vision was framed and so was our Constitution. India was declared a sovereign, socialist, secular, democratic republic State ensuring justice—economic, social, political; liberty—of thought, expression, belief, faith and worship; equality—of status and opportunity and promoting fraternity.

I really doubt if our policy makers, the leaders of various political parties, the so-called guardians of our Constitution, know the meaning of these words which describe the identity and ideology of our nation.

Introspect and you will see images of people like Mahatma Gandhi, Lal Bahadur Shastri, Sardar Vallabhbhai Patel, Pandit Nehru, Subhash Chandra Bose, Dr Rajendra Prasad flashing through your mind—leaders who laid the foundation of independent India on the building blocks of patriotism, honesty, hard work, faith, selflessness and courage.

It was their courage that helped them cross the insurmountable hurdles, swim against the current rule, and, win an independent nation for us and restore our pride and respect.

But what can I say about today? What is the reward for honest, courageous and selfless national service by people like my brother, Satyendra Dubey and Manjunath? Brutal murders, endless tears in the eyes of parents, the family and loved ones. And then starts the drama of promises and retribution.

The world starts praising, giving awards (posthumously) but who works to eradicate 'corruption', that brutal murderer? No doubt we have come a long way since Independence. The standard of living has risen, there are technological advancements, the country is striving to achieve economic stability. We are a developing nation which is empowered to frame its foreign and national policies keeping in mind the interests of its people. But so long as power is vested in the hands of leaders who are drenched in corruption and hypocrisy, the outcome will always be the heart-rending deaths of our IITians, IIM students and many more unheard and unknown sons of our motherland.

Why is today's youth so frustrated and directionless? What is the reason for the brain drain? Why does an honest officer face several transfer orders until he's dumped in an unworthy office? Who are the role models for today's young generation? Why are Silicon valleys not in India? Why are anti-social forces thriving?

It's high time we introspect. All prevalent problems point to the same direction—the depth to which corruption has seeped into our system, weakening its very roots. Our vision of empowered India refers to empowerment at each and every level—the empowerment of every Indian. Every Indian should be empowered to work with honesty and to seek safety. Our present education system needs to be reformed. Instead of changing the school syllabus to match ideologies and whims and fancies of every passing government, we must try to elevate facilities in schools as well as research institutes to international standards. Raising educational standards will not only increase the literacy rate but also reflect in the scientific and technological advancements of our nation.

As we watch tears rolling down a mother's eye, it is time we realise the need to give up selfish motives and work towards a better India. An India free from corruption, free from racial prejudices, no more stained by the blood of her devoted sons. Where the brother of a Satyendra Dubey has pride and not just anger to assuage his grief.

KANCHA ILAIAH
DALIT RIGHTS ACTIVIST

Textbooks That Teach Dignity of Labour

As a child when I followed my illiterate shepherd father, neither my parents nor my village social forces knew what India meant, where its borders began and where they ended. This was true of many village communities all over India.

Whether the social mass in the village India was free or was bonded was decided on the caste position within the village but not based on the nationality of that mass. The nationhood of India was not existent for them. For them, the notion of nation had no meaning whatsoever.

If somebody was born in an upper caste, he/she had more freedom and more respect of self and of the other than those who were born into the lower castes. If somebody was born in a Madiga/Chamar family, he/she was born bonded and untouchable. His/her self was untouchable to all the castes above that one. For any village being, the social location in the caste system gave both power/wealth or powerlessness/poverty. For a long time the nation with its power or powerlessness did not touch our lives.

The real villages were not like Karl Marx's imagined villages. They were neither self-sufficient independent entities within themselves nor were they socially and economically connected to one another so intimately. They were messy places in plains adjacent to forests. The connection between villages was limited. People's connections were within their respective castes even of other villages. Social life was stifled and economic life was primitive and precarious.

With a government school coming into the villages in the early sixties, the nation began to connect with the village. Child education became a symbolic dream of their nationalist modernity. Education landed in our village like a helicopter at election season. In any early formative linguistic state, a beginning of modern education in a newly fashioned nationalist language—Telugu, Kannada so on—setting aside the caste-tribal languages in which social groups were communicating with each other, was a cultural long jump.

School brought into our life symbols of nationalism—quite innocently the religious symbols of the dominant castes, as they wrote the lessons in the image of their culture: the culture of Hinduism. A Muslim child was to learn that culture as his/her—though not of his/her—nation's. Rama and Krishna were put in our lives as national heroes but not as religious heroes of a particular religion. The Rig Veda and the Bhagavad Gita were said to have been the most inspiring nationalistic books.

The born bonded children—I mean the Dalit children—were not yet entering school but here and there, there were Muslim and Christian children in the early days of education. If a Dalit family became Christian, the nationalist teacher would allow that family's child to sit in the class as touchable. But while teaching about Hindu gods as nationalist images there were no doubts in the mind of the teacher that religion and nation were two different things. If there was a Muslim or Christian teacher he/she could not dare to say that the Quran or the Bible was a nationalist book too. Thus, nationalism and Hinduism became synonymous. So who got empowered morally and ideologically in that environment? A Hindu nationalist. Neither a Muslim nor a Christian nor a Dalit-Bahujan self got constructed as nationalist. Naturally, hardly any sense of power was instilled in their minds.

But that nationalism had no social basis of establishing a level playing field wherein the caste and religious barriers could be erased and a secular self could be created for all human beings, where humanism could operate on a larger social scale.

In those days, we did not realise that by reading those textbooks we were going to produce a crippled mind that would push us into a culture of indignity of labour. We hardly understood that labour was basically responsible for the advance of science and technology, as our parents who were involved in labour were constantly abused as foolish. We too developed hatred towards labour. We too thought that labour and education were inimical.

If we failed in our further studies we had no place to go back to because shepherding, tilling, pot making, shoe-making and so on were not supposed to be taken up by the educated as they were not considered nationalist professions. Many of us did not realise that that mode of nationalist education was going to make us powerless in an otherwise imagined India of empowerment.

Our education in a regional language slapped us on the face to say that 'you are misfit in an Anglicised universal India'. The prospects of power came here via a convent school that an ardent Hinduwadi would also go to, preferably to a school of St. Joseph or St. Mary. We suddenly, at that late age, realised that national empowerment takes place through self-empowerment and that comes through English. And it was operating through a theoretical twist, of course, that English had come here through a conspiracy of Macaulay and we should be careful in allowing everybody to learn it. To enter into that linguistic domain and to learn the tongue-twisting theory, we were too old in terms of age and too weak in mind.

A nation cannot become empowered if an exceptional being like Dr A.P.J. Abdul Kalam who could become a scientist having gone through the hardships of a Tamil education or like Dr Manmohan Singh who is said to have studied under streetlights—perhaps in the Punjabi medium to start with—and has become an economist of his stature and moved into that position. Nowhere have exceptions empowered a nation. Only when the social mass gets an empowering education can a nation get empowered.

As of now our education system has not produced a social mass that can translate their parental and communitarian historical science and technological experience into modernist science and technology. The religion-centric nationalist education kept all the religious identities on the national table to drive daggers into each other. The caste-centred cultural spheres made us treat each caste as an enemy of the other. A real secular self, with an inbuilt sense of the dignity of labour, is yet to be born.

A scientific temper that can challenge our very neighbour, China, if not the west, may spring up if we recognise English as the necessary national language to be taught on par with every regional language in every state from class one to every child. We can—and must—take out all forms of religious content from textbooks and teach the dignity of labour on a compulsory basis. Perhaps India will then begin to empower itself.

R.A. MASHELKAR

DIRECTOR GENERAL, COUNCIL OF SCIENTIFIC & INDUSTRIAL
RESEARCH, & PRESIDENT, INDIAN NATIONAL SCIENCE ACADEMY

Stem the Brain Drain, Inspire Growth

India's future is in IT, not in IT as in Information Technology, but in IT as in Indian Talent. Giving every opportunity possible to Indian talent to reach its real potential would truly empower India.

What happens to Indian talent today? 50 per cent of Indian children go to school. 30 per cent of them reach the 10th standard. 40 per cent of them pass. Thus, 6 per cent of our children go past the 10th standard. This is only a tip of the iceberg, of which only a very small part shines. A huge part of the iceberg remains submerged and dark. To me, India will be truly empowered when we let the entire iceberg shine by lifting it.

I too belonged to that submerged part of the iceberg. I was born in a very poor family. My father died when I was six. My illiterate mother did menial work to bring me up. I went barefoot till I was twelve. I studied under streetlights. Yet I was empowered again and again.

I studied in a free municipal school. Access to free education through public funding was the first empowerment in my life.

On finishing primary school, I sought admission in a secondary school. I required 21 rupees as admission fee. My mother did not have the money. A lady, who herself was a housemaid in Mumbai, gave her savings to us. One 'have not' sharing with another 'have not' was a powerful lesson of empowerment early in my life.

I stood 11th amongst 1,35,000 students in the state in the Maharashtra State Board exam in 1960. I was about to quit school, since my mother could not afford my college education. The Sir Dorabji Tata Trust gave me a scholarship of 60 rupees per month until my graduation. Thus, my next empowerment came through the philanthropy of an industrial house. My school teachers empowered me. Principal Bhave taught me physics in school. One day, he took us out in the sun to demonstrate the method of finding the focal length of a convex lens. When the sun rays were focused on the paper, it got burnt. He turned to me and said, 'Mashelkar, if you focus your energies, you can achieve anything in life.' That gave me an inspiration to become a scientist. It gave me the philosophy of life; focus and you can achieve anything. Empowering India to me, therefore, means growing millions of Bhaves, who will inspire young Indian kids.

I was teaching and researching in England in the early seventies. Indira Gandhi was the prime minister. The news of Nobel laureate Khorana not getting a job in India had done the rounds. She asked the then director general of CSIR, Dr Nayudamma, to go abroad, pick up the brightest and the best and offer them jobs on the spot.

Nayudamma came to London in 1974. He met me, among others. He offered me a position at NCL in Pune. There was no application, no formal interview, no bureaucratic hurdles. I came back to India, thanks to a science leader, who was trusted and empowered by a prime minister.

India cannot be truly empowered until the best of its talent stays in India and contributes. Why does talent leave India? An Italian Nobel laureate, Riardo Giacconi, who settled in the US said, 'A scientist is like a painter. Michelangelo became a great artist because he had been given a wall to paint. My wall was given to me by the United States.' To empower scientists, it is necessary to give them a wall to paint.

This year, I became only the eighth scientist from India to be elected to the US National Academy of Science since 1863. After the Nobel prize, this is one of the highest honours. Every scientist aspires for it. The honour came to me this year because a visionary CSIR leadership had empowered a young Mashelkar by giving him his wall to paint thirty years ago.

My lessons from my life are simple. A society that gives an opportunity for education to everyone, that has inspiring teachers, that has philanthropic industrialists, that has visionary leaders in all walks of life and that gives talent every opportunity to reach its real potential—becomes truly empowered.

G. MADHAVAN NAIR
CHAIRMAN, INDIAN SPACE RESEARCH ORGANISATION

Intellectual Capital Is the Change Agent

To me, India empowered means that every adult in this country is able to earn his livelihood with honour and dignity. Every adult has a say in governing the country in a democratic set-up and each one's voice is heard and cared for. Every citizen becomes an asset and contributes in his own way to nation building.

All these can be achieved only by literacy and healthcare and providing infrastructure like communication and transport, even to the remotest areas, and creating employment opportunities to use the varying skills and talents of our citizens.

Having been associated with the Indian space programme since its inception, I would say that India has shown the capability to build its own satellites for communication, television broadcasting, meteorology and resources survey and management as well as to launch them using its own launch vehicles like the Polar Satellite Launch Vehicle and the Geosynchronous Satellite Launch Vehicle.

The fact that India is capable of achieving self-reliance even in the most advanced technologies like space and, more importantly, use these capabilities for the upliftment of society at the grassroots level shows that India has the potential to become an empowered nation.

The recent initiatives like tele-education through EDUSAT for formal and non-formal educational services, tele-medicine networks that connect speciality hospitals in major cities to rural and remote areas and the Village Resources Centres that help farmers on various aspects like land-use, water, agriculture, weather, market information, etc. can help in empowering our society at the grassroots level.

There is a need to focus our attention on the development of the younger generation. Traditionally, Indians have very high intellectual capabilities. The inherent intellectual talents of our youngsters have been proved in the IT field and in intellectual competitions like international mathematics and astronomical Olympiads or even in intellectual games like chess.

What is required is to harness this highly capable intellectual potential for productive nation-building efforts. Creating the right environment through a progressive and modern educational system designed to bring out the talents of the pupils, inculcating a scientific temper, improving their knowledge base and skills as well as moulding them to become disciplined, committed and patriotic citizens can make India an empowered nation in the coming years.

JAYANT V. NARLIKAR
EMERITUS PROFESSOR, INTER-UNIVERSITY CENTRE
FOR ASTRONOMY AND ASTROPHYSICS, PUNE

Exciting Research Out of Labs into Universities

I visualise an empowered India as a nation that is materially and mentally in the 21st century. Thus, it's counted amongst the advanced nations as far as progress in science and technology is concerned and is able to make effective use of its natural resources. Its citizens will have the mindset to take rational decisions not influenced by pseudo-science or by notions two-three centuries back old time.

I have always been impressed by scientific and technological achievements of an exceptional order in areas like space, atomic energy, information technology etc. coming from India. At a personal level, I felt a sense of achievement when the Inter-University Centre for Astronomy and Astrophysics I was asked to set up in Pune attained an international reputation for excellence within seven years.

Unfortunately, we are not doing enough to attract the younger generation to science. Our school syllabi and examination system are geared to encourage and reward rote learning rather than comprehension and originality. Our productive scientists in research institutions do not come forward to teach university courses. We need an avenue where undergraduates and postgraduates in our colleges come in contact with teachers who are doing exciting science.

There is a need to encourage and attract bright young scientists in our research labs and universities. We have to shed the mindset that universities are simply glorified schools and that only research institutes can do research, in complete isolation from students. When students see exciting research being done in their colleges, some of them will be motivated to stay and do the same.

MEDHA PATKAR
SOCIAL ACTIVIST

People in Control of Their Resources

Even after 57 years of independence, one has to dream of a 'strong, capable and confident India', that is yet to come true. If this is a message not just for some bright, young school children standing in front of you in an elite school in a mega city, then you can't escape questions—what strength, what capability and what confidence, in doing what? All these virtues or qualities together can be termed 'empowerment', which in turn is to be spelt out within a value framework.

The empowerment (not only of the rulers or the state but of civil society, the common people in India), one can say, lies in their capability and readiness to make the best use of resources—human, natural and financial, to meet the needs of all. Needs, not desires, minimum or optimum, include food, water, shelter, health and livelihood as a means to the end.

One can say this process of harnessing resources, production and distribution of the value added is to be necessarily equal and just, if one's goal is not just power and privilege to a few and deprivation and destitution to the others!

India has a huge resource base and a favourable matrix of flowing rivers, deep aquifers, millions of hectares of land, forests (though more or less degraded), rich minerals, aquatic wealth, as also more and more citizens with human power. It has to apply its vision to use these to make a country where no one will be hungry or thirsty, unemployed or underemployed, shelter-less or even illiterate.

The power of all this cannot be limited to the electoral power of the elite but must be extended to include the real people's power which lies in their ability to choose of appropriate technology, and putting into place mechanisms for ensuring distributive justice as also the democratic process of planning, and the making of these choices itself.

This requires, on one hand, people standing united at whatever level they work together, beyond caste, class and gender divisions, with a deep faith in human equity, commitment to national integrity and the required tolerance to attain and maintain unity.

It also demands that the State behaves, not misusing its political mandate to divide and rule or misappropriate people's resources, not creating any conditions for human injustice, in any form, traditional and customary, caste-based or modern. If the State doesn't or fails to do this, then the test of empowerment lies in challenging the State itself.

Satyagraha, in its various forms, is the test of both empowerment of the citizenry in critically assessing the the State's performance, in asserting their rights and that of the State in responding to the same.

The beauty of such a bifocal vision of an empowered nation state is that it does involve struggle, it may lead to a social movement but ultimately doesn't aggravate but helps resolve the power conflict.

With such a dream in our hearts, where do we stand today? Events after events and various politico-economic analyses give us a clear indication that we have reneged on the values of equity as well as self-reliance. The arson and murder of Dalits in Gohana, farmers committing suicide in a vast region from Andhra Pradesh to Punjab, the eviction of thousands of slum dwellers, deaths of adivasi children due to malnutrition amidst a comparatively richer natural resource base, or degraded, waterlogged lands, dead cattle, dry rivers and empty public exchequers.

Each of these examples are signs of unacceptable, undemocratic decisions and actions by the State, and at times, by inhuman anti-social groups instigated by unholy politics. The still distant ways of empowering the Dalits to counter atrocities include universal and egalitarian development measures, granting them rights to livelihood, as also effective measures of positive discrimination, such as reservations.

Empowering farmers and labourers against the agrarian economy crisis that India is still facing could only be by giving them the right kind of status and space, as well as value for their agricultural produce, the natural capital invested, and labour inputs.

The owner-cultivator category, if respected and supported (why call it a subsidy when in every sector, much of the infrastructure-to-production process has the State's massive support), can sustain itself and agriculture could emerge as a sector accommodating vast human power.

The choice of technology to deal with the worsening crisis is thus obvious: organic farming, self-reliant multiple cropping, as also equitable land distribution. Empowering farmers and farm labourers can't be done by providing an international market.

The global market powers that the rulers ally with in the name of our green producers, are all out to exploit our seeds of sustainable biodiversity, change our laws and patent our products and processes. Their profiteering ways fill the godowns but keep the stomachs of the toilers in the field empty.

The challenge to this has to come from the organised farmer force but when our elected representatives in power are ignoring the dreadful impact of market intrusion beyond limits, it is to be opposed at every forum— economic, social and political. The agreements against agriculture and agriculturists in India, signed behind curtains and beyond the borders at WTO fora, need to be questioned and so does Monsanto's way of genetically modifying food and economically exploiting natural wealth.

A large section (93 per cent) of our working masses are called 'unorganised' but they too, as victims of disparity in wages, and who are denied the security and support of the State, are up against it. Their empowerment lies in demanding and attaining equity through comprehensive and fair labour laws.

But the trend is the opposite. Even the so-called organised workers in banking, insurance, education, and in the private and public sectors are being thrown out simply by allowing foreign capital and corporates to take over. Their profit rules above our people, as our ruling elite further their own petty interests.

The modern kings, striking their postures at democratic fora such as the parliament, making unscrupulous alliances with the corrupt and criminal, shaking hands with international capital, are all out to turn a vast majority of this country into bonded labourers and disempower them. The sell-out of our minerals, our aquatic wealth and the impact of this is devastating not just on the displaced and destitute, but also to our independence and our future.

Empowerment lies in asserting the sovereignty not just of ministers but of people—as was the vision of Gandhi and Ambedkar. Social control over resources can lead to not statist power but a democratic socialist Indian power.

This vision of self-reliance, of both the State and the society, can be worked out to the last detail and tried in small, yet replicable ways all over. It doesn't suggest isolation in the global context but it has to begin with the real social units—our communities—and the democratic processes. It rejects the unlimited greed of a consumerist lifestyle or competing with war-mongering, pompously rich nation states out to expropriate and destroy not just their neighbours but the world.

First rights to our land, water and forests will then be granted to our adivasis, Dalits, grazers, fishworkers and farmers according to the principles of land to the tiller ownership of the means of production and gram swaraj—all of which have much in common.

The individual-community conflict can be resolved by the 'Gramdan' model, with some improvement. These democratic fora will work with technology and not without it, to sustainably harness the resources. Our waters can be tapped but beginning with mini and micro watersheds. The principle of subsidiarity, enlarging circles with diminishing rights and powers will be followed not only in watersheds but also in administrative units.

Living a simple, self-reliant life is not being against prosperity. It needs empowerment from the moral to the physical. This approach is not against science, it stands for the scientific method but does not misuse science and technology. It upholds the values of equity and sustainability which can and are to be ensured only by popular participation and direct democracy.

S.Z. QASIM
SCIENTIST,
LEADER OF INDIA'S FIRST ANTARCTICA EXPEDITION

Science and Technology Can Drive Social Change

It is to the credit of our planners and those responsible for the formulation of India's science and technology policy that they have grasped the far-reaching implications of technological developments, which are now being accelerated in each plan. The tenth Five Year Plan has witnessed some highly encouraging trends in the development of national capabilities in new frontier technologies. However, the utilisation of the economic potential of the new technologies must be fully realized in the Eleventh and subsequent plans.

Because of the vision and foresight of Pandit Jawaharlal Nehru, our development plans have always recognised the vital role of science and technology in the social and economic transformation of our country. Our universities and institutes of national importance now annually produce 3,00,000 or more people trained in different scientific and technological fields. National expenditure on science and technology, including industrial research and development, is now more than 1 per cent of our GNP. However, because of the unprecedented explosion in scientific and technological knowledge in the developed countries, the technological distance between the rich and the developing countries is not becoming narrower.

The exploitation of modern scientific knowledge and technological advances is now the main source of economic growth in developed countries. The new technologies have far-reaching implications for the comparative advantage of countries in the international competition for global markets. Developing countries cannot remain just silent spectators while this new industrial revolution sweeps the industrialised world.

The ongoing science and technology resurgence is being called the fourth Industrial Revolution and for this we need a properly planned strategy in the emerging global order so that we can achieve whatever we envision in time.

The most fortunate thing about the new industrial revolution is that it is largely dominated by skilled people and not much by heavy machinery. In other words, it is more software-oriented than hardware. For example, the phenomenal growth in information technology has resulted in an exponential increase in software demand. This means large employment generation for skilled people to use computer programming effectively. Modern technology is more oriented towards system configuration than the development of hard and robust machines. This has provided a lead to India where the scientific and technical manpower pool is so large that even with limited financial resources, intellectual input can compensate the reduction in hardware. This is the reason why software export from India is one of the largest foreign exchange earners for the country today and our computer programmers are very much in demand throughout the world.

The outcome of science and technology as an instrument of socio-economic change depends a great deal on the proper articulation of the complex linkages that exist between the management of technology, the economy and wider polity. An effective strategy for the management of technical change must be based on a careful analysis of the country's social and economic objectives, and the various resource constraints it faces. From a long-term perspective, a country like India, suffering from an acute scarcity of land and natural resources on a per capita basis, must give high priority to the development of technologies which can overcome these resource constraints.

Degradation of land and water resources constitutes a major threat to the sustainability of the growth process in several parts of our country. Science and technology has a major role to play in meeting this threat. In particular, in the planning of science and technology, special attention has to be paid to raise the productivity of dry land agriculture. Demand for commercial energy is likely to increase rapidly in the process of development. Commercial energy is highly capital-intensive and our dependence on imports for meeting our requirements of hydrocarbons is quite considerable. Technologies designed to conserve energy and those like solar, wind energy and sea power which are based on the use of renewable resources must, therefore, receive priority. Similarly, the acute shortage of drinking water in coastal areas and on islands (Lakshadweep/Andaman & Nicobar) can be adequately fulfilled by producing an endless supply of bacteria-free, potable water from seawater using low-temperature desalination technology, as has been installed on Kavaratti Island by the National Institute of Ocean Technology (NIOT), Chennai. In inland areas, recycling technology of used freshwater can provide an answer, as is being done in several European countries.

The limited natural resource base of the country also implies that we will have to rely on international trade much more in the future to meet our requirements of hydrocarbons and other scarce raw materials. We cannot finance these imports without a dynamic export sector. It is only through a competitive manufacturing base that we can build up an expanding export sector.

Exporting in the globalised economy of the modern information age will require adequate access to new information technologies, new micro-electronic devices for quality control and an updated system of design and engineering capabilities, as well as modern infrastructure of telecommunications, banking and other financial services.

Flexible manufacturing systems of clusters of computerised numerical control machines are transforming production processes in the world. They save on labour and other inputs, inventory and warehousing costs and facilitate the production of multiple, highly custom-tailored, small batches of products on the same set of equipment. As a result, these technologies threaten to erode the competitive advantage of developing countries even in such traditional labour-intensive industries as textiles. Our export strategies must take all this into account.

It is therefore necessary that planners and all those concerned with the management of education and scientific and technological research should face up squarely to the challenge of making that technological leap. Clearly, there will be a need for larger resources. But there is an equally urgent need to review the efficiency and effectiveness of the existing structures for the management of science and technology. The government's strong commitment and practical support are indispensable, but this should not lead to excessive bureaucratisation of scientific and technological research. In particular, we've to ensure that our research institutions provide an environment conducive to the pursuit of excellence and creativity.

We need specialised institutions for technology development, but their management strategies must have built-in safeguards to promote and nurse creativity. We must ensure that the institutional structure of research and development is sufficiently geared to the needs of the production system.

Economic policies have an equally important role to play in the process of technological transformation. In an age of rapid technological change, the inducement to invest in new processes and products is greatly affected by the prospects for reasonable price stability and the stance of fiscal policies. A stable macro-economic environment ensures that higher productivity, rather than speculative gains, becomes the major determinant of corporate fortunes.

For strengthening the socio-economic sector with science and technology, we have to be grateful to the founding fathers of our republic for giving us a political framework based on democracy, respect for fundamental human rights and the rule of law. We have deliberately chosen the difficult path of ushering in a social and economic revolution within the framework of an open society and polity. We can take pride in our achievements since Independence. But we can hardly be complacent.

ARUNA ROY
ACTIVIST

Tune in to the Voice of the Deprived

We all want to matter, from the poorest, most marginalised to the most powerful individual and community. We want our views to be heard, our pain and suffering addressed, our hopes and aspirations to be acknowledged. The motivational power of this universal desire to be relevant has always encouraged me.

Democracy theoretically offers every individual an equal voice in deciding our collective future. That is empowerment. But it is a long voyage from theory to practice. It is along this journey that we can nurture individual and collective motivation with compassion and understanding, or sow the seeds of our collapse through indifference, shatter dreams and silence voices. Our 55 year experiment with democracy has been a mixed bag.

In India, both the sanctity of public space and individual freedom coexist with the attempt to curtail it. But the danger is in the lack of protest when there is a deliberate attempt to limit these spaces.

We get into narrow sectarian debates and forget that in the denial of others' democratic rights lies the beginnings of the end to our freedom. We also want to put our heads into the sand and not see the deprivation, poverty and oppression that exists all around us.

The demolition of urban slums, driving away of the urban poor, the continuing oppression and marginalisation of women, Dalits, the ghettoisation of minorities are not merely the denial of a visual presence. They are the festering sores of our body politic which will turn into our Frankenstein.

The biggest horror for any individual or community is exclusion. In the consequent spread of alienation and intolerance we sow the seeds of our own destruction. We must make and protect the spaces for dissent, even of the most poor, alienated, and marginalised. We must ask ourselves what we can do to change those conditions. It requires confidence and political maturity to listen to these voices. When we do so, we will have an involved and empowered India.

In a sense, democracy is at its best when it is kept simple and straightforward. The vote is only an affirmation of the people being sovereign in a democratic framework. The challenge in one sense has been to return in more meaningful ways to having a system of governance 'of, by and for the people' in a practical manner.

Public action has come out of these basic and cherished ideals. Action which connects a concern for oneself with a concern for others eventually strengthens one's own sense of well being and peace. Democracy gives us all a right to act. Many of us are in fact denied the right to act, because of caste, class, religious and gender prejudices. Others who can, do not act. They neither perceive their role nor even think of a social agenda.

We have an obligation to enable those who are denied access to shrinking public spaces. Also to push those who can, but do not, into some sort of limited public action. Imagine 1 per cent of Indians in intelligent public action—it is a crore of people who can change this country. We could be a part of the process of change and feel immensely empowered.

Important moments of my content have come out of collective action. Whether it was in 1,000 women protesting against rape, innovating in methods of expressing their emotions, or in a dharna, where after struggling together for months and years, a change is acceded to. Campaigns have repeatedly demonstrated the power of collective participation to change the direction of governance.

My own involvement with many campaigns shows that even laws with far-reaching consequences, like the Right to Information Act and the Employment Guarantee Act, can come about through the involvement of ordinary people in the conception, formulation and implementation of law and policy. They also result in simple practical entitlements for democratic action.

I do not see empowerment in the disappearance of problems, but in the strength and ability to deal with them. As you reach the end of a campaign and achieve something, in the seeds of that achievement lie the problems of the future: maybe even of the present. Democracy primarily needs common sense. Ordinary Indians have it in plenty. Provided we perceive it, give it respect, respectability and credence.

We need to nurture a social ethos where religion means compassion, kindness and acceptance of another's faith. Where plurality is respected and success brings humility and not arrogance, appreciation and not rejection.

If the national movement was one massive act of concerted public action, it cannot peter away into a memory of recalled glory. What a million small and big efforts have shown in post-Independence India is that this continues to exist. Unfortunately, it is no longer central to public, political concern. Politics has been narrowed to its most limited definition, and allowed the justification for inaction.

In a democracy, politics is everybody's business. Our political lives only begin with a casting of the vote. The damning of 'politics', and making it a bad word in our lexicon, has given us the luxury of cynicism and inaction.

For too long we have only blamed others. We cannot rely on one leader, ensconced in an artificial halo (of electric lights), to bring about change. Empowerment is the recognition of our collective political responsibility. We need to use the power we have, with intelligence and courage.

SRI SRI RAVI SHANKAR
SPIRITUAL TEACHER

No to Blame Culture, Yes to Courage and Change

To me, India is empowered when at least 80 per cent of its people are empowered. As most of India's population lives in rural areas, just a few urbanites being empowered will be unfortunate for this country. India will be truly empowered when people at the grassroots start feeling confident about themselves, their way of life, their tradition and their language.

A Frenchman is proud of being French or speaking French, but here in India for a Kannadiga, Telugu, Maharashtrian or Tamilian, pride depends on how well versed he or she is in English or any other foreign language. Their pride is in eating pizzas, owning branded jeans and shoes and the foreign trips they make.

There is nothing wrong in adopting good things from other cultures. The problem is, creativity and entrepreneurship die out completely when you don't take pride in your own culture and lose self-esteem.

The most effective yardstick of empowerment is the willingness of people to take responsibility. We need to move away from the blame culture. Instead of blaming the elected government, religious leaders, police and even the weather, people need to take responsibility for creating not just a prosperous but a happy society as well.

Many societies in the world are prosperous, but they are miserable to the core. To me, India empowered means a crime-free, humane society. A renewed focus on its core areas of strength will make India realise its true potential.

India has the best potential for tourism which needs to be exploited. India has one of the best scientific talent pools in the world. India also has youth power. The ancient Indian knowledge of yoga is a rage all over the world. From Kashmir to Kanyakumari, India is bestowed with rich spiritual literature and philosophy. Ayurveda has the potential to make India a leader in holistic healthcare.

India should be proud of its diverse cuisine, dance and music, rich textiles, embroidery, jewellery and embellishments, which have been widely appreciated all over the world. As the saying goes, India is sitting on a huge pile of wealth, not knowing its worth. Real empowerment will happen when the people of India realise that they have the power to change.

M. SHANMUGAM
FATHER OF S. MANJUNATH, THE IIM GRADUATE AND INDIAN OIL CORPORATION OFFICER WHO WAS KILLED IN U.P. FOR REPORTING AGAINST MALPRACTICE AT A PETROL PUMP

In the Line of Duty

My son Manju told me several times that he had received threats while doing his duty in the Lakhimpur area of Uttar Pradesh. My advice to him had always been to get out from the area or to quit the job if there was a threat to his life. But my Manju was not one who knew fear, he would not give up without a fight. Even with me he was loving but fearless.

Now as I grieve for my son, I think it's not just Lakhimpur or U.P. or any other state that's a difficult place for an honest person. Corruption is everywhere, in every state, in every district. The media have exposed corruption so many times—but have things changed in this country? No. Everywhere there is lawlessness. I am sorry if I sound despairing.

India will be empowered if honest people like Manju, who act against illegalities, who don't take bribes are able to work in this country. Their lives should be safeguarded. In India, people believe that if you act against corruption, you will not survive, that you are in danger. That has to change.

From what I have heard since my son's death, there have been around five IIM-Lucknow graduates who joined oil companies in India as sales managers. After seeing the ground situation, three of them are said to have left. One IIM-L student, who was earlier in BPCL and was a friend of Manju's, visited us after his death. She told me, 'Uncle, I have seen the malpractice. I could not do anything, I left.'

Take my own case. I am nearing 58 years; until I was around 35, I followed a principle that I wouldn't use bribery to get any work done. I obtained my driving licence, my house-building permit without paying a bribe. I was made to run around for nearly a year for the khata (ownership) certificate for my house, but I refused to pay a bribe.

I realised then the amount of time and energy I had spent to get the khata. If I had paid the Rs 50 that the clerk at the government office asked me to do on the first occasion, I would have got my khata much sooner.

Like President A.P.J. Abdul Kalam said, we are confident of driving without a licence in this country because we are sure that if we pay Rs 50 to the policeman who stops us, we will get away. Only a small fraction of people in this country stand by a no-bribe policy. That fraction has to increase.

We need a nation that respects its laws 100 per cent. We need a nation where those who break the law pay for it, not slip through the loopholes. What has happened in the Satyendra Dubey case? It took months before the police said they had nabbed the alleged killers, one of them even escaped. What happened to the complaints he made?

Our country is moving forward. We now encourage multi-national corporations to do business out of India. We are constantly in touch with people from developed countries, we know how they live, what they believe in. We must respect the law like they do in their empowered countries.

For, until there is respect for the law, honest people have to be very careful. I told my son that when he faced problems, he should act like other officers. He said there had been no one at Lakhimpur for a while. Even if there were some, I know Manju was his own man, he hated to follow others' examples. What he thought and decided was usually the final word.

India empowered to me is when any son's or daughter's final word isn't a dying declaration in the line of duty.

DEVI SHETTY
CARDIAC SURGEON; CHAIRMAN,
NARAYANA HRUDAYALAYA HOSPITALS

Ensure the Best, Insure the Future

It is almost a tradition in South Kanara of Karnataka for young people to join medical school and soon after graduation, go to Europe or the US for post-graduate training. I did exactly the same and in the year 1989, left Guy's Hospital in London for Kolkata (then Calcutta) to start the B.M. Birla Heart Research Centre, a super-specialty heart hospital for the Birla family, which eventually became one of the pioneers in the emerging field of cardiac surgery.

The transformation from Heathrow to Howrah was remarkable. As late as 1989, getting disposable gloves and disposable slag for a heart operation was a major event—leave alone other expensive materials for the surgery.

In a short period of time, I could see the entire industry change as professionals like us started demanding things and the industry started supplying them.

I understand it is difficult for people to believe but I am proud to say that today, certain materials used in heart surgery made by Indian companies are sold at a slightly higher price than their competitors from the west. And we Indians prefer to use these materials not because they are made in India but because they are better, they are the best.

Where do we see high-tech healthcare leading to in a country like India? Are we anywhere close to the largest and the best in the world or do we have a chance? The answer is simple. Within the next 10 years, India will have the best mass healthcare programme in the world. Every procedure on the human body will be done in a different manner and how it will be done will be defined by a doctor in India—and these changes are not going to take a lifetime. All the ingredients for this major transformation are already in place; it's just a matter of time before somebody puts all the pieces of the jigsaw puzzle together and comes up with an end product.

India trains close to 20,000 doctors a year. Karnataka has over 600 nursing schools. There are streets in Mangalore which have one or two medical colleges and half a dozen physiotherapy and pharmacy schools. All these are going to pay rich dividends to the healthcare delivery system.

Healthcare is an interaction between man and machine. The scarce commodity in healthcare is technically-skilled people which we produce in abandon, and that's our asset.

Our only missing link was the paying capacity of poor patients. But with the experience of 'Yeshasvini micro health scheme' launched by the Karnataka State Cooperative Societies in association with our organisation and the Family Health Plan, the problem was solved.

So we now know that with a modest amount of Rs 5 a month, we can provide wonderful health care, as shown by Yeshasvini which covers the health care of 2.5 million farmers for just five rupees a month.

Now this scheme is in the process of being launched in Maharashtra, Andhra Pradesh, Rajasthan, Tamil Nadu and various other states. Once poor people realise that just as they pay for rice, kerosene, and milk, they also have to pay a tiny amount every month for healthcare, the problem of healthcare delivery in this country will be solved.

Healthcare is one of the largest employment generators for people coming from the lower socio-economic strata. The National Health Services of the United Kingdom—of which I was once an employee—is the third-largest employer in the world after the Chinese army and our Indian railways.

Just for taking care of a few million people's health in the United Kingdom, they have hired the third-largest organised work force. You think about a situation where half of our country's population carry a smart card of micro-health insurance and we are talking about employment for, perhaps, the largest organised work force in the world. For, investment in healthcare not only creates a healthy nation but also creates millions of job opportunities.

M.S. SWAMINATHAN
AGRICULTURAL SCIENTIST

Make Hunger History through Gram Swaraj

India's independence was born in the backdrop of the great Bengal famine. This led Jawaharlal Nehru to say in 1947, 'everything else can wait but not agriculture'.

In free India's tryst with destiny, achieving freedom from hunger was thus accorded high priority. On the occasion of the fiftieth anniversary of our independence on the midnight of August 14-15, 1997, the then president, K.R. Narayanan referred to our democratic system of governance and the Green Revolution as the two major achievements of the first 50 years of freedom from colonial rule.

What should we consider as our principal achievements on the occasion of the 60th anniversary of our independence on August 14-15, 2007? In my view, providing every child, woman and man in our country an opportunity for a healthy and productive life through concurrent attention to nutrition and education should be our overriding priority.

We no longer experience famines, unlike in the colonial period when serious famines occurred almost once in five years. However, food security at the level of every household, defined in terms of access to a balanced diet and clean drinking water, is still a far cry. Over 250 million children, women and men go to bed each night partially hungry.

According to the mid-term appraisal of the Tenth Plan by the Union Planning Commission, we are off-track in terms of achieving the UN Millennium Development Goal of reducing the incidence of hunger by half by 2015.

What is worse is the widespread incidence of maternal and foetal under-nutrition, leading to the birth of babies characterised by low birth weight (LBW). Such LBW children face even at birth, handicaps in terms of brain development and cognitive abilities.

Denying a child the right to realise its innate genetic potential for physical and mental development is the most cruel form of inequity. Any nation which undervalues its human resource and over-values its material resources like land and buildings will always remain poor. This is the basic cause of the Indian enigma, where excellence in many areas of human endeavour and science and technology co-exists with extensive poverty, deprivation and inhuman living conditions for 25 per cent of the population.

This is not a god-given destiny, but entirely man-made. How then can we shape our destiny in the direction of making hunger history and gram swaraj a reality?

Hunger has three dimensions—chronic under-nutrition arising from inadequate purchasing power; hidden, caused by the deficiency of micronutrients in the diet like iron, iodine, zinc and vitamin A; and transient, caused by earthquakes, tsunami, drought, floods and other natural calamities.

The hunger hot-spot areas in our country are largely rainfed with poor infrastructure and communication. The present conditions of food insecurity prevailing in the earthquake affected areas in Jammu and Kashmir as well as in Pakistan are examples of transient hunger.

Where there is a problem there is invariably also an affordable and implementable solution. The National Rural Employment Guarantee Act will help reduce chronic under-nutrition. In my view, this should be developed into a Food Guarantee Act by August 15, 2007, combining the features of the Food for Work and Employment Guarantee programmes. We must increase consumption if we are to induce our farmers to produce more. Enabling small farmers to enhance productivity will help eradicate hunger considerably.

Unlike in industrialised countries, where 2 to 3 per cent of the population depends upon agriculture for their livelihood, over 60 per cent of our population depends on crop and animal husbandry, fisheries, agro-forestry and agro-processing for their daily bread.

The National Commission on Farmers (NCF) has suggested methods of enhancing small-farm productivity in their first two reports submitted to the government of India in December 2004 and August 2005. Improving soil health, particularly addressing micro-nutrient deficiencies in the soil, besides improved water conservation and management will help greatly bridge the prevailing wide gap between potential and actual yields in most cropping systems.

Hidden hunger caused by micro-nutrient deficiencies can be overcome through an integrated food-cum-fortification approach, including multiple fortification of salt. Transient hunger can be eliminated through a national grid of community grain banks operated by local women's self-help groups. Priority in the location of the grain banks should be given to areas where communication tends to be disrupted during the monsoon season or during natural calamities, as in hilly areas and islands.

There is no time to relax on the production front. Both absolute and factor productivity (i.e. response to fertiliser, water, etc.) are going down. The rate of growth in food production is now much below that of the population growth rate. The multiple role of agriculture as the backbone of our food, livelihood and ecological security systems as well as of national sovereignty is yet to be widely realised.

Farmers in industrialised countries operate large farms supported by heavy inputs of capital, technology and subsidy. In contrast, the 25 per cent of the global farming population living in our country suffers from serious constraints in the areas of technology, input supply, services and public policies, particularly in the areas of pricing, marketing and rural infrastructure.

Our agriculture is increasingly becoming a gamble in the market and without arrangements for assured and remunerative marketing, farmers will lose interest in farming. There is a need for an integrated strategy which involves attention to defending the gains already made, extending the gains to dry farming areas and making new gains through farming systems diversification, value addition and enlarging home and external trade.

Defending the gains will involve proactive research to meet the challenges of climate change and the incidence of new diseases. In particular, we should immediately strengthen our capacity in biosecurity as suggested by the NCF last year. The H5N1 strain of bird flu virus can kill millions of both poultry and human beings. Alien invasive species of pests, pathogens and weeds can do immense harm to our crop and animal security.

The challenges are formidable but they can be overcome if we use the power of democratic decentralisation through panchayati raj institutions. Every gram panchayat can develop and operate a community food and water security system. By harnessing the tools of the internet and community radio, every village can become a knowledge centre.

Knowledge connectivity should become the backbone of the Bharat Nirman movement. Fortunately, a national alliance, consisting of all the stakeholders, assisted by an international support group, has been formed to make Mission 2007: Every Village a Knowledge Centre a reality.

Complex problems can be solved only by disaggregating the analysis as well as the action plan. This is where the over 3 million elected members of panchayats, including over a million women members, can become the torch bearers of an India empowered movement designed to make hunger and illiteracy problems of the past.

NARESH TREHAN
CARDIOTHORACIC SURGEON

Create Healthy Villages in the Other India

Enough of enumerating India's problems. We need to enumerate solutions. We all know that there are two entirely different, parallel Indias. There is a disturbing divergence between the two. One India is progressing towards becoming a developed nation. The second India, rural and 70 per cent of the country, is being bypassed in this process. It may have improved in that mass famines are rare. Most people have a roof over their heads, they are clothed and have food. But, beyond that, they are exactly as they were two decades ago.

The fundamentals of basic necessities have been largely met but other basic necessities such as their environment and health are still wanting, they have almost no healthcare and only poor education. There is a divergence instead of a convergence.

Enough thought has been given to it. Enough has been written about it. The problem is understood many times over. But the implementation is missing. The time has come to take ownership of solutions and implementation.

On the one hand, we are saying that India's GDP is growing at 6 to 8 per cent, which by any standards is a healthy growth rate. But, because we are starting at such a low level, if we are to catch up with the rest of the world, we have to drive the engine at a growth rate of 12 to 14 per cent.

It is politically hazardous for governments to promise 12 to 14 per cent growth because if it reaches 6 to 8 per cent, then you are considered a political failure. So the government is cautious. Officially, the government is saying 6 to 8 per cent is acceptable but in actuality it is necessary that the government push the drivers of growth, such as tourism, the software sector, industry etc. The government must assist them to achieve 12 to 14 per cent in the next five years.

More important than this is to take charge of the second India: the rural population. It is essential to first create healthy villages. The definition would be: clean drinking water, sanitation, public toilets, waste disposal, hygiene education, vector control and schools, essential to eliminate the disease burden on the rural population.

One model like this already exists. Hero Honda, CII and Escorts Heart Institute adopted the village Joniavas. Joniavas has 2,500 residents and abuts the back wall of Hero Honda's Dharuhera plant in Haryana. Joniavas was adopted as a pilot project.

The audit undertaken showed any village you may have been to. The sewage from the village dwellings flowed freely in the front and back lanes, in between homes. The backyard of each home was a garbage dump and the hand pump from which the whole village used water was right in the middle of the sewage dump. There were several water bodies replete with breeding mosquitoes. The school had no wall around it. There were no toilets for the children. The girls would not go to school because of the fear of having to relieve themselves in public. The road leading to the village had slush that was six inches thick.

After the audit, work was carried out with finances from Hero Honda; Escorts Heart Institute and CII provided technical knowledge and supervision. Over a two-month period, a pucca drainage system, garbage disposal system and a potable water pump were installed. A wall was built around the school. Toilets were provided for the children. The mosquito breeding was destroyed. A compacted earth road was built going into the village. The primary health centre was activated with constant motivation and supervision. The total cost was Rs 12 lakh.

The responsibility for maintenance was undertaken by the sarpanch with two volunteers. There is monthly supervision by Hero Honda, CII and Escorts Heart Institute. Now multiply this 1,00,000 times over and we have a beginning for a healthy India. Reduction of the disease burden on the rural economy could have a great multiplier effect. The rural population will earn more, spend more and the whole economy will move forward and this provides an added incentive to industry.

The next step. President Abdul Kalam has raised a workable and brilliant proposition. The president proposed the linking of such transformed villages to form a critical mass of 50,000 villagers to create a new rural model. This would mean pulling together between thirty to forty villages and linking them with metal roads and public transport.

They would have access to one proper hospital, one college, shopping facilities and an entertainment complex. This means that all the villagers would have access to one major hospital in their vicinity, as well as all the other benefits of a small town. This will open up opportunities for telemedicine from the local hospital to city hospitals.

All this can become a reality with an extensive network of public and private partnership, which has proved to be a powerful resource. The outpouring of public participation in the tsunami relief efforts showed this amply. We need to convert disaster relief to a process of continuous participation from corporations, health care providers, voluntary bodies and (extra)ordinary citizens who are ever willing to find ways and means to fulfill their social obligations.

It must be made mandatory that every major industry adopt a village close to their factories and manufacturing plants, where a large proportion of the beneficiaries will actually be their own employees and their families. This is not a one-way street. Industry will feel the benefits.

So stop the whining and complaining which seems to have reached epidemic proportions in India. Address what you can do, in whatever form, to make it work for all of us. A broad-based participation by all the stakeholders of our society is essential. Only then can we truly accomplish the targets of resurgent India.

SADHGURU JAGGI VASUDEV
SPIRITUAL TEACHER

Technology for the Common Good

A nation is not its land and buildings—it is its people. If we as a nation have to rise and be empowered, the first and the foremost thing we need to do is to empower the people.

Empowerment does not mean amassing of material wealth or technology, but is entirely an inner process, a spiritual process. Without the necessary sensitivity, inner balance and the faculty of discrimination in individuals, widespread negativity and perversions creep in. This is how a human being or an entire culture sinks to its depths.

Never before has mankind been as comfortable as it is today. The kind of comforts and conveniences that even kings did not have a hundred years ago are now available to the common man. Today our pursuit for these is so vigorous that the very life of the planet is being threatened. Yet, it cannot be said that we are any happier than our forefathers. This is because people try to create an outwardly perfect life, but the quality of our lives is based upon our interiority.

Modern technology has tremendous capability for both—creating well-being or total destruction. Without bringing in the dimension of spirituality that lends an experience of all-inclusiveness in individuals, it will surely lead to destruction not just of humanity but of the planet itself.

After all, whatever any human being is doing, whether it is pursuing money or pleasure or god, he is only seeking his own well-being. Spirituality only expands this innate urge to include the whole humanity within oneself. This is the only way that human well-being can develop.

Developing the spiritual core of humanity does not mean propagating any particular religion. Unfortunately today, most religions have been reduced to mere belief systems. And belief systems are bound to clash with one another. Spirituality means to raise the body, mind and spirit to its true potential. Once this is established other challenges can be handled rather effortlessly. When we strive to create human beings functioning at their ultimate potential then his general well-being is naturally taken care of.

In every society, it is necessary that there are at least a handful of people whose passion in life is beyond their own well-being. Every society needs those individuals who will go on planting mango trees without thinking whether they will get to eat the fruits or not. Of all the degenerations we have suffered, this is the most damaging, as the nation is now deprived of its greatest strength—producing exalted beings who are rooted in a different dimension of existence and whose very presence is a blessing to the planet.

One example that the world is familiar with and whose fruits we continue to eat is Gautama Buddha. As a prince perhaps he would have had a few more wives and children and ruled over his little kingdom, but as an enlightened master, in many ways he has changed the course of life on the planet. We value this culture not because we happened to be born into it, but because this culture had perfected the technology of producing such beings.

When I was 12 or 13 years of age I happened to come across some literature in which Swami Vivekananda said, 'Give me hundred truly dedicated people and I will change the face of this country.' At that time it seems there were 330 million people in this country, but he could not find a hundred truly dedicated people. I thought, what a tragedy!

A man like Vivekananda is a phenomenon, he doesn't happen every day. When he arrived, we could not give him even a hundred people in this vast country. It seemed like a great tragedy for this culture and this country. From that day I always thought in my life I must create at least those hundred people the man dreamt of. For 20 years I have gone around working for this and today, I can proudly say, we have created many people who place the well-being of the world around much above their own—life or death, these people will fulfill what has to be fulfilled.

Today, I can proudly say that in homes and the marketplace alike we have created people whose vision and experience of life are rooted in the harmony and unboundedness of life rather than any narrow perception of the limited. I can proudly say that it is not just the urban and the privileged, but even the impoverished, whose struggle for existence is a daily process, that are able to walk the inner path to well-being. But this is far from fulfilling what is needed.

There was a time where in a society a few people were spiritual and the rest of the people went to them for blessings and sustained their lives. Today, with the tools of science and technology, we have brought ourselves to a self-threatening situation where everybody in society needs to turn spiritual, otherwise there is no survival for this world. With the kind of equipment and capabilities that we have, it just takes one fool to blow it up. And there are any number of those fools standing in queue to get to the top.

So spirituality is no more a fancy pursuit. It is an absolute necessity for our own survival and the planet's survival that every human being brings in the spiritual dimension into his life. Unless some sense of oneness touches the people, especially the leadership on the planet, self-destruction is a live threat.

Sceptics are quick to ask, 'Is such a thing possible?' I want to tell them, do not think of the future of the world on the basis of existing realities. Existing realities on the planet could be changed in a moment, because existing realities do not take into consideration people's will, they do not take into consideration people's commitment, they do not take into consideration the love in their hearts.

Existing realities are just looking at the number of people that died on the planet today, the number that were slaughtered today, the number of bombs that exist on the planet, but statistics cannot consider what is beating in the human heart. If only we can stoke that, if only we can stir up what is happening in individual hearts, miracles are possible.

It is not far away, we just need to work for it. With the spiritual legacy of this land, with the spiritual processes that are available to us today, it is definitely a possibility. If we dedicate ourselves to making this happen around us, we can see in our own lifetime something tremendous and dramatic happening on the planet.

P. VENUGOPAL

DIRECTOR, ALL INDIA INSTITUTE OF MEDICAL SCIENCES

Made in India, Make It Work for India

I am a born optimist. To me India was empowered at the midnight hour of 15 August 1947, when its first prime minister, Pandit Jawaharlal Nehru delivered the historic 'tryst with destiny' speech in the Indian Parliament. The freedom that came to the people of India at this golden hour was further strengthened with the coming into force of the Constitution on 26 January 1950.

India, the biggest democracy of the world, carries the unique distinction of empowering its every citizen irrespective of his/her caste, creed, religion, status or region to participate in the process of government formation.

To me, the most important and empowering day for the people of India would come when they would have complete freedom and the ability to make 'informed judgments' about their destiny.

The scourge of poverty, disease, illiteracy and ignorance, problems of health, sanitation, clean and safe drinking water are interlinked. We have to make concerted efforts to eliminate them to gain full empowerment.

As individuals, we Indians have outstanding capabilities. Most western countries, including the US, are driven by intelligent brains which were produced, nurtured and trained in India. The same individual excellence needs to be harnessed to deliver outstanding results as a team within the country also.

There were numerous occasions in the past when we Indians have felt empowered. Indians felt empowered when Dr Hargobind Khurana, Dr C.V. Raman, Dr S. Chandrashekhar, Gurudev Rabindranath Tagore and Mother Teresa received the Nobel Prize. Indians felt empowered when our hockey team won gold medals in the Olympics and our cricket team won the World Cup. Indians felt empowered when Rajyavardhan

Singh Rathore got a silver medal in the Olympics and our young ambassador Sania Mirza joined the exclusive club of the top fifty tennis players.

Indians felt empowered when our doctors and engineers astonished the world with their brain power on numerous occasions. Therefore, it is time we Indians rose above the narrow confines of hatred, greed, arrogance, pettiness and selfishness and joined hands to make India a great nation, a place that it very well deserves. No government can deliver unless every citizen considers it his national duty to perform at a level best suited to whatever area of activity he is involved in.

As an individual, I felt highly empowered the day I performed my first heart transplant operation on 3 August 1994. But after having achieved this, I realised that disease is the worst enemy of humanity. God has given us the ability and brains to win any war against diseases, including HIV/AIDS. It is in this direction that we doctors have to play an extremely important role and set the highest standards of professionalism. The research in the use of stem cells for fighting incurable diseases needs immediate attention. The president of India has already unleashed formidable thinking forces in the field of nano-technology.

The list of possibilities is endless and so is our ability to deliver. We Indians are second to none and we should take a vow to empower all our fellow citizens in the best possible way we can because that will bring about the real empowerment of the country.

CORPORATE VOICES

ANU AGA
DIRECTOR, THERMAX LTD

Be Accountable and Demand Accountability

For India to be really empowered, the two most important ingredients to my mind are: better governance and greater sensitivity in terms of responsibility of citizens.

Let me start with a story. When god created the earth, all the countries accused god of being partial to India because he bestowed it with a substantial landmass, which was largely free from extremes of climate, and had intelligent and hardworking people and abundant natural resources. God appeased all the nations saying, 'Don't worry, I will see that I give India a larger share of corrupt people!'

The Indian experience reflects the metamorphosis that our politicians go through once they come into power. Before being elected they make promises to resolve our problems but once they have gained power, one gets the feeling that their concentration shifts towards politicking and personal gain.

It has been mentioned by Rajiv Gandhi and by Dr Alexander, ex-governor of Maharashtra, that 80-85 per cent of government spending on social causes does not reach its targetted people because of massive corruption and inefficiency. The fault also lies with society: for not being ourselves accountable and for not demanding accountability. We tend to justify our passivity by pleading helplessness and by merely grumbling and fault-finding.

The corporate world also has its share of the unscrupulous. A few years ago, the *Indian Express* ran a series of articles 'Loot and Scoot' and named individuals who had let down their shareholders and their banks and yet lived a lavish lifestyle. Corruption has engulfed us, and all citizens, corporates and individuals, are affected by it. Out of fear or lack of will to fight it, many people put on the facade of being honest.

We need to generate corporates and individuals who have the courage to openly state that given the situation in which we live, they cannot be honest. The same feeling of helplessness is also experienced by honest bureaucrats and politicians. Hopefully a dialogue can be initiated between society and these politicians/bureaucrats, to seek avenues through which meaningful change can indeed be achieved.

Another suffocating area for citizens and corporates is the plethora of archaic legislation and the ambiguity surrounding the laws of the land. This empowers the corrupt enforcers of these laws to cause no end of harassment and litigation, and saps creative energy.

A basic question that faces us is: where is the accountability? Accountability of government, of corporates and of individuals. We need to face this squarely—in the words of John Kennedy: 'Ask not what the country can do for you; but what you can do for the country.'

On the economic front, it is true that in the last few years industry has performed well. We have got over the fear of China and some companies are daring to go multi-national. Several reforms that are still in the pipeline need to be passed with alacrity so that corporates can realise their full potential and the huge entrepreneurial resource can be fully tapped. If we are to compete with countries like China, who by the way have already entered the Indian market with their labour, corporate India cannot be left to compete burdened by huge disadvantages.

India to be strong, needs to remain united. And to be united, India needs to follow the secular path so that all communities feel safe and secure. A feeling needs to be generated that first we are all human beings, and that we are all proud and happy to be Indians. This can only be achieved when people-power openly and strongly condemns and rejects politicians and religious heads who exploit situations for their own vested interests.

As far as sensitivity is concerned, we have made ourselves numb and indifferent to the suffering all around us. If we see a person lying on the street we do not bother to help and assume he is a drunkard. The plight of thousands suffering under floods or droughts makes us, at the most, write out a cheque but in no way do we want to get involved to mitigate the situation.

We want other countries to help us financially or to send volunteers but we do not tap our own resources to the fullest. There is the huge untapped resource of housewives and students, who have the time and the ability to reach out. They need to be self-motivated to act. Each one of us has a role to play—remembering the old saying that it is 'little drops of water that make a mighty ocean'.

We can be proud that India has a lot going in its favour. It is a well-respected and powerful nation. In some areas we have made great progress, and the world has started taking notice of us as a major emerging powerhouse. We can accelerate this process if each one of us examines ourselves to determine the areas in which we can make a difference, and then passionately acts to achieve this. Let us do this with a positive attitude—to ourselves first become accountable, and then strive for improved accountability from the government and society.

MUKESH D. AMBANI
CHAIRMAN & MANAGING DIRECTOR,
RELIANCE INDUSTRIES LIMITED

Finding the Dhirubhai Within

India is its people, a billion plus. India is a civilisation rooted in antiquity. Empowerment of India requires deepening the basic values of our civilisation—inclusive, pluralistic and universal—so eloquently summed up in a simple, but profound concept: vasudaiva kutumbakam.

Empowering India means empowering every Indian, specially the youth who comprise the majority. Provide them access to world-class education, technology and skills and they will seize the opportunities looming large on the horizon, and win for the country the race for global leadership in the knowledge age. Education and health are, therefore, on top of my empower-India agenda. Quality education and sound health of every man, woman and child is where empowerment of a society begins. India empowered is an educated India, a healthy India.

I am proud of the quality of the minds of our young men and women. They have entrepreneurship, initiative and self-confidence. This is why India continues to amaze the world. It is among six countries that launch satellites, and among the three countries that have built supercomputers on their own. Our workers, managers, doctors, and professionals have demonstrated their prowess in all parts of the world.

When fetters are removed, Indians perform and flourish because their mind is creative and they have the spirit of enterprise. You empower India when you remove the constraints and let our youth realise their full potential. India's rapid growth requires energy—from natural endowments under the earth and above it, from oceans and seas, wind and sun, and, also, from fission and fusion. India empowered is India energised.

And I use 'energy' in its multiple meanings. It also connotes the creative energies of the nation. Nature has blessed India generously with land, water and abundant sunshine. India's farmers are hard-working. They are endowed with wisdom distilled from the experience of several millennia. Less than 40 years ago, India imported 9 million tons of foodgrains to support its people. Today, it has a surplus foodgrains stock of 60 million tons. The Indian farmer has achieved this miracle because the fruits of science and technology were placed in his hands. Empowering India requires bridging the distance between laboratories and farms.

India will be fully empowered only when poverty is completely banished. The technological revolution has made this goal achievable within our lifetime. It is no longer necessary that a large number of people be kept poor so that a few may become rich. On the contrary, the sharper the reduction in poverty, the greater is the growth of disposable incomes and more rapid is the addition to the middle classes. This acceleration demands more and better goods and services and sets in motion a virtuous cycle. Therefore, for empowering India, our policies and actions must reflect the inexorable linkage between growth and employment, between investment and improvement in the quality of life of the common people.

India will then also become a major resource for food and flowers, textiles and automobiles, health and education and research and innovation for the whole world.

India must keep her windows open so that the fresh breeze from the outside may come in. At the same time, we must not be swept off our feet. Should you find that this is what Mahatma Gandhi said, please remember that in the last one thousand years, he did more than any other single individual to empower India and her people. As President Kalam has said, an India empowered is an India that can stand up to the world. Not only as a military power, but also an economic power, a technological power and above all, in the power of mind and spirit.

For me, my father remains an eloquent example of what empowerment means. India was empowered when the son of a school teacher became a Dhirubhai Ambani. Empowered India means enabling every Indian to discover the Dhirubhai within.

SUBROTO BAGCHI
CO-FOUNDER & COO, MINDTREE CONSULTING

Empower Labour to Empower Itself

I was born in 1957, 10 years after India's independence. At that time, despite Mahatma Gandhi's call for emancipation, it was the Harijan men and women who went door to door to collect human excreta in a large tin or an earthen pot that they would then carry on their head to another location. These men and women were paid by the municipalities to do this work.

I have seen the practice as late as 1969 when, as a little boy, I watched them come and go. 22 years after independence—how could we remain blind to this unimaginable act of human beings having to carry on their head the excreta of fellow humans as their profession? Can you imagine that among us today are their progeny, who would much rather not remember that such professions existed in a free country? You might say, this was only in the past. Think again as you drive to work today. It has just barely changed.

Look closely at the men who hang from the back of the scavenger trucks in our metropolises. Clothes smeared with dirt—face blackened with garbage. These men, bare foot and barehanded, pick up wet garbage from dustbins, load these trucks and travel with the garbage to its final destination. They do not have the ignominy of carrying human refuse on their head, but the risks to their health are just as real.

58 years after independence, we are just as insensitive to the phenomenon as were our parents who found the previous arrangement as convenient. The role of the municipality has changed—it has outsourced the entire thing to a contractor and it is the contractor's job to manage the process. In what way is the man doing the work different from you and I? It is just the accident of his birth that places him where he is.

To me, empowerment means liberating India from this convenient social exploitation. It is a disgrace to me and my social conscience. It is a disgrace to the system I have built. It is a disgrace to the words government and democracy. Earlier, the 'untouchables' had names and faces. Today, they still exist—but they have been granted constitutional anonymity.

Now I want to talk to you about the other untouchables—our women. When I first started travelling outside India, I realised that most women on streets in India, while going about their daily work, walk with their eyes downcast. Everywhere else in the world, they look straight ahead. However educated she may be, if she is alone on a road, if she is travelling on a train, wherever she might be—the Indian woman looks down. It is a necessary defence against Indian men. You will not see this in any developed country.

58 years after Independence, our women—of whom we are born—do not walk safe. A young Japanese woman who wanted to discover India once stayed with us. One day, I asked her what she liked about India and what was that one thing she did not like? She told me the usual things all tourists say they like about India. The one thing she said she did not like made me hang my head in shame. She said, if you are a foreigner and a young woman and you happen to travel alone in India, every one concludes that you are available for sex! She was disgusted. I have met many educated women of various ages who come to India as visitors. They all make the same observation.

Finally, in my empowered India, people will be valued not just for mental work but for the physical work they do. People who perform physical work will be paid respectable wages that make basic comforts in life as accessible to them as they are to you and I. One day, I got down at the Orly airport in France and was picked up by a cab driver. The man was as well-dressed as anyone else. We got chatting on the way as he was driving me to a hotel near Versailles where I had a conference to attend. Next to my hotel stood an even more beautiful hotel and pointing it out to me, the man said, that his wedding had taken place there. I was simply amazed.

When will it be in India that a taxi driver in Mumbai or New Delhi can dress up half as well as you and I? When can he take his family to enjoy the same holiday destination that you and I go to? When will it be that the maid who comes to clean the house can dress up half as well as you and I without being suspected of thievery?

To me, India will be emancipated and empowered when the man scavenging on the municipal truck will work in sanitary conditions comparable with any developed country and is paid half as well as an entry-level software engineer. In an empowered India, women will not have to lower their eyes when they walk past a stranger, lest they be presumed to be available for solicitation. In that India, we will not underpay people who work with their hands and make a living with their skills. Until such time that we do not recognise the importance of these things, we will not be an empowered nation.

RAHUL BAJAJ
CHAIRMAN, BAJAJ AUTO LTD

Cheer the Winners

A society moves forward when the capable and the deserving are supported in their desire to move ahead. A society that does not support its weak is inhumane and uncivilised, but the achieving societies that deliver a better life to their people are those that cheer their winners. As Blake said, 'Great things are done when men and mountains meet, this is not done by jostling in the street.'

A nation is empowered when its weakest citizen can function without fear or favour. We may be better than some despotic countries but we daily experience a nation enslaved. Our minds are still colonised and we are being treated, and behave, as subjects not citizens. Be it Gohana or when a citizen interacts with a government functionary or rides potholed roads or suffers power cuts.

Our governments post-Independence have largely been thwarting achievement. The numbers game of electoral democracy puts a premium on appealing to the lowest common denominator. Communalism and casteism are cancers which sap our strength. A society should want everybody to be strong, give equal opportunities, but what we urgently need is faster growth of the cake. That comes from supporting the achievers or at least not hindering their progress.

We have many strengths: be it democracy, growth, inflation, foreign exchange reserves, human resources or demographic profile. Also, we are the world's fourth largest economy by purchasing power parity. But our per capita situation and our human development indices are abysmal. Our physical and social infrastructure is abysmal. Our quality of governance is the pits. As someone put it, 'we are a first-rate people in a third-rate system.'

In the world today, people don't compete, companies do. While the individual is very important, the economic agent is the corporation. Only the corporation has the economic and technological muscle to compete in the present and to invest in the future. Only healthy companies can provide the secure future we seek and work for.

We live in a globalised world. We have to and are competing with the best in the world. Our systemic inadequacies, be they of infrastructure, labour policy, corruption or red-tape, only weaken the domestic producer against his foreign counterparts. Foreign companies investing in our country, adding value, creating employment are good for us. But Indian companies are better.

It is the tragedy of our country that the previous statement may be contested. In no other self-respecting country in the world is this the case. We must stop instinctively mistrusting business. Business on the other hand should improve upon its actions such that it gives ground for people to trust it.

We are achieving what we are achieving in spite of our governments. Unfortunately, it would be realistic to assume that this will continue to remain so.

In our families, companies and civil society we have to create and sustain values, attitudes and behaviour that are necessary for enterprise to take root and develop. The root of enterprise is an unflinching belief in merit. What works and who delivers have to be the overriding criteria. Not that there should not be other criteria, but they can only influence say 10 per cent of the outcome. 90 per cent of the outcome must be determined by merit. Also, ends have to be as important as the means, within an ethical framework. The job must get done. Excuses are endless.

If India is to be empowered, it will be empowered by the people. Within our spheres of influence we have to push the envelope. We have to build our networks and communities. We have to find our political vices. We have to resist the temptation to succumb to the easy way, be it of cutting corners or paying a bribe. Pandit Bhimsen Joshi once said, in a very different context, that what is good is difficult and difficulty is what one tends to avoid. We have to try to live by the higher than all laws, our internal moral law.

We have to set goals for ourselves that expand our delivery. We have to broaden our goals to include nurturing and strengthening institutions that develop our social capital, like educational and health care institutions. Whenever we see someone struggling to achieve, we should help him or her in whatever small way we can. We have to support, celebrate enterprise wherever it exists.

Most of us are paying 20 per cent or more of our incomes to the government and get little more than the electric lamp on our streets in return. Let us give one per cent of our incomes to those in need or trying to achieve something.

I have Tagore's 'Where the mind is without fear' in my office. I have yet to discover a better vision for our country. Each day I read it to get the strength to cope with the absurdities of today and to work for a better tomorrow

KUMAR MANGALAM BIRLA
CHAIRMAN, ADITYA BIRLA GROUP

Revamp Education for Excellence

What can empower a nation that, in recent times, has earned the credibility of becoming an intellectual capital of the world? The answer, for me, is obvious. It is education. Education that is value-based. Education that imparts roots and also gives wings. What can be more empowering than that?

I am not an educationist, although this is a subject that is close to my heart. Therefore, I cannot offer an expert opinion on the need to revamp our country's educational system in the urban context. My point of view finds its genesis in my own experience as a student, as a parent, and as someone who is exposed, in one way or another, to the educational systems that exist in other countries around the world.

The only way to convert the liability of having a population of over a billion is to educate them. This in turn, will empower them to dream of building a new India, as it hurtles forward towards an exciting future, one we cannot even imagine.

First, our education system puts our students on a process-line. It is like a car assembly plant, where the same model is produced day in and day out. It assumes a standard set of skills and the same competency across the learners—an assumption that is fundamentally flawed.

I dream of an education system for India that would help each student reach her or his maximum potential, implying that each individual is running a race with himself or herself, to be the best she or he possibly can, to hone the talents she or he has, such that they are empowered with a strong sense of self, and to acquire new skills that will help build as all-rounded a personality as possible.

This is obviously contrary to the trend today, with students under tremendous mental stress, having to compete with each other to secure some obnoxiously high marks, to, in turn, find a place in a premier institute in the country.

Fundamentally, what is needed is an attitudinal shift that recognises that a country as large as ours will have to differentiate by creating an educational system that has options to cater to the different aptitudes and capabilities of students. An incident in south Mumbai of a 15-year-old jumping to his death from a high rise brought this issue to the fore. Does our educational system add as much value as it creates stress for parents and students? Does it equip students with 'real' and contemporary skills that can make them winners in the real world?

Several countries have adopted models that generate options for students as early as during their secondary education days. The result, a more productive and happy workforce that can contribute its might to the task of nation-building. This calls for a change in the mind-set for our society at large, and for parents in particular, who need to break out of the mould of wanting the more conventional career paths for their children.

The number of career options by themselves that are available today are far more than ever before. The faster our education system is revamped to recognise this, and the sooner parents accept this, the better it would be for a country that needs every productive mind to work at its optimal best.

What is urgently required to implement this—an education system that differentiates, and one that gives a menu of options to students to choose from—is a revamping of our system of education at a national level. It calls for a panel of experts who believe in the need to contemporise our education system, who can put their heads together and create a charter of a system that will be a paradigm shift from the existing one.

A collaborative effort between the government, the corporate sector and appropriate NGOs can turn this seemingly impossible dream into reality. Given their several preoccupations, no government in recent times has given education a directional change in the required way.

The results, undoubtedly, would be astounding. I cannot believe that there can be a better way to empower India than this.

MICHAEL F. CARTER
FORMER COUNTRY DIRECTOR, INDIA, THE WORLD BANK

Resource Allocation Is the People's Prerogative

In Nehru's immortal words, India has a tryst with destiny. Its billion strong people are its most valuable resource. With their enterprise, savvy and skills, they are justifiably striding assuredly onto the world's stage.

Yet, think what could happen if all of India's people, including the poorest, those with disabilities, communities from backward castes and tribes, and above all women were truly empowered with a direct role in the management of resources? If they had the confidence to demand the quality of infrastructure and services they rightfully deserve. From the building blocks of education and healthcare to the foundations of power, water and transportation, they could unleash an economic force so powerful that it would dramatically alter the face of India.

In the nearly 60 years since Independence, India has held steadfastly to its democratic traditions. Empowering all its citizens to ensure the efficient use of public funds and to hold their leaders accountable would deepen this further into a truly participatory democracy, unleashing the country's vast untapped economic potential. Given the immense size and diversity of India, and the sheer scale of its challenges, strong participation at the grassroots is the only answer.

In the global knowledge economy of the 21st century, while nations are rapidly greying, India's youth—set to grow in numbers for many decades to come—can be a unique asset. But, before these young people can become productive citizens in the world of tomorrow, they must be fully empowered today. And a good education is undoubtedly the most powerful tool to do so.

While many more of India's children now go to school, over 10 million primary age children still receive no schooling at all. Secondary school enrollment—at only about 35 per cent—is lower than in countries at similar levels of development. And while India can be justly proud of its world-class educational institutions, many of its children receive instruction of far inferior quality.

The government has made elementary education a fundamental right for every Indian child and has launched the nation-wide Sarva Shiksha Abhiyan to support this effort. But, ensuring that such a gargantuan system—the second largest in the world after China—actually delivers is a major challenge. One of the best ways to make sure that it does so is to empower parents and local communities with complete information about what is being spent and give them a voice in how schools function.

'May you live for a hundred years,' is a traditional Indian blessing. Good health clearly empowers. Yet, tragically, while modern medicine can easily fight diseases like diarrhoea and malaria, many of India's children are undernourished and needlessly die from preventable illnesses, keeping infant and maternal mortality rates stubbornly high. And, medical expenses are a major factor in driving Indian households further into poverty.

The answer lies partly in better health services—but also in better access to clean water, better nutrition and better roads. And, in all these areas, experience suggests that improved service delivery will only be achieved if those affected have a direct say in how resources are allocated.

The Chinese say that women hold up half the sky. Yet, women and girls often have fewer opportunities, and almost half of India's women cannot read or write. Empowering women can give them greater choice in determining how many children to have and when to have them, reducing fertility rates, and leading to well-nourished and better educated future generations. Projects in rural Andhra Pradesh, for example, have shown that when women from disadvantaged communities are given a voice, they are able to chart a bold new future for themselves and their families.

Although the country is rapidly urbanising, the majority of India's people still live in the villages. Despite large expenditures on rural development, the stubborn reality of rural poverty persists. Farmers are unable to demand and get better prices for their produce, and the poor have limited access to infrastructure, services, credit and markets.

Changing the face of rural India means empowering the rural poor with the information and the market power that are the keys to increasing income. Thus, empowerment to me is the most important word in India's development dictionary. India's people are its strength. Once empowered, they will be able to better grasp today's opportunities and enable a resurgent India to take its rightful place in the world.

Y.C. DEVESHWAR
CHAIRMAN, ITC LIMITED

India Inc and Last Mile Connectivity

An empowered India will be a nation in which we have been able to successfully eliminate the scourge of poverty. An India in which we have been able to wipe every tear from every eye, the mission that Mahatma Gandhi inspired us with.

India means basically rural India, because India lives in its villages. Over 72 per cent of India's population lives in rural India. India's villages are home to 75 per cent of India's poor. The bulk of the population of rural India subsists on agriculture. Therefore, in order to tackle the problem of poverty in India, specially in rural India, we will have to consistently enhance the international competitiveness of Indian agriculture.

One important step in this mission is to enable, and consequently empower, even the smallest marginal farmer in the remotest recess of India's rural hinterland to use technology, especially information technology (IT). It has been demonstrated beyond doubt that if we enable India's farmers to creatively leverage IT, the resulting power of information and knowledge will help them compete successfully in the Indian and world markets.

Nearly 87 per cent of India's 6,40,000 villages have population clusters of 2,000 people or below. In spite of a network of roughly 3.6 million rural retail outlets, there is no active marketing or distribution of products and services in these small villages because of uneconomical 'last mile' logistics. Nearly 35 per cent of India's villages are yet to be connected by roads. Tele-density in rural India is barely 1 per cent. Apart from being geographically dispersed, these villages, as economic units, do not have the means to support the scale of investment required to upgrade last mile connectivity.

A large segment of India's rural population subsists on less than $1 per day. Ironically, this is less than half the subsidy provided to each head of cattle by the Organization for Economic Cooperation and Development (OECD). Grinding poverty is so badly crippling that the poor do not even have the awareness and the ability to hoist themselves out of the morass of penury that they are sunk in.

For the same level of income, a rural wage earner's propensity to consume is only half of that of an urban wage earner. This is because agriculture, the predominant source of livelihood for the bulk of the population of rural India, is still fraught with a lot of uncertainty and risk.

The fragmentation of farm holdings, over-dependence on monsoons and the lack of sophisticated inputs and knowledge trap the Indian farmer in a vicious cycle of underdevelopment. To initiate the process of an economic turnaround, we need to provide cost-effective last mile connectivity, which will consequently lead to productivity-led economic growth.

In the new India I envision, village communities will be vibrant economic organisations. These villages will induce a virtuous cycle of consumption of goods and services, economic growth, education and development. But economic development and the growth of the Gross Domestic Product (GDP) will not be the sole indices for measuring progress in an empowered India. The quality of life will not be determined solely and wholly by the return earned on economic and financial capital.

The return on environmental and social capital will be equally important. An empowered India that will not short-sightedly pursue economic growth at the cost of environmental and social capital. Economic growth and sustainable development are not necessarily the same. Right from the time of the Industrial Revolution, we have witnessed unparalleled material development. But this material development has come at a heavy environmental and social cost. More natural capital has been destroyed after the Industrial Revolution than ever before in human history. In the last half century alone, the world has lost a fourth of its topsoil and a third of its forest cover.

In the past three decades, one-third of the planet's natural wealth has been consumed. At present rates of destruction, the world will lose 70 per cent of its coral reefs within our lifetime. We will also drive about 25 per cent of marine life to extinction. In fact, very little of natural capital will be left at the end of the next 150 years. The challenge of India's development goes much beyond the upgradation of human capital. Let us imagine that India now joins the ranks of the OECD as a developed country with similar levels of per capita consumption of energy. The country will then annually: (a) consume 8 billion kilo-watt-hours of electricity—over 60 per cent of world consumption; (b) discharge 12 billion metric tonnes of carbon dioxide and other greenhouse gases into the atmosphere—which amounts to nearly half the world's emissions; (c) deplete fossil fuels by 180 quad British thermal units—about 45 per cent of the world's consumption; and (d) create non-recycled solid waste to the tune of 6 billion kilograms from the transport sector alone. This simple extrapolation demonstrates the devastation that economic growth can wreak on the environment.

That is why the world community is desperately seeking to drastically reduce energy consumption through a combination of resource efficiency and the use of renewable energy sources like solar and wind energy, apart from developing alternative technologies like hydrogen fuel cells. The threat of environmental degradation was poignantly highlighted way back by Mahatma Gandhi in his reaction to a question related to India's economic development. He said, 'It took Britain half the resources of the planet to achieve prosperity. How many planets will a country like India require?'

There are several other serious issues related to other sources of natural capital that India needs to pre-emptively address. Let us take water. As per the ministry of water resources, the total water requirement for India is projected to be around 1,180 billion cubic metres by 2050. Only 1,122 billion cubic metres of usable water resources are currently available in India. Today, 282 out of India's 602 districts are classified as 'moisture deficit'. Hence the critical need for effective water management and vastly enhanced efficiency in water use.

Take the case of soil. The Indian Council for Agricultural Research (ICAR) estimates that the annual loss of topsoil in India is over 16 tonnes per hectare—equivalent to a crop loss of nearly 13 million tonnes. India's wastelands have increased from 22 million hectares in 1980 to over 35 million hectares today, representing about 18 per cent of total arable land mass. Declining forest cover is a major reason for soil erosion. Only 11 per cent of our land area has a crown density of 40 per cent or more, and therefore qualifies to be classified as forests. The desirable forest cover is 33 per cent.

The development model that India pursues will have to help the country go well beyond attaining its economic objectives. It will also have to simultaneously enable the nation fulfill its social and environmental aspirations as well. India will have to seriously engage with the broader issue of ensuring sustainable development.

Sustainable development means that economic progress will have to be achieved in tandem with environment enrichment and social development. Sustainable development is about the triple bottom line—straddling the three dimensions, economic, social and ecological. It means creating economic wealth along with social and ecological wealth.

The widening disparities of income and consequent social tensions, and the alarming depletion of natural resources have been engaging the attention of global leaders. This global concern has resulted in the evolution and formulation of the 'Millennium Development Goals' by the United Nations (UN). All the 191 members of the UN, including India, have subscribed to these goals.

The UN has set 2015 as the target deadline for the achievement of these measurable goals. That is possible only through public-private partnerships. Several other initiatives such as the United Nations Convention on Climate Change (better known through one of its milestones, the Kyoto Protocol), and the Global Reporting Initiative (GRI) are manifestations of global concern over environmental destruction and social regression.

The more developed countries of the west have realised that the limits to development are not defined by financial capital but by natural capital. They are now beginning to get their environmental act together. With increased awareness, these countries are beginning to place a premium on products that use sustainable inputs, processes and technologies. For example, organic tea commands a 20-25 per cent premium over non-organic tea. Indeed, countries have begun to use environment and labour standards as non-tariff barriers to trade.

The challenge of evolving and executing a holistic and inclusive growth strategy is greater for a developing country like India with its resource crunch. India needs economic growth with social equity. At the same time, India needs to also enrich its environmental wealth. The urgency for tackling sustainability issues cannot be overstated in the Indian context.

The India of tomorrow should have an appropriate regulatory framework to ensure the sustainability of its national development. These regulations should protect the country's biodiversity. They should also help conserve India's land, air, water and forest resources. They should also enable the conduct of all economic activities with the least adverse impact on society and the environment. Regulations should also progressively upgrade standards in keeping with evolving technologies. But regulations alone will not suffice, as they tend to prescribe only minimum acceptable standards.

In the India of the future all organs of society will play a proactive and constructive role in mutual partnership to realise the national goal of sustainable development. The role of Indian business enterprises in this regard is critical, particularly because the corporate sector deploys a chunk of social resources in the pursuit of its growth objectives.

From the point of view of sustainable development, we can classify all business enterprises into three kinds: the first are those companies that single-mindedly pursue the goal of creating shareholder value above everything else. These companies exist from quarter to quarter. Focused solely on their quarterly returns, these companies leave a deferred and gargantuan environmental and social burden for future generations to take care of. Every such company is like an albatross hanging around society's neck.

The second are those companies that pursue the objective of creating shareholder value, but take care to comply with regulations. To some extent, these companies slow down the damage to natural capital. The third are the business enterprises that are willing to go the extra mile. These companies go well beyond the dictates of regulation. These organisations do not view the creation of shareholder value as the sole and supreme goal. They understand that creating shareholder value is merely a means to realise the broader purpose of creating value for society. They are driven by a superordinate goal. They are inspired by a sense of a larger purpose. They demonstrate a 'Commitment beyond the Market.' The business-scape of tomorrow's India should be strewn with enterprises that demonstrate exemplary social conscience and integrity. In the emerging India, the concept of trusteeship should extend beyond shareholders to society at large.

NARESH GOYAL
CHAIRMAN, JET AIRWAYS

Affordable Air Travel for Everybody

I have watched with fascination (and to a limited extent participated in) the progressive liberalisation of the Indian economy and with it, that of the Indian civil aviation industry since the early 1990s. This process of liberalisation has slowly, but surely, unleashed a vast potential travel market, both for business and tourism, and an opportunity to travel by air for increasingly larger segments of the Indian population.

I am indeed delighted that the Indian policy makers have fully recognised the huge contribution that the expansion of air connectivity, both within India and with other countries worldwide, makes to the growth of the Indian economy, in generating employment and developing subsidiary industries. Earlier this year, the World Travel and Tourism Council estimated that currently the Indian travel and tourism industry, directly and indirectly, accounts for 5.5 per cent of the country's total employment and 5.3 per cent of the country's GDP.

The opportunities available need to be viewed in conjunction with several aspects of the growth that is taking place in other segments of the Indian economy and society. India is fast emerging as a centre of financial and economic activity, a base for doing jobs for other countries at lower costs. Notwithstanding the current shortages, I see enormous scope for India, in the long run, to be an exporter of technically qualified and trained personnel for the aviation industry, e.g. aircraft maintenance and avionics engineers, pilots and technicians. But to be able to do this successfully, the country will need to build many more schools and training academies and set up new training facilities that are truly centres of excellence, so that India can become the centre for meeting the needs of qualified and trained personnel worldwide.

I do not need to emphasise how small a proportion of my fellow Indians today (or indeed ever) have travelled by air. I know that we must take cognisance of the ground reality, that the vast majority of us are not as yet economically empowered to be able to even think about such possibilities. Nevertheless, even if we were to restrict ourselves to the affluent middle class and upwardly mobile segment of the Indian population of probably more than 300 million, the present size of the Indian air travel market of around 18-19 million passengers is clearly a minuscule portion of the total available market. In fact, when you take into account the travel cycle of the average domestic passenger, particularly the Indian business traveller—who constitutes between two-thirds and three-fourths of the total air travel market—of around at least three one-way trips per year, the number of individuals travelling by air within India works out to only around 6 million.

The opportunities are, therefore, vast and successive governments in recent times have given due recognition to the need to implement policies and create an environment that promotes and assists in the growth of the Indian aviation industry. The policies also give recognition to the need to simultaneously create opportunities for the rapid integration of the Indian civil aviation industry in the global air transportation industry.

The government's policy decision in early 2005 to allow privately-owned Indian carriers to operate in the highly competitive and rapidly expanding international travel market into and out of India is also a step in the right direction. Supported by the progressive liberalisation of India's air services agreements with other countries, this policy will go a long way in making the Indian carriers more competitive with the well-established foreign carriers serving the Indian market, improving the air links between India and the rest of the world and contributing significantly to the promotion of tourism in India. That this is really important for the country does not need any reiteration, more so when we recognise that the foreign tourist inflows into India were only around 4 million in the financial year 2005 and that around three quarters of the passenger traffic to and from India is being carried by foreign carriers like British Airways, Lufthansa, Singapore Airlines, Emirates, etc. I firmly believe that the coordinated and parallel marketing efforts of Air India and Indian Airlines and the privately-owned domestic carriers will enable our country to regain its rightful share of the air travel market into and out of India and assist the tourism ministry's promotional efforts in the growth of in-bound tourism.

For all these policy initiatives to succeed, however, it is extremely important for the parallel efforts initiated by the government to modernise and improve the supporting infrastructure to be pursued on a war footing and completed in the shortest possible time. We have the distinct advantage of adopting the best features of all the new airports and terminals that have been built all over the world in recent years whilst designing and building the new facilities in our country—for example, the new airports in Hong Kong, Kuala Lumpur, and of course, Singapore and Dubai, to name only a few. We don't need to reinvent the wheel, and we surely have enough talent in our country to design, develop and build the best world-class facilities.

Equally important is the need for policy makers to recognise that the Indian aviation industry faces crippling and very high input costs and that unless urgent and active steps are taken to reduce the tax burdens, improve the productive use of the limited resources that are available and thereby bring the cost structures in line with those prevailing worldwide and in neighboring peer countries, the dream that I have talked of earlier of making air travel affordable to a significantly larger number of my fellow countrymen may never materialise. I strongly urge the government to recognise the role that it has to play to be able to fulfill its own policy objectives, in partnership with the private sector and with the active participation of all the players in the travel and tourism industry.

India has a long way to go to be able to come anywhere close to reaching international standards in large segments of the travel and tourism industry. What is encouraging, however, is that all of us have at last woken up to the potential and the possibilities and that slowly, but surely, we are jointly marching towards achieving the goal. No longer is air travel regarded as elitist or the domain of only the privileged or an industry that must cross subsidise other economic activities and modes of travel.

For me, the empowerment of India in the travel and tourism segment will only have taken place when the Indian carriers have demonstrated to the world the standards and qualities of performance that India is capable of; when we have developed India as an entrepot for international cargo traffic flows by air; when the Indian carriers have succeeded in developing many more tourist destinations in India and in selling India to the world, making it a competitive and attractive destination for shopping and exporting Indian culture worldwide—in other words, making India known for its new spirit, for its entrepreneurship rather than its apparent poverty, grime and dirt.

I am very optimistic that we will succeed, that the right environment is being created gradually—though it needs to be speeded up—and that the travel and tourism industry will be an important engine for the growth and progress of India, in particular for the creation of additional jobs and in bringing the country together. There are many crucial areas that need to be tackled. I am confident that we will do this successfully and that we will win the battles and also the war. For me personally, it will not be, as Shakespeare wrote, 'love's labour lost' but rather 'love's labour regained'.

K.V. KAMATH
MANAGING DIRECTOR & CEO, ICICI BANK

Building World Class Physical and Social Infrastructure

India today is at the cusp of a paradigm change in its growth trajectory and its position in the world. The global competitiveness of Indian industry and the role our knowledge capital is playing in the process of globalisation and structural change in the world economy are the visible signs of India's empowerment.

So what is powering India and what must we do to keep up this momentum? Our current economic success rests on the series of initiatives taken by India for over a decade and the entrepreneurial talent that economic liberalisation has fostered.

Over the last decade, India's entrepreneurs have leveraged our knowledge capital and our ability to assimilate and develop technology. Through this process we are not only creating value for ourselves but are adding value to other nations and societies.

By sublimating our knowledge capital into wealth creation, we have demonstrated a new growth paradigm, where our people, not just our mines, land, factories and physical production facilities, are our key economic resource.

This is now extending from technology services to medical research, healthcare, biotechnology, design and other knowledge-based sectors. Maintaining and enhancing the momentum in these areas requires continued investment in education, at all levels, to ensure that our young people have the knowledge and skill base needed to make the most of the vast array of opportunities before us.

The last few years have seen Indian industry make a strong recovery. After a prolonged and often painful process of restructuring and repositioning, Indian businesses have emerged leaner, more efficient in terms of process, quality and financing, and competitive on a global scale.

We are seeing Indian companies across sectors investing overseas and entering new markets through acquisitions or greenfield ventures. Indian companies now have the confidence to compete with international players in markets outside India. At the same time, global corporations are seeing India as a supply and manufacturing base.

The ability of Indian businesses and professionals to conform to and sometimes exceed international benchmarks is a key outcome of the process of allowing free domestic and foreign competition across various sectors. Indian companies have been able to drive down costs and achieve higher and higher levels of efficiency.

India's mobile telecom service tariffs, the lowest in the world, and the increasing affordability of domestic air travel are just two examples of how we are redefining the cost to the consumer while ensuring profitability and shareholder value creation.

This process of growth and development has been backed by a sound financial sector and robust regulatory framework. The Indian financial sector has kept pace with the needs of the growing and increasingly diverse economy, offering high-quality services to businesses and individuals alike.

The availability of efficient financial services is a key driver of business efficiency and the ability of people to meet their needs for housing and other lifestyle aspirations. We have successfully created institutions to regulate the capital markets, the financial sector and other sectors like telecom and power, ensuring good corporate conduct and healthy private participation in various spheres.

Going forward, there are two key areas that require close attention. The first is the development of world-class physical infrastructure: power generation and distribution, roads, ports and airports. These are essential enablers of growth. The second is the extension of the benefits of growth to larger sections of the population.

We must engage many more of our people in the economic mainstream, by giving them access to the tools they need to participate in the nation's development. A key element of this process is access to financial services for the under-served segments of the population in both rural and urban areas.

Currently, vast numbers of our people do not have access to formal sources of credit or the protection of life or health insurance. They continue to depend on informal sources for their financial needs and their livelihoods are exposed to risks ranging from unfavourable climatic conditions to disease and non-availability of affordable, efficient healthcare facilities. This is a challenge that must be addressed jointly by the government and private participants in the economy.

We have already shown our ability to adapt technology and business structures to the unique needs of the Indian market. We must take this to the next level by creating sustainable propositions for rural India and the low-income segments of the population, energising their latent potential as drivers of growth and widening the scope of the upward socio-economic mobility that India is witnessing.

India is already empowered. Key sectors of the economy are on a self-propelling growth trajectory. We must now unlock the remaining shackles and unleash the power of every Indian to play his or her role in the full realisation of India's potential.

KIRAN KARNIK
PRESIDENT, NASSCOM

Information Pagdandi to Bridge Divides

Knowledge is now the currency of power. No longer does power flow out of the barrel of a gun; rather, it flows from the barrel of a picture tube (TV or computer screen) or the barrel of a pen. Since knowledge derives from information, true empowerment depends crucially on the availability of information. To me, India informed is India empowered.

An informed country means an aware citizenry: individuals conscious of their rights, recourse and responsibilities; of the pitfalls of jingoism, the mindlessness of fanaticism and the dangers of dogma. Aware also about their heritage and culture, of compassion and caring; imbued with tolerance and the scientific temper. Though cliched, this laundry list of virtues is certainly desirable, and information will aid its attainment. Empowering India means to me the empowerment of the disadvantaged, and this requires that information be available at the grassroot level.

It is in this context that I see the pagdandi as empowerment. Literally, a foot path, it takes shape as each individual chooses a route for going from one point to another. Over time, depending on the number who adopt a particular route, it develops into a pagdandi. Thus—to put it in the jargon of the day—it is user-created, need-driven, and a path of choice.

Conceptually, one can think of an 'information pagdandi'. Though very different from 'information highway', the two are not necessarily in conflict; in fact, they integrate well, just as many small streams ultimately create a mighty river.

What has the information pagdandi to do with empowerment? A great deal: without it, true empowerment is well-nigh impossible. Empowerment is not merely about the right to elect 'leaders', not even when one sees the image of a citizen going into the voting booth, undeterred by armed disrupters. Ballot over bullet is a strong re-affirmation of a robust electoral democracy, but does not lead to full empowerment. A free and fearless vote once every five years (or more frequently) is good only for a temporary high. True empowerment requires moving beyond electoral democracy to participatory democracy; and it is here that the information pagdandi enters the picture.

Participatory democracy, wherein citizens are involved in the process of decision-making, requires informed choice. It also means monitoring of projects, processes and finances of the government by the community. All this requires access to information on a continuing basis.

The Right to Information Act, though not ideal, is a huge step forward in terms of the right to get such information from the government. However, to actually access it we need the pagdandi. In some cases, this may mean a bulletin board; in many others it may involve technology—a photocopier, community radio, local TV or a computer. A computer, though expensive, is fast, versatile and efficient; it facilitates comparisons, transmission and analysis of data, as also quick and widespread sharing of information.

Many assume that technology is beyond the grasp of the poor, the illiterate and the disadvantaged; therefore, sophisticated devices like computers cannot be used by them. Experiments like NIIT's 'hole-in-the-wall' have nailed this lie, by showing how illiterate slum children learn the use of a computer, without any instruction, purely by the discovery method. Anyone who has seen a roadside mechanic repair a tractor or car will concur.

Yet, one does not necessarily need a computer to access data. Sophisticated back-end computerisation can simplify access—through interactive voice-response systems, for example, available via telephone. Meanwhile, computer systems that convert text to speech (and vice versa) are helping overcome the literacy barrier. The creation of community facilities, with free or pay-per-use access, is demolishing the economic barrier. With these developments, and hopefully the expansion of community radio and local TV, information can be easily obtained by anyone anywhere in the country.

The elimination of inequities of information availability—and, thereafter, knowledge—can be a major means of combating social discrimination and economic disparities. New information and communication technologies have demolished distance, making geography history. They can also be a 'digital bridge' across social and economic divides, empowering the disadvantaged through information and knowledge.

To return to the pagdandi, it is always a two-way road, like the new infocom technologies, thus ensuring that information and knowledge flows are not one-way.

This is crucial to empowerment, providing a tongue to those who have only had ears, giving a voice to the voiceless. What better metaphor, then, of a model for development than the pagdandi: a path based on need, chosen and created by self-organisation and consensus, used by and open to all? What stronger means of empowerment than the information pagdandi, providing information access to all, ensuring two-way communication, creating knowledge communities that are decentralised, autonomous and yet linked into the wider world through the information highway? To empower India, more power to the pagdandi!

JAGDISH KHATTAR
MANAGING DIRECTOR, MARUTI UDYOG LTD

A Four-Wheeler for Every Family

Four wheels here do not represent just a car. They represent a robust and thriving industry. Likewise, 'four wheels' is not a reference to my own business. Rather, it is a reference to my area of influence, my own personal medium, through which I as an individual can hope to contribute to an empowered India.

I believe that more than anything else, it is business and industry that will empower India. We do need more education, more roads, more power, more healthcare. We require the State to deliver in areas where it has failed to do so. But we have known and discussed these requirements for a long time.

Even when they come, they will only be the essentials. What Indians would also want for their true empowerment are more industry, more enterprise, more competitiveness, more jobs, more commerce, more opportunity, more choice—we want them all quickly.

Cars are a powerful way to build a thriving and robust industry and generate opportunities. In economy after economy, cars have proved to be the force multipliers. They have been the nucleus around which have grown other sectors of the economy. In the US, Japan, Europe and now in China, the car industry has ignited booms in commodities, in manufacturing, in transport, in road construction, services. Above all, it has fostered entrepreneurship. To aspire to put every Indian family on four wheels is to aspire for a prosperous, competitive, confident India.

Every new car that rolls out of a factory in India generates 5.3 jobs across the economy, says an ICRA study. Apart from the service sector, cars create these jobs in manufacturing where they provide even the semi-skilled and the less educated an opportunity to live with dignity. The prosperity that the car industry brings is rarely confined to a state or region.

Maruti's sales and service network, for instance, directly employs nearly 30,000 people across 1,100 Indian towns and cities, an example of the sheer breadth and reach of the opportunity that the car industry can create. Four wheels is empowerment in another way. It gives ordinary people the privilege of mobility. Gives them more control over their lives, more options, more leisure, more exposure. It fosters warmth and togetherness. I am discovering now that if we do the hard work of reaching out to new areas and customer segments, then even gardeners, mechanics and engine drivers can be persuaded to buy cars. For hundreds of thousands of others—small businesses, taxi operators, transporters—four wheels signify more than leisure; they are instruments of livelihood and sustenance.

Even so, the most important empowering role of cars is in the way they are providing mobility to women. More than half the people who have enrolled at Maruti driving schools in the last seven months have been women. They are women from all walks of life: working women, students, entrepreneurs. More than half of them are housewives. All these women can now go to work in a car, go to a hobby school in a car, go shopping in a car, drive on their own to visit friends and relatives. I see this as a tiny step forward on the long road to empowerment.

I am glad that people and governments in India are increasingly seeing the empowering role of four wheels. Governments no longer sniff at cars as elitist or as luxury items. They appreciate the car industry's potential as an engine of growth and competitiveness. That explains the steady reduction in the tax burden on cars. Of the three priority areas of the present government—agriculture, manufacturing and employment—the car industry is a key participant in two of them.

Many ordinary folk also no longer shun cars as expensive status symbols they can do without, and embrace them for the improvement cars bring to the quality of their life. That explains why the customer base of cars has deepened and widened across the country. I have chosen four wheels as the weapon for India's empowerment also because it is the area where I personally can make a contribution. That is an important consideration for me. I am comfortable offering a prescription for empowerment which, while relying on other people and entities to discharge their roles, has a role for me as well.

For India to be empowered, each of us has to treat our skill or area of action as more than a livelihood. We have to treat it as a means to make our own contribution to empowering India. We have to resist talking about the darkness, and focus on where and how to light a candle. Only when we take responsibility will we pave the way for empowerment. Trying to put every Indian family on four wheels is my way of contributing to an empowered India.

NAINA LAL KIDWAI
CEO, HSBC INDIA

Nurture Entrepreneurship in Villages

An empowered India is an India where every Indian can hold his or her head high. To be proud to be Indian, with a strong sense of belonging and identification with India. It is about an India that enables every man or woman to rise to full potential, irrespective of caste, creed or religion, or based on birth and domicile.

As Prime Minister Manmohan Singh has said 'we need harmony rather than uniformity'—the very diversity of India is our strength. We need to move from the zone of discrimination or favouritism to facilitation. That is, it is not just about creating quotas and reservations but enabling every person to be empowered to demand and realise rights.

It is about being heard—to have a voice. To use that voice to shape the future. Needless to say, we need governance structures and education to enable this.

Empowerment is about the ability to make choices. An India empowered must enable everyone to have a choice. To go beyond the drudgery of eking out a day-to-day existence, barely affording a day's meal, to being able to save. Empowerment is about aspirations and also the ability to fulfill them. In this respect, I believe microfinance and entrepreneurship at the rural level are key.

I have seen the success of organisations such as SEWA in achieving this—the pride of the woman in the village who has dared social norms and has started earning for her family, supporting them and being able to make choices. To be able to choose what to eat, to wear, to send her children to school, to educate herself and not have to spend all her savings on health bills—60 per cent of the typical rural Indian family's earnings is spent on health. We need more such success stories. More such people

266 NAINA LAL KIDWAI

like Ela Bhatt who make a difference, who selflessly empower a million women in our villages.

I have been fortunate in having choices, in having an environment that allowed me to dream the dream, and empowered me at various critical stages to fulfill those dreams. Empowerment is about national pride. I love my country and I am here by choice because there is no other place I would rather be. I have travelled and have had the option of working anywhere in the world but have chosen to be here because this is where I belong. I am proud to be from a country which is identified with global and timeless leaders such as Mahatma Gandhi and Nobel laureates such as Mother Teresa.

The future of the business and corporate world is going to be influenced greatly by stakeholder groups. These groups include customers, employees, investors, suppliers, as well as community groups, media, NGOs and regulators. We are going to increasingly see these groups demand better governance and, more importantly, ethical governance of corporations.

Stakeholder groups, as is already happening in many countries, are going to play a crucial role in ensuring corporations in India address the interests of their customers, employees and shareholders, and also the environment in which they operate. Fortunately, we already have excellent role models in India in companies such as Infosys and Wipro which have established the highest standards in the world and are great global benchmarks.

ANAND MAHINDRA
VICE-CHAIRMAN AND MANAGING DIRECTOR,
MAHINDRA & MAHINDRA

Think National, Act Local

India Empowered is a grand phrase, but to me the greatest manifestation of an empowered India is when there is a clear and measurable change for the better in people's daily lives, whether they are paanwallas or prime ministers. Hence, we need to discard old shibboleths and ask ourselves one simple question: what is the best delivery mechanism to make a difference to people's lives? What works?

What seems to be working is permitting people to take responsibility for handling their own issues and improving their own lives. We witnessed an outstanding example of this during the disaster in Mumbai, christened 26/7. Left to themselves without much official help or interference in the offing, people just banded together and effectively did what needed to be done.

There were no aam janatas, no darbars, no confabulations with political heavyweights. People sized up the situation and tackled the problem in spite of the lack of official 'help'. When it came to the crunch, it was the spirit of the local community that triumphed. And I have no doubt that if they had been involved in creating disaster management plans, life in Mumbai would not have broken down at all.

I am not encouraging governments or civic bodies to abdicate their responsibilities. But I am advocating that the principal role of these bodies is to create a template and provide facilitating conditions and then let those who are most closely affected implement the solution most suited to their needs. It's a question of structure, scale and involvement.

And I find that without thinking too much about it, we are doing it more and more. Mohalla committees restore peace in riot-affected areas; Advanced Locality Management (ALM) bodies take over the responsibility for sprucing up their neighbourhoods; village panchayats run by women, who see the management of the village as an extension of the management of their households, run very well.

Localised methods of rainwater harvesting, built and managed by the people most affected, are transforming many areas of Rajasthan, so much so that there is no water shortage in Gopalpura, one of the most drought-ridden villages in Rajasthan, while there is not enough water in Cherrapunji, the wettest place on earth! Why? Because the villagers themselves have figured out ways to treat water with the respect it deserves.

The common success factor in all these examples is that burning issues are effectively tackled because the implementation is on an intimate, involved and human scale. So if you want to empower India, empower its people to deal with the issues that most impact them. Gandhiji realised this when he summed up his economic ideas by saying 'We cannot serve humanity by neglecting our neighbours'.

It is fashionable to deride Gandhi as retrograde and anti-industrial. But increasingly Gandhi is appearing to be simply ahead of his time. He was arguing for economic activity that made the most rational sense for the people directly affected by it. With issues of sustainability threatening to overwhelm the world today, it is perhaps time to explore Gandhian thought once again, as his admirer Schumacher did when he wrote his seminal work, *Small is Beautiful*.

Schumacher gives an interesting example of the way a traditional economist would look at freight and infrastructure, versus an economist who looks at it from Gandhi's perspective.

A traditional economist would advise that longer the haul, the lower the freight rates should be because this encourages scale specialisation and 'optimum use of resources'. However an economist promoting sustainability would encourage local short-distance transportation and discourage long hauls, because the latter would promote urban migration, concentration of employment and the growth of a rootless and uneconomic way of life.

Anyone who has lived in Mumbai long enough to see how it is under siege from the onslaught of rural migration, would have very little difficulty is seeing the sense in this. Real empowerment should result in making life better, not harder and more arid.

And as I have questioned before, should we not pay attention to managing existing infrastructure, thus reducing the angst in people's lives, rather than focusing solely on mega projects which come with a set of implementation challenges? Perhaps we should start thinking on a smaller scale in many areas of our national life.

Decentralisation is more complex than simply breaking up a larger unit into smaller units. It's rather the idea of 'smallness within bigness'. As I have seen in the course of running a business, for a large organisation to work, it must behave like a related set of smaller organisations. Big ideas can be spelled out at the top, but it is small and dedicated groups and task forces that best implement them.

What works for a company also seems to work for a city, and what works for a city may well work for a nation. Think national, act local may well be the slogan for the future.

Empowerment has to have empowerment at the point of impact—which is the daily life of every Indian. It's a simple concept with complex consequences—a shift in our concept of appropriate technologies, a shift of scale from sweeping to human, a shift from business for pure profit to business for people. There can be many differing views on scale, but ultimately what really works for human betterment is what counts. Small is not just beautiful; small can actually be big, if you want to bring about change that matters.

ARUN MAIRA
CHAIRMAN, THE BOSTON CONSULTING GROUP, INDIA

Enable the Software of Democracy

India empowered to me is every Indian having access to the means to improve his/her own life: when every Indian can plug into the education system; when healthcare is available and affordable for every Indian; when access to employment opportunities is unconstrained by caste and religion; when everyone has access to information; when women and men with entrepreneurial spirit, who historically did not have the means, can obtain finance for their enterprises even if they have no collateral other than their integrity.

India will be empowered when those who have—power, money, property—use their assets for their own profit, but in a way that also empowers those who do not have to also have access to the means to improve their own lives. India empowered to me is communities of people taking charge of their surroundings, combining their resources and capabilities and working together to make the improvements they need.

India empowered to me is the spirit of partnership in which people work towards a larger goal they all aspire to—their vision of pahalé India. India empowered to me is the realisation of Gandhi's vision of freedom where the historically downtrodden are able to rise with dignity and their own efforts.

India empowered to me is the realisation of India's tryst with destiny. Nehru and Gandhi had the same love and concern for India's people. However, their visions of the means to achieve India's tryst with its destiny differed. Nehru had a top-down model, leading from the commanding heights. As his vision played out, people began to wait for government to solve their problems. Their own initiative diminished. They became dependent, not free.

India will be empowered when people—in civil society, business, and government—do not wait for someone else, but take the initiative to find the partners they need to achieve their goals.

As India aspires to accelerate its growth, improve its infrastructure, and catch up with China, many yearn for a strong, central leadership that can align diverse interests, lay down the law, and drive implementation. However, the model of power emanating from the centre to drive people is not practical for India any more. It may work in other countries where their histories provided them, sometimes through violent revolution, a central authority that people dare not question. Though India once had, it does not now have a single, strong, nation-wide party and may not have one for years to come.

Nor should we wait for a charismatic leader to emerge whom all will trust and follow without protest. Power in India must be with the people and the power of people will drive change through multiple points of action. India will be empowered by the light coming from millions of 'Fireflies Arising', each bringing its own light, rather than light shone on them by a floodlight from a tall post.

India empowered to me is an active and responsible civil society; it is companies with the daring and smartness to compete with giants from other countries and who also act responsibly to strengthen the social and natural environment of India; it is government which has finally shed its colonial culture of babu bureaucracy and has developed instead the capability to provide power to people and communities to develop themselves. It is about 'participative governance', and not merely 'government', driving change.

A nation drives forward on four wheels: the front wheels of the economy and the physical infrastructure and the rear wheels of the society and the political system. China is pulling itself with power through the front wheels, by rapidly improving its infrastructure and powering its economy. Its hope is that the power in the front wheels will drag it out of any swamp in which the rear wheels may get mired when pressures for political change increase.

India's vehicle drives on power through the rear wheels of democracy and society, which push the vehicle forward for improvements in the economy and infrastructure—as the people of Bihar have done in the 2005 assembly elections. Big trucks, auto engineers say, are safer in the long run with rear wheel drive.

India empowered to me is a country that derives power from its traditions and also adapts and innovates. Building on India's centuries' old tradition of tolerance, highlighted by the emperors Ashoka and Akbar, and on Gandhi's idea of non-violent change, we must evolve an appropriate technology of democracy to govern our vast and diverse nation.

The Constitution, with its legislatures and other formal institutions, along with the system of electing representatives to these institutions, is the 'hardware' of democracy. However, it is the 'software' of democracy— the processes of dialogue in these institutions, as well as the public participation in the debate—that brings democracy to life. We need to improve the software to make Indian democracy fully effective and make India a shining example to the world of an inclusive, equitable, vibrant, free-market democracy.

SUNIL BHARTI MITTAL
CHAIRMAN & GROUP MANAGING DIRECTOR,
BHARTI ENTERPRISES

The Corporate Sector Must Turn Around Agriculture

This is a resurgent India, an India on its journey to take a pre-eminent position on the world stage. India's march to becoming a global power is evident and inevitable. What is more important is to ensure that all of India's one billion plus people develop confidence in their own infinite capacities to help themselves and lead lives on their own terms.

I witness this phenomenon sweeping the entire country. On a recent trip to the country's hinterland, I was pleasantly surprised to meet a family where the husband has taken up a job in Mumbai while his wife and two children live in the village. The wife today keeps in regular touch with her husband thanks to a mobile phone, which the family owns. The phone is ensuring rapid flow of information and also resources for the family. The family no longer depends on the village postmaster to write and post letters to Mumbai. From a society where material comforts were meant only for the wage earner, a mobile phone for the woman in the family is an instrument of empowerment. It is heartening to see people of this country themselves leading this change.

Empowerment is not a moment of epiphany. It sometimes involves a simple direction of helping people help themselves. In Punjab, for example, where we started contract farming for our agri-business, we deliberately involved the women folk in the villages to work in the fields. We have seen that almost 95 per cent of the women folk in these villages have started working. Their children are being looked after in a creche being run by the co-operative society of the village. Today, both the members of a family are earning, which means a double income. Also as high as 90 per cent of the daily wages of women reach home, which translates into a promise of a better future for children in the village.

In an empowered India, every Indian should be able to earn his livelihood with honour and dignity without being worried about where the next meal is going to come from. For this to happen we need the development process to be well-rounded and to engage all sections of society, whether in the urban or rural areas. The focus should clearly be on educating the poor, providing healthcare and ensuring mass employment. Even a small increase in the income levels in the rural areas will ensure a much better standard of living for crores of people. It will also ensure higher consumption of goods and services, which in turn will have a catalytic effect on the growth of the overall economy.

India is today at the forefront of the technology and knowledge services revolution. The standards of education in the country have improved and manpower training is leading to improvements in the skill sets of the work force. Today India's human resource commands an enormous repute in R&D and technology. The enormous growth witnessed in telecommunications, aviation, information technology, pharmaceuticals, biotech and other sectors is empowering the country on a platform of performance and excellence. We are today confident of competing with the best in the world in any sector or industry.

The country's march to progress can only be sustained if the country as a whole is involved in the process of development. Agriculture continues to be the backbone of the economy and for a country which has all the makings of being a global powerhouse, agri business needs to be attended to with alacrity. I believe that the corporate sector needs to play a greater role in turning this around. The vibrancy of agricultural exports observed in the recent years is most encouraging and provided it gets sound investments and a stable policy, there are enough indications that the agri trade will turn the corner.

In the last 58 years, as a nation, we have had insufficient progress on infrastructure development and are still way behind other countries even in the developing world. The government has rightly put infrastructure on the forefront of its economic policies. What is needed now is a set of speedy and concrete on-the-ground actions for fast-track implementation of all the proposed infrastructure projects—ports, roads, airports and power projects.

An efficient and rapid flow of information is a catalyst for economic and social development. Vision 2020 conceives of India evolving into an information society and knowledge economy. IT and telecommunications will be the springboard. Telecom and IT are improving opportunities for people across different social strata. A whole range of information-based industries and applications have come up, creating new sources of employment and earnings with welfare-enhancing consequences for both the poor and the wealthy. There is a need to further expand the country's IT and telecom infrastructure to keep the momentum going.

India has the potential to lead the world. With a right mix of policies and resources, an empowered India will be a reality.

BRIJMOHAN LALL MUNJAL
CHAIRMAN, HERO HONDA MOTORS LTD

Bijli, Sadak, Paani, Vahan

Before I outline my vision for the India of tomorrow, I would like to briefly go back in time to the years following our independence from the British Raj in 1947. People of today's generation would not possibly be able to imagine how difficult those days were. India had just got freedom from centuries of foreign rule, but the country was divided and the aftermath of Partition brought about unimaginable human tragedies affecting millions of people in the subcontinent.

It was the political leadership of the time and the inherent resilience of the Indian people which saw India emerge from those turbulent days to be one of the most stable and vibrant democracies in the world.

We gained independence but inherited empty coffers from the British in 1947. The precarious financial health of the government at the time did not allow India to grow at a fast pace. We would not have lagged behind the rest of the world if the British had left the economy in better shape. Hence, India continued to be a closed economy for decades after independence, and economic growth was slow for years.

Despite all that, the country even in those days could produce scientists and engineers of calibre. We established world-class technical and management institutions, medical colleges and hospitals, built dams, national highways, nuclear reactors and research institutions in various parts of the country.

To me, therefore, when we talk of India empowered, we should draw our inspiration from the common Indians who had the courage and vision to withstand the traumatic days following the Partition. We, as a country, not only survived those days, but emerged stronger to compete with the best in the world and achieve success in various fields.

The achievements of those days would look small compared to the pace with which the western world progressed during that time, unless we look at our achievements with this perspective. Personally, I have lived through those days and understand what odds the country was up against. Sitting on the lawns outside Parliament House on August 15, 1947, I witnessed the Union Jack come down and the Indian tricolor go up—a moment I will cherish forever. But the next few months were the most traumatic times of my life, as I experienced first-hand the horrors of Partition.

Thankfully, today's generation is much better off. For their benefit, I would try to articulate what India for the future would mean to me. In the 1970s, India's development needs at the micro level were succinctly summarised in a catchy slogan: roti, kapda aur makaan. In recent years, another slogan has been coined—bijli, sadak aur paani; this ostensibly seeks to capture India's economic priorities as it tries to integrate with the rest of the world.

It astonishes me to see the word vahan (transport) missing from these important themes. And I am not saying this as a two-wheeler manufacturer, but as someone who has grown up in small towns with hardly any mode of public transport. In a country like India with a population of over one billion, the right to own one's own mode of transport should be a legitimate right. That's because for many in India today, owing a personal vehicle— whether it is a cycle, a scooter, a motorcycle, a tractor, a truck or a car— is not just a vital mode of transport but an important convenience, a means of livelihood and an expression of economic freedom.

To understand why this is vital in a country like India, let's look at India's urban transport system. Even in developed countries, people without their own modes of transport tend to struggle. But in countries like the US, UK and Singapore and many others, people at the bottom end of the economic pyramid are at least guaranteed an efficient and streamlined public transport system. This enables the people to utilise their valuable time for productive work.

The transport demand in most Indian cities has increased substantially, due to increases in population as a result of growing migration from rural areas and smaller towns. Yet, the public transport system in most Indian cities is in a mess. A study conducted by IIT Kanpur some years ago revealed that dedicated city bus services operated only in seventeen cities and rail transit existed only in four out of thirty-five cities with a population in excess of one million.

This accentuates the importance of private transportation. What does it mean for us in the transport business? Without doubt, given the vast disparities of income, it is imperative to be able to create and deliver value all along the transport chain. In other words, we should be able to offer products that are affordable and accessible. This is a lesson that we in the Hero Group have had to learn. And we are still learning it the hard way as we've evolved from making bicycles to motorcycles and diversified into areas like IT, etc.

Today, we might be India's largest maker of bicycles and motorcycles, yet we've still barely scratched the tip of the surface in terms of market penetration. In spite of the fact that cycles are India's cheapest mode of personalised transport, the annual sales of bicycles are pegged at only around 11 million. Likewise, the auto industry derives much pride from the fact that the two-wheeler industry crossed sales of 6 million in the financial year 2004. Yet, in a country of one billion people, these are not figures that we should be proud of. Clearly, we need to set our priorities right.

Private transportation is no substitute for public transportation; it can never be. But until India's public transportation systems—in rural and urban India—become a viable option, it is critical to make private transport more accessible and affordable to India's masses. Of course, as the head of a two-wheeler company, I am interested to see that this happens, but there's also a strong national interest. To my mind, you can give someone food, you can give him clothes, and you can even give him a roof above his head, but if he or she does not have access to his or her own mode of transport to reach the workplace, the person will never be fully empowered.

Broadly, in the Indian economy, however, there are encouraging trends as well. The economy has more than doubled in real terms since reform began in 1991. The commitment to the reform process by successive governments at the centre has helped ensure healthy growth. Our thriving and young middle class is also fuelling consumer demand. All these factors have made the rest of the world sit up and look at India as an investment destination.

On the other hand, for the vast majority of India's 1.1 billion people— more than a quarter of whom live in poverty—even such transformative growth can't come fast enough. The burgeoning services sector, for example, accounted for more than half of the country's GDP in 2003 but employs fewer than one quarter of its workers. Some two-thirds of all Indians work in agriculture, where growth is slow and prospects are limited.

India is not just about its cities. The real India lives beyond the cities and urban landscapes. We must ask ourselves whether we have even been able to provide roti, kapda aur makan to the teeming millions living in our villages. Why do we ignore the little children in dusty clothes begging at traffic signals in our cities? To that extent, isn't this slogan of the 1970s still valid in 2005? If India lives in its villages, then it is the responsibility of all of us to make that real India empowered. And it needs willpower, vision and commitment to achieve that.

N.R. NARAYANA MURTHY
CHIEF MENTOR, INFOSYS TECHNOLOGIES

Leaders Must Dream Big

Empowerment, at Infosys, is about providing opportunities to individuals to achieve their aspirations, while ensuring that community objectives are met. Thus, to me, an empowered India is a country that provides opportunities for every child to achieve its potential, through education, health care, nutrition, shelter and employment.

At the same time, we must ensure that these children advance the interests of the country. Given that today we rank extremely low on the Human Development Index, such empowerment seems a distant dream. However, I am confident we can achieve this dream if we accomplish a few things. What are they? To achieve this dream of empowerment, we must take tough, unpopular and unpleasant decisions.

The tragedy of India is that we shy away from bold and tough decisions because we do not want to displease anybody. To push these decisions through, we need strong political leaders. We need leaders who have the courage of their convictions: the courage to dream big, to take difficult decisions and to make sacrifices.

Our leaders have to be people who can straddle several worlds—the urban and the rural, the modern and the traditional, the rich and the poor, the educated and the uneducated. They have to appreciate the aspirations of all these worlds. They should not believe that development is a zero-sum game, with gains to one world meaning losses to another.

I often hear my politician friends talk how the IT sector has created a great divide between the haves and the have-nots, and how that should be checked. Sadly, they believe that the solution is to restrict the growth of the IT industry, instead of encouraging the creation of a larger number of such jobs.

Our leaders have to believe that the only way we can solve the problem of poverty is to create more jobs and shift a large number of people from agriculture to manufacturing and services. They must be open-minded, and willing to learn from the experiences of leaders across the world. They must aspire to benchmark India globally.

They must be action-oriented—we have become too much of a rhetoric-satisfied society. Success is all about execution. Leaders today must espouse meritocracy, at least within their own caste or community, since caste has entered the DNA of our society. They must become role models for honesty, modernism, quick action and openness.

How do we achieve this? The only solution is for the top leaders of every political party to demonstrate leadership by example. Leaders across political parties must come together and resolve to promote these values for the good of the future generations. This is tough and seems impossible. However I, for one, believe in the adage that a plausible impossibility is better than a convincing possibility.

There is no other way in our society. In the beginning, we will see a few good leaders being cast away quickly. But, once we see this behaviour from a generation of successive leaders, it becomes the norm. For example, at one time it appeared impossible to stem the mass defection of Aaya Rams and Gaya Rams from one party to another. The practice came to an end because all our political leaders came together and stopped it.

We must have a bureaucracy that is competent, fearless and action-oriented. The major skills for economic development are simulation, planning, estimation, business plan preparation, project management and execution excellence. Our bureaucrats are very good people but are very poor in these skills, if the performance of government funded projects is any indication. Thus, they have to be trained in these skills.

We must create an environment within the bureaucracy where high-performers have incentives to perform without fear. It is best if we abolish the current tenure system and move to a five-year contract system and a promotion system based on performance. Every good deed from a bureaucrat must be appreciated and rewarded.

On the other hand, institutions like the CBI which have been used more as terrorising instruments than for catching the guilty must be wound up. Our philosophy of 'suspicion before proof' has to change to 'proof before verdict'. If we persist with these changes for a few years, we will see wonderful bureaucrats emerge.

Finally we, in the corporate world, have to change as well. We have to become men of steel, and stop crawling when politicians ask us to bend. I see umpteen cases of such behaviour even today. We have to learn to stop asking for sops from the government. For instance, I cannot understand how CEOs of companies that make thousands of crores of profit ask for tax exemption, just because they are in the export business. We must accept that we are in the export business because it is a lucrative business.

When we ask favours from the government in order to create asymmetry in the market vis-à-vis our competitors, we become drawn into the system of corruption. In addition, we must work assiduously towards reducing the social and economic divide in our society and gain the goodwill of the people. We have to learn to put the interest of the corporation ahead of personal interest.

In the end, we, the fortunate elite of this society, have to take responsibility. No matter what our vocation is—politicians, bureaucrats, corporate leaders or academicians—we have a responsibility to show courage and lead by example, to make this a better society for future generations. I know of no simpler mechanism to achieve change than this.

A.M. NAIK
CHAIRMAN & MANAGING DIRECTOR,
LARSEN & TOUBRO LIMITED

March Ahead with a Global Mindset

India is at an inflection point in its economic development, and we have every reason to feel optimistic about its future status as an economic powerhouse. We can only achieve our dreams if each of us decides to participate in and contribute to this movement of development of our nation.

For India to grow at a sustained rate of over 7 per cent, it will require the manufacturing sector to grow at 12 to 13 per cent. We need to recognise that manufacturing has been the engine of growth for all developed economies. While the manufacturing sector in India contributes just 17 per cent to our GDP, it contributes over 50 per cent in China and over 40 per cent in Thailand.

Every rupee invested in manufacturing adds four rupees to our GDP. Besides, it results in the creation of employment even at the lower education levels of our population and thus results in wider distribution of prosperity in the economy.

It was estimated that offshore manufacturing to low-cost countries would increase from USD 1,400 billion in 2002 to USD 4,500 billion by 2015. India has the potential to garner USD 300 billion of this. Harnessing this opportunity can transform the quality of life of our population.

In the 1960s, based on manufacturing capabilities and cost structures, manufacturing activities shifted from the US and Europe to Japan for mass produced items like consumer electronics and cars. This was facilitated by world-class infrastructure and labour productivity. Later, the production of such products shifted to Korea driven by the same factors. In the last 15 years, China has emerged as the centre for mass manufactured products, based on their labour reforms, discipline and world-class infrastructure.

While in the past India has missed several opportunities to develop into a manufacturing centre, it has the potential to become one of the manufacturing bases for the world, especially for products that have high engineering design content. Indian companies are also becoming globally competitive in some sectors like auto components.

For the manufacturing sector to grow significantly, we need to develop good infrastructure in our country, and our government needs to make the necessary policy changes to further increase the role of the private sector. Joint government and private sector participation in the development of roads, ports, airports, power utilities and urban infrastructure will result in faster execution and higher quality levels.

Investments in manufacturing and infrastructure have a multiplier effect on our economy. Good infrastructure will also facilitate the dispersal of manufacturing units away from the major cities and will enable quick and reliable movement of manufactured goods to markets in India and abroad.

Labour reforms are also required to stimulate investment in our economy. If investors have the option of easy exit when businesses do not succeed, they will be forthcoming in investing more in India. Thus, labour reforms will actually result in the creation of more jobs.

We need to recognise that as an integral part of the global economy, we all need to develop a global mindset. Enabling policies will go a long way in attracting capital to the manufacturing and infrastructure sectors.

Indian engineers have been recognised the world over as being amongst the best. While many of them contribute to the enrichment of foreign companies, the benefits of this talent do not trickle enough into our own economy. The manufacturing and infrastructure sectors compete for talent against the IT and ITES, FMCG and the banking sectors. Unfortunately, students do not consider manufacturing and infrastructure sectors as preferred career options. The short supply of talent to the manufacturing and infrastructure sectors could jeopardize our ability to achieve a 12-14 per cent growth rate in manufacturing and to build world-class infrastructure for our country.

While the rapid growth of the BPO and ITES sectors have created large employment opportunities for the lower band of our workforce, of serious concern is the loss of our engineering talent to multinational companies setting up offshore engineering centres in India that results in a 'virtual brain drain'.

While most young people aspire to jumpstart their quality of life with high-salary jobs, we need to systematically make them conscious of the long-term benefits in participating in building a rich and powerful India.

As Indians, we have a responsibility to bequeath to our children a country that is well-developed and economically strong and where we are proud to live. India needs our talent: this is critical for our national and economic development.

NANDAN M. NILEKANI
CEO, PRESIDENT, MD, INFOSYS TECHNOLOGIES

Reduce the Knowledge Gap between the Ruler and the Ruled

The daily death rattle in Iraq reminds us how fragile and inchoate is the arduous process of giving birth to democracy. We in India have become used to the institutions and processes of our democratic republic. Yet even as we celebrate the world's new found admiration for the way we have managed the diversity of our people and channelled their aspirations, there is a gnawing feeling that the job is only half-done. And even as we believe that the natural province of the argumentative Indian is a free society, we look for answers to make India truly empowered.

Some search for panaceas that involve great leaders coming on their white steeds delivering salvation. Others take refuge in ideologies often flawed and fundamentalist. Some more hark back to a more moral, simpler era. Yet the answer is not there so much as in making our governance more open and responsive.

To truly empower India, we need to reduce the knowledge asymmetry between the ruler and the ruled. Once the opaque veils on our state are raised, the citizen will be truly in charge. The sunshine that we bring to bear on the inner working of government will ensure that both the incompetent and the corrupt will have far less chance of getting away with it.

To do this, we have to bring together the two great proven successes of independent India, our democratic tradition and our mastery over information technology. The process begins by using technology to automate and streamline the processes by which we take decisions, use funds and deliver services to the people. This automation is usually seen as a way to streamline processes, improve public delivery and reduce corruption.

But the most important function of automation in a governance scenario is to create a window into the inner working of the government. If the citizen is able to get visibility into the inside functioning of the government, on how decisions are made, on how money is spent, on who the beneficiaries are and what were the outcomes, it stands to reason that the quality of decisions will be far better, the system will become accountable and the citizen will be far more empowered.

However, technology is not enough. The natural tendency of the state is to use information not to empower its people, but to exercise more control and repression. If technology is implemented by itself, all it does is transfer the levers of power from one set of people to another. Hence, any effort to implement technology must have a concomitant goal mandated by law to disclose to the people all the information that has now been made possible by the use of such tools.

The third leg of this process is creating a forum for citizens to engage with the State on the basis of this vastly new knowledge of the State's functioning that is available. The actual mode of citizen participation may vary, based on which tier of government it is, and the nature of governance. But citizen involvement is vital and it is going to be far more effective, since it will be with information and data whose integrity is accepted, rather than in an atmosphere of distrust.

The final piece of the puzzle is the right to information. This is what will allow the ordinary citizen to ensure that he can prise open information from the hands of an unwilling State. The Right to Information Act is often touted as the magic pill that will be the panacea for all our ills. But unless it is preceded by technology-enabled knowledge systems, mandated disclosure and structured citizen participation, it will be a damp squib. Having right to information without the first three will be like giving every child a right to education without having built any schools.

Is all this doable? Absolutely. When independent India was conceived it was done in an analog era of paper and pen. It was built on top of a foundation of set of bureaucratic processes left by the British. Our founding fathers could not have anticipated the swift advances in technology that allow us to wire every nook and corner of the country, that would make computers and software cheaply available and bring the liberating power of the internet. Nor could they have known that in this new information-intensive era, Indians would have a natural aptitude, and play a leading role.

The marrying of our democratic and governance mechanisms with the liberating power of IT is the key to reducing the knowledge asymmetry that exists between the State and its citizens. This gap between what the

State knows and what the people are told is the root of repression, corruption and inequity. It is this complete opacity that allows those who have subverted the State to use it for their own ends. Eliminating this asymmetry and setting the foundation for an open democracy is what will truly empower India.

P.R.S. 'BIKI' OBEROI
CHAIRMAN, THE OBEROI GROUP

Getting Ready to Welcome the World

I am happy to say that the government which took charge in May 2004 demonstrated a high level of commitment to the travel and tourism industry. For me, India empowered is a government which realises the great economic potential of the tourism, tour and hospitality trade. I am happy due recognition is being given today and it comes from the highest quarters of this government. I believe we have now begun to move in the right direction.

Tourism is an industry which plays a pivotal role in the economy of a country as it is one of the biggest employment generators—the tourism industry has a multiplier effect in the job market where it creates jobs for seven people after it touches just one person. Is there any other economic sector which hires people who have retired (there is no age bar for guides) and cuts across the gender and age divides?

The tourism industry is also a window to the world from which even India can be viewed. India is a unique destination and deserves easy access for visitors. I can say with some pride and gratification that we have successfully removed constraints for an open sky policy for international airlines. In fact, at the WTTC meet in Agra recently, I got into a big row with the government saying that domestic airlines should also be allowed to fly abroad, as it increases seat capacity.

Both Indian Airlines and Air India have had the luxury of protection from the government for far too long. Today, I am happy to say, we have more international flights than ever before, and this will not only encourage tourism but also have a positive effect on foreign investment.

Now, that's the good news. The downside is that a lot still needs to be done to develop and improve infrastructure in the country to boost tourism—from upgrading airports to developing more hotel properties at the dozens of tourist destinations all over the country.

Our airports are in a deplorable state, they are disgraceful and the worst in the neighbourhood. And I do not mean just the major metros, but in also highly visited tourist destinations like Jaipur and Udaipur. These airports actually reveal that we are an underdeveloped, Third World country.

For instance, while we have upgraded the Agra airport to an international airport, the facilities available there are worse than those at a camel fair. I must add here, that in the enthusiasm to open the skies, I do not welcome the idea of charters as the tourists spend no money in the country as everything is already paid for at home. After all, the person who spends $20 consumes the same amount of water as the person who spends $200!

Another crucial area where government intervention is required is to make available government-owned land more cost-effective to develop new hotel properties. We need more hotels—Delhi has a dismal 5000 luxury rooms available today.

I had proposed that the government give its land on a long-term lease to hoteliers where they pay a nominal fee per annum, equivalent to say 5 per cent of the value of the property, over seventy-five years or more. Unfortunately, the government wants to sell its real estate at commercial prices and get the money upfront.

I am not saying that the government give us land and lose money, but with this long-lease arrangement, it is possible that the government makes money too.

Other areas where critical attention is required: clean cities and tourist spots, taking care of our monuments and heritage.

And, most importantly, simplifying the visa regime. Perhaps the most ridiculous argument the bureaucrats give for stringent visa controls is our security concerns. Which country in the world does not have security concerns today? In our neighbourhood itself, Sri Lanka, which has had a scary security environment, has the least visa controls for tourists. I think, for India to be truly empowered, the government must be empowered against its own bureaucracy.

Where will the vast army of visa officials go if visa regulations are relaxed?

DEEPAK S. PAREKH
CHAIRMAN, HDFC LTD

Fortune Favours the Prepared Mind

It has been aptly said, albeit in another time and era, by Louis Pasteur that 'fortune favours the prepared mind'. Those who can claim to be the masters of the universe, the barons of business, the creators of wealth and abundance will be those who lead their employees to imbibe new skills, transcend traditional parameters, create knowledge-awareness and constantly provide training as a means to learn and empower.

It is a fragile yet effervescent business environment, those who adapt to change rapidly and courageously will be the winners in any developed or developing economy. Indian industry has largely responded to global assimilation, to the need to be a global Indian company, to attract foreign investment to partake in the world-pie that is on offer for those who have a taste for adventure!

These corporate czars who seek new dimensions to traditional business practices are the future empowerers, the future strength of India's knowledge workers and the makers of India's undeniable place in the world economy. Policy-makers in the government will need to internalise this pace and stand solidly supporting the economic agenda that India has cut out for itself.

Leaders of the government in countries such as China, Japan, South Korea, Indonesia, Eastern Europe are proactive to change and a capitalist method of enriching their population has been a dramatic reversal from previously held protectionist beliefs. These drivers of change are the true empowerers and emperors of the world.

I have been a vociferous proponent of unshackling the economy and introducing financial sector reform. My big moment that followed after the foreign exchange crisis in 1991 was reform in the banking sector and the foray of private-sector banking that emerged in the Indian economic arena. Soon to follow was private-sector insurance that allowed several initiatives to take hold, effectively giving much needed competition to state-run insurance initiatives.

These changes saw India surge forward in the global financial services arena, with hitherto revolutionary ideas infused with hitherto unseen capital inflows in a truly emerging business environment. This has been a personal 'big moment' that has translated into many initiatives HDFC has incorporated into its fold as a financial services company.

VIVEK PAUL
PARTNER, TEXAS PACIFIC GROUP

Empower Youth to Drive India's Progress

More than half of India is under 25, more than a third under 15. That means more than half the country does not know what the Emergency meant, has never experienced a war with Pakistan and knows Kashmir only for its violence, not its beauty. To nearly a third of the population, Indira and even Rajiv Gandhi are historical figures, gone before they were born. For as long as this group has lived, India has had nothing but coalition governments that changed prime ministers eight times in sixteen years.

India cannot be empowered until this youth boom feels empowered and they approach life with the zest of a Bunty and Babli. They see themselves as capable and at least as good as any counterpart around the world. They have great ambitions and are willing to work hard to achieve them. They do not see a humble upbringing or being raised in a village or a small town as an impediment.

They do not expect some authority figure to hand them something, they simply seek opportunity. This youth boom puts India at a historic moment of transition. As India adds more to the global workforce than any other nation in the world over the next decade, and as this cohort exercises its propensity for consumption, it can power India to a developed country status in just a couple of decades.

US investment bankers talk about how India will become one of the world's largest economies in a couple of decades and follow the path that Japan did in the seventies and eighties. The stock market scales new heights every day. This rosy haze can hide the fact that this success is far from guaranteed. In fact, it is quite the opposite.

As the pace of reforms has begun to slow down, so has the economy, and with that, job creation. Sure, the economy is growing and adding jobs, but is it enough? As this youth boom comes of age, if there is not enough opportunity for them, it is not that India will simply achieve some fractional portion of its full potential. There will be a tipping point, below which youth unemployment can create enormous social pressures, pulling the nation into the same mire that held it back, as redistribution becomes more important than creation, and the flicker of 'chhoti si asha' is snuffed out.

In fact, a study by the Boston Consulting Group indicates that within the next decade, half of India's unemployed will be its educated youth. We cannot allow that to happen.

In simple arithmetic terms, if one half of the group is under 25, and the current jobs are pretty much held by those over 25, then India needs to double its employment! We need the economy to grow at over 10 per cent; 6-7 per cent growth is great relative to the past, but not enough to serve the future.

The BPO/IT industries, for all the limelight they bask in, generate a negligible 0.2 per cent of the employment. Employment growth and opportunity will come only as the Indian economy inflates. India cannot skip the industrial revolution, it must accelerate through it.

This means India must remove the strictures that have held back the manufacturing and traditional service industries. It takes no advisory panel or commission to determine that India needs to reform labour laws; needs to liberalise the regulations that govern application of capital, particularly foreign direct investment; invest in education, healthcare and infrastructure and fund it not by running up debt but by cutting back on all the unproductive spending on money-losing state-owned enterprises and unnecessary subsidies; needs to hire enough judges to clear the decades-long backlog in the courts; and to cut the 30,000 statutes that tie down progress.

India cannot make glacial progress on only a couple of these—we do not have the luxury of time. India must move quickly and now and on all these areas.

Easier said than done—despite some of the world's best leaders, progress has slowed as politicians are frozen by their concerns about balancing coalitions and bureaucrats, by the dogma of the past. Economic empowerment must move away from New Delhi and state capitals to the natural mercantile energies of countless thousands of Indian entrepreneurs across small towns, large cities and villages.

As the economic uplift touches every part of India, social empowerment will surely follow. Empowerment is not given—it is earned. Democracies depend on their citizens to govern themselves, to look for pratinidhis instead of netas. Self-governance is not easy and takes time.

Look at the cradles of modern democracy—it took the US almost 50 years after its independence to give the vote to 3 per cent of its population and at that time even the UK had only 3 per cent of its population with the right to vote. In the US, it took almost 100 years to have universal suffrage.

India started its democracy with a big leap granting the universal right to vote, and now with over half a century of experience, is seeing the upsurge of true empowerment of its peoples. There is a blossoming of opportunities for citizens at every level to participate in movements, be they in the spreading of participative democracy, local education improvement, women's empowerment through micro finance, land reform, etc., and each of these is making the apparatus of the state more accountable.

While there are many success stories, India still needs thousands of local champions to take on the leadership mantle. As the famous quote says, 'Never doubt that a small group of thoughtful, committed people can change the world. Indeed, it is the only thing that ever has.'

Await not empowerment, but seize it and get others to do the same. This youth boom has little voice today to protect its interests, it needs us all to be activists and history will not forgive us if we waste their dawn.

AZIM H. PREMJI
CHAIRMAN & MANAGING DIRECTOR, WIPRO

An Education Worthy Enough for India

5 8 years after independence, one question remains in my mind: why did we struggle for independence? For close to three centuries, British colonial rule was the norm for our countrymen. Even before the British, our nation had only known the rule of kings, monarchs and emperors. Having barely experienced any other form of governance, what then triggered the powerful independence movement?

I think the answer lies in understanding that the independence movement was not a struggle against the British. Rather, it was a struggle for an idea of India—a democratic ideal that first existed in the minds of a few and then sparked an entire nation. Paraphrasing from our Constitution, this is the idea of a society where the spirit of brotherhood reigns among the people of India, transcending all diversity; a society that protects nature and has compassion for all living creatures; a society of humane citizens; a society that strives towards excellence in all spheres of individual and collective activity.

This, my friends, is a lofty and worthy vision for our country. However, in the decades since Independence, are we any closer to realising this idea of India? The independence movement cannot remain static history—it needs to be re-ignited. We cannot let that precious flame of national consciousness die when millions of our countrymen continue to languish in economic and social poverty.

In this day and age, I wonder how many of us can truly relate to these words of Gandhiji: 'I will give you a talisman. Whenever you are in doubt, or when the self becomes too much with you, apply the following test: recall the face of the poorest and the weakest man whom you may have seen, and ask yourself if the step you contemplate is going to be of

AN EDUCATION WORTHY ENOUGH FOR INDIA   297

any use to him. Will he gain anything by it? Will it restore him to a control over his own life and destiny? In other words, will it lead to swaraj for the hungry and spiritually starving millions?'

I think this cry now falls on ears that do not necessarily listen, and it is likely that one key reason is that we have not succeeded in developing a spirit of compassion and social action among our citizens. We need to revitalise our social consciousness, and I see no answer that does not begin with the state of our schools; for education is the fundamental process for triggering social progress and reform.

Thus a seemingly simple question, why did we fight for independence, now transforms into something more specific: what kind of education will help our children develop into spirited citizens—citizens who are critical, creative and caring; citizens who will drive social improvement? This is a large question, and I am not qualified to offer an answer. At best, I have a few ideas, some of which I present to you.

To begin with, I am clear that such a citizen cannot come forth in a classroom that is not democratic. In our schools, students are usually treated as beings who need to be didactically tutored, disciplined, and moulded. Students are 'told' what to do, how to behave and what they must know. It seems to me that the first step is to make classrooms more open, friendly and democratic. A classroom is where the student is an active and equal participant in the teaching-learning process and is continuously formulating, questioning, thinking, experiencing, challenging, reconstructing—and thus learning.

My own experience is that a good teacher can impact a child deeply— simply because children learn by observing and trying to emulate adults. Therefore, the second requirement is to have teachers who are good role models. It is essential that our schools have teachers who are competent and committed; who are constantly learning; who are good listeners; who care about their students and about the world. And we have to help the teacher become this, and she has to try and become this.

The third step is to recognise that schools are important spaces for social learning. Here, the child learns how to relate to her classmate, to the person who keeps the school clean, to the authority of teachers, to the stray dog, to the tree in the playground. And if the child learns to treat each being with love and equity, then the child will grow up learning to live in harmony with herself and with respect and care for her world.

I am certain each one of us can come up with many more such ideas. However, if these ideas need to bear fruit, if our schools have to change, then it is imperative that each one of us is driven to action—as a parent, as an educator, as a student, or as a concerned citizen. In our own small way, and in our own backyard, we have to raise a clarion call. Only then will enough critical mass catalyse to stir our societal juggernaut from its inertia.

I would like to end with the words of Swami Vivekananda: 'Our duty is to encourage every one in his struggle to live up to his own highest idea, and strive at the same time to make the ideal as near as possible to the Truth. Education is not the amount of information that is put into your brain and runs riot there, undigested all your life. We must have life-building, man-making, character-making assimilation of ideas. If you have assimilated five ideas and made them your life and character, you have more education than any man who has got by heart a whole library.'

SAM PITRODA
CHAIR, NATIONAL KNOWLEDGE COMMISSION

Technology Will Usher in Change

In a society still riddled with century-old prejudices, stereotypes, the caste system and rituals, we need continuous intervention of a force that is non-political, non-judgmental, non-denominational and rational to empower people. To me technology is that force. Technology is a great social leveller. It brings access to modern tools and methods to increase productivity and efficiency at reduced costs. It is an entry point to bring about generational changes. It is by no means an end in itself. It is about designing more efficient tools for the country's carpenters or hand water pumps that would draw more water for less effort or rural classrooms that use more modern teaching tools than blackboard and chalk or public toilets designed to cater to a large population or better brooms for municipal conservancy workers or water carriers that would not sit atop a rural woman's head for miles. It is about better health service, improved education, affordable housing, transparent government, more jobs etc.

In the 1980s, when the Rajiv Gandhi government began addressing India's many challenges using technology, there was widespread derision. The general political consensus in the country then was that we were all westernised Indians who were completely disconnected from India's real issues. We were dismissed as 'computer boys'. Some two decades later, our faith in technology as an instrument of transformational change stands vindicated. ICT (Information and Communications Technology) success has given us confidence, connectivity, major new companies and around $150 billion in foreign exchange reserves.

Being born underprivileged, precisely among the kind of people we are now talking of empowering, technology opened doors for me. It erased my caste and empowered me to upward mobility. When people talk of technology they invariably think in terms of computers, satellites, aircraft and other gadgets. To me technology is problem solving at personal, community and national levels. It is about doing things differently. It is about change in mindsets, processes, products and preferences. Technology is about opportunities and experiences.

India desperately needs to create technological leaderships at all levels. While the information technology entrepreneurs have been justifiably celebrated in the country, we need similar stories in other fields. It is heartening to know that some segments of India's politics and administration have begun to understand the importance of technology. They have also begun to understand that if they do not keep up with the pace, technology will make them redundant.

In the 1980s when we introduced computerisation of the railway reservation system, certain quarters of India's establishment reacted with unvarnished anger. They thought it spelled doom for hundreds of thousands of railway employees. Little did they realise that while technological intervention can be disruptive in the short-term, in the long-term its benefits far outweigh the loss.

In spite of the examples, many confuse new technology with labour displacement as opposed to labour retraining and readjustment. We must remember that technology has played an important role in our green revolution, milk revolution, space, defence, telecom, railway reservations, energy, medicine etc.

The STD-PCO revolution has been much celebrated in India, but I remember the amount of resistance and cynicism it met with when we first introduced the idea. Most people saw it as just a telephone booth when, in fact, it was an instrument of societal change. It made access to information for millions of Indian citizens easier and cheaper than ever before and in the process empowered them.

As India emerges as an information technology centre and its economy firmly establishes itself among the world's top five, I think the time has come for yet another round of transformational change using technology. The platform which has the potential to unleash such transformational change relates to building new knowledge potential to respond to the needs of the 21st century. This requires reforming our education system from top to bottom to improve quality, quantity, access and relevance substantially. We cannot be happy with our peak performance at IITs and IIMs. We must improve by lifting thousands of schools and colleges where students do not learn enough to be able to find suitable employment.

It also requires new focus on our research and development institutions with emphasis on innovations and entrepreneurship to create and manufacture products and services for our people at affordable prices. The big challenge is to improve knowledge production, dissemination and applications for agriculture, health, industry and government.

With the forces of globalisation, privatisation, liberalisation and free market it is important to recognise that we must change our age old processes and practices with new knowledge and new understanding of the ever changing competitive nature of the global market.

True knowledge can empower people at all levels. It can make people aware of their rights and responsibilities. It can also provide them tools and techniques to be productive and meaningful in the information age. To achieve this, the best brains in the country will have to focus urgently on solving problems of the poor and the underprivileged at the bottom of the pyramid.

To me the key to empowering people is to provide knowledge, tools, technology and techniques to change their mindset from negative cynicism to positive optimism with hope for the limitless opportunities in this ever changing world.

SUBIR RAHA
FORMER CHAIRMAN,
OIL AND NATURAL GAS CORPORATION (ONGC)

Stable, Quality Energy: A Dream Come True

For me, India will be empowered when darkness is not a compulsion of the night. This will be a time when there is no uncertainty of outcome at the press of a switch. A time when the poorest of the poor student can do his homework in the light of a lantern for which kerosene was not purchased at black-market prices. A time when taps do not run dry because there was no power for water pumps; patients do not die because there was no power for the hospital. This will be a time when women and children do not trudge miles every day collecting water and wood. This will be a time when the 'fuel mafias' in coal, cooking gas, kerosene etc. go out of business.

The president, in his address to the nation on the eve of the Independence day in 2004, had articulated his vision of energy independence for India by 2030. I believe in his vision. We have the resources not only to become energy independent but also to become, in a matter of the next decades, a net exporter of energy to the rest of the world.

What we need is the zeal to transform these resources into efficient, economic and environment-friendly power. Hopefully, things will change. Otherwise, the BRICS idea will remain a pipedream. The debate on manufacturing versus services will be pointless. Without power, India will not be empowered.

The key issues are known—pricing anomalies and theft, whether outright theft, adulteration or diversion. Genuine concern for the poor can be realised only through cost-efficient operations. Because of the inherent contradictions in our policies and practices, the economy continues to be burdened with huge avoidable costs. Ultimately, the tax-payer has to pay for all these inefficiencies. The hard fact is that the benefit of subsidised pricing does not reach the intended beneficiaries.

In many socio-economic aspects, we have outlived the inflexible approach of a closed economy. Energy is perhaps the only area where the dogmas of the past blind us to the realities of the globalised market-place. Partial or incomplete reform is perhaps worse than no reform at all. In a controlled economy, the accountability lies with the State alone.

In the transition phase, the State and the corporate investors keep going round in complicated circles, without reaching anywhere. The fuel resources do not get converted into power because investors are not motivated. The value of power is not appreciated, resulting in unbelievable wastage due to obsolete conversion technologies and indifference to conservation.

For decades, we have been talking about an integrated approach to energy planning and investments. For decades, we have accepted the need for mass transit systems. For decades, we have realised that indigenous coal must be processed through environment-friendly technologies.

There has to be a day when we actually get down to decisions, investments and implementation. This will not happen unless the 'vested interests' are tackled head on. Like everything else in the process of governance, the initiative must come from political will.

India Empowered will be when all children, whether born to the rich in the metros or the deprived in the hamlets, will be assured of a uniform quality of education through a national network sustained by uninterrupted availability of stable, quality energy.

KIRAN MAZUMDAR SHAW
CMD, BIOCON

People as Agents of Change

An empowered nation is synonymous with national pride. Pride to me is the most powerful ethos that defines empowerment. India's private sector, led by information technology, telecommunications, biotech, pharmaceuticals and many others, is empowering the country on a platform of performance and excellence.

A *BusinessWeek* report comparing India and China indicated that while China outperformed India in terms of foreign investments, India outperformed China by a factor of two when it came to returns on investment in almost every industry sector. The India factor is now a force to be reckoned with and something that is building national pride through amplified job opportunities which are reversing the brain drain.

Apart from industry, success in other areas like sports, entertainment, the visual and performing arts and heritage are also great contributors to pride and empowerment. Today's youth is inspired by successful icons, be it business, sports or the performing arts.

Sania Mirza's successful debut on the world stage has empowered many an aspiring tennis player to pursue professional tennis. Indian cricket, though at an all-time low, has brought global visibility to India's leadership position in the game. Today, Rahul Dravid and Sachin Tendulkar are as sought after as Bollywood stars. Likewise, Narayana Murthy and Ratan Tata are revered across all sections of society.

A visit to Malaysia left me with a lasting impression of what nation building and empowerment is all about. Only a few decades ago, Malaysia was a country that suffered a deep inferiority complex from its highly advanced and progressive neighbour, Singapore.

As a Bangalorean, I remember feeling mighty proud of Dr Mahathir

Mohamad's revealing statement that he would like to develop Kuala Lumpur as Malaysia's Bangalore! Today, it is just the reverse: Kuala Lumpur is a city of the future that has left Bangalore far behind. The infrastructure is impressive, the people are confident, the economy is booming and there is an immense sense of national pride and, more importantly, the political will to move on and build even further on this success. What Malaysia has demonstrated is the power of political will to transform an uninitiated mindset into a progressive, dynamic nation on the move. Against this backdrop, I despair at the abysmally slow pace of change in our country. I am envious of countries who have outpaced us in development.

If there is one class of people who are not empowered, it is our politicians and bureaucrats who do not seem to have any inclination to bring about progressive change. They are unable to rise above archaic and petty politics to make any visible difference to the communities that elect them.

However, amidst this gloom, there is also hope. There is a noticeable change taking place in various ways where men and women are gradually building an ethos of empowerment through a deep sense of purpose, willing to overcome challenges because they want to change this country in a manner that every Indian can be proud of.

VENU SRINIVASAN
CHAIRMAN & MANAGING DIRECTOR, TVS MOTOR COMPANY

Islands of Prosperity in a Sea of Poverty

We need to look at empowerment in terms of people who have been left out by the post-1990 economic liberalisation and reforms—the people who do not consume because they don't have the power to; and who do not therefore participate in the economy or its growth.

They have to be economically active first before they can contribute anything to society. Having worked in rural and forest areas, my way of looking at it is that out of these groups, the first priority are the scheduled tribes followed by scheduled castes.

They form a sizeable minority and a disproportionately large percentage of them live below the poverty line. The scheduled tribes come to my mind as one of the most neglected parts of our society, living far away from the society in forest areas, beyond the reach of health and educational institutions.

Even where there are such institutions, we know very well that doctors do not go there, teachers do not teach there and the administration is apathetic to them. Most importantly, there is huge conflict between them and the forest departments.

There needs to be a major overhaul of the Forest Act in order to allow these people to partake of some of their own resources in an eco-friendly and sustainable way in the forests where they live. They live in areas extraordinarily rich in natural resources such as iron ore or bauxite; and they see the exploitation of these resources by businesses with absolutely no benefit to them other than providing them low-paid, unskilled employment.

This results in disenchantment and frustration, which leads to violence and extremism besides further alienation. There is nobody ready to listen to their tale of woe and provide them with any resolution of their grievances and problems. Therefore, this I would consider as one of the biggest opportunities or gaps in our society in terms of empowerment.

If this issue is not addressed, an entire region in the heart of India, including northern Andhra Pradesh, Orissa, eastern Vidarbha, Chhattisgarh and Jharkhand will continue to remain as disturbed areas of our country with no possibility of integration with the mainstream.

The second group of people who have still not benefited sufficiently from the progress of the past few years are the scheduled castes. They suffer continuing discrimination and oppression in rural areas even in the so-called more advanced states of our country. The other backward castes are more integrated into society and stand a better chance of access to all the governmental concessions and benefits, leaving the scheduled caste people far behind.

Again, the education and employment opportunities for these people have lagged far behind the other sections of society. Unless something drastic is done to address both these categories of people, we cannot really see an empowered society in the real sense in India.

The third area is women from rural areas who are poor. They are the thrice handicapped. Undernourished and oppressed by widespread male chauvinism, they are also often illiterate. There is also female foeticide and infanticide, still continuing in spite of rules and laws that have been amended from time to time. In this particular case, the solution has to come from the development of self-help groups in a big way and institutions such as the Grameen Bank of Bangladesh. There have to be some kind of formal micro-credit programmes on a massive scale, which focus on these poor rural women.

My vision for an empowered India thus will be a society free of discrimination on the basis of caste, creed or gender and where all sections of society are fully involved in the economic progress of our country. Going back to the words of Abraham Lincoln, I believe a house divided against itself cannot stand. India cannot hope to remain a prosperous country leaving behind such a large segment of our own people. Having islands of prosperity in a sea of poverty is not the sustainable way to grow.

RATAN TATA
CHAIRMAN, TATA GROUP

Time for India to Shift Gear

Over the last two years, India has been attracting increasing global attention as a 'nation on the move'. Its high growth rate and its evident sustainability, its global prominence and potential in the knowledge-based industries, its pool of skilled manpower and its low-cost manufacturing base, coupled, very importantly, with confidence in its political leadership, have all gone towards giving India a new position in the global economic scene.

Having received this level of recognition and acceptance, it is essential that India should leverage this momentum and enhance its position in the region. The greatest mistake that could be made would be for us to become complacent and to allow our economic momentum to slow down.

The UPA government's 'Common Minimum Programme' spells out the broad agenda agreed upon between the coalition partners but, as the name suggests, it is a 'minimum programme' and perhaps this needs to be supplemented if India is to be empowered to fulfill the hopes and aspirations of its people.

As a great believer in India's potential, I believe strongly that our country could make even greater progress if:

- Only the highest standards are set and demanded on all initiatives. Most projects or initiatives are conceived and executed with several compromises, often resulting in substandard results. We should demand the highest international standards in whatever we undertake.
- All policies are framed and strictly implemented for the national good, rather than being modified to appease powerful vested interests or political ideologies.

- Investment in infrastructure is given the highest priority. Our ports, airports, road networks and power systems are outdated and inadequate to meet the needs of the country. They are also far behind the infrastructure of several countries in the region. There is a desperate need to update, upgrade and build capacity for the future.
- Knowledge-based industries are identified by the government as India's future strength and dominance. This would call for creation of many more vocational schools and good institutes of learning in IT, biotechnology, the sciences, medicine, as also substantial incentives for home-grown research and development in the corporate sector. India has one of the world's youngest populations today and will by 2030 have the largest working age population in the world. We should leverage this advantage by enlarging the skill and knowledge base of this enormously valuable resource.
- A 10-year economic vision is announced with measurable goals, and which has the 'buy-in' of all political parties. This 'vision' would need to be executed without bending to vested interest groups or ideologies. Its execution should reflect concern for the environment and for depletion of the country's non-renewable resources.

Such a plan could have major goals for tourism (which would create tens of thousands of jobs, justifying investment in national infrastructure and being a large earner of foreign exchange), ferrous and non-ferrous metal capacity goals (leveraging India's mineral resources) and some major national projects, such as, possibly, a gas pipeline from the Middle East, a limited-access national highway system, national water harvesting, drinking water projects and the like.

This is the time for India to shift gears and for our leaders to view India in the global context—competing and excelling in the global arena. We can no longer compare ourselves with our own past history, nor be satisfied with growth and improvement in small increments.

This is the time when India must set major goals and mobilise all its resources to achieve these goals through bold and sustained initiatives. We need to empower our people and subordinate individual vested interests in favour of initiatives for the good of the nation. It will be such actions alone that will enhance prosperity in our country and raise the quality of life for our people.

All of us should be proud of what India has become and the manner in which it has emerged from over forty years of protection. We now need to put our shoulders together to enable India to take its place amongst the successful economies of the region.

THE ARTS, SPORTS

VISHWANATHAN ANAND
CHESS GRANDMASTER

Don't Wait for a Chance, Make It Happen

In 2001 at the Kremlin, in the highest realm of chess, I, the lone non-Soviet player there, was in a game against Vladislav Tkachiev. At a certain moment, I made a move and saw about 1,500 Russian hands clap in unison. In chess, these kinds of gestures are very rare when a crowd applauds in the midst of a game. To be acclaimed by the critics in their land for your talent is heartwarming. For me, it was a moment when I felt proud to have the tricolour beside my board.

The answer to what my country can achieve and my role in it lies with Neeraj Mor. A lad from Haryana who learnt chess from the NIIT Mind Champions Academy portal, Neeraj Mor represents the Indian of the next generation. Adept in computers and with a perseverance to achieve, he has shown that chess has no language or geography. Only success and defeat. For me, Neeraj represents GenNext in India.

In 1984, I travelled abroad for the first time to play. It was there I met Ivanchuk, Dreev, Gelfand and Piket; people from my age group. At that event I realised if I had to be in the top 1 per cent of my sport, these are the guys to beat; if I do that, I will always be the best player from my country. I think in sports, sometimes, we value titles in name and not in spirit. If we have to be a global force in sport, we have to set our eyes on absolute performance.

Sometimes we tend to be content with what we have and fear risking unchartered paths. In sports, there are small windows when you have to prove your worth. If you let that moment pass, it never comes back. As 15-year-olds start playing with the world elite, we need to understand that opportunities never come. They get made. We are excellent in postmortem analyses but we do not have a proactive strategy. I think China understands that very well.

In chess, the internet and computers have changed the way the game is played. Talent and players have to adapt. Change is never rewarding at the first try. But it is what will bring victory in the long run. Instant success never happens. We tend to idolise a person after one achievement or demonise them for the same reason. I think assessment has to be objective and always with a global perspective.

Education is an important component of life. It is not just academics but social skills that are extremely important. It is quite sad to see young children forced to leave school to learn chess. I went through university, reading Archies and listening to Madonna while being World No. 5, and never felt I had to give up any of that to be a chess player.

When you represent a sport, what you do influences the sport. In certain sports you have to achieve at the highest level to keep your sport in the public eye. Maybe that has made India a chess force to reckon with. Chess has come a long way since the eighties when I first started out. We were all in the race to become the first Indian Grandmaster. Now India is an accepted chess nation. We are ranked 15th in terms of our absolute strength. An excellent statistic that traces the spectacular rise of talent in the game. We have quality grandmasters who are getting stronger.

Chess is one of the few games where gender is not a division. India has produced world-class players of both sexes. I think this has helped overcome preconceived notions and girls should be encouraged to participate more in school-level events. After all, it was my mother who showed me how to play chess.

What needs to change is the official bureaucracy in the form of various sports associations. Most officials forget that they represent the players. Their prestige comes from the players and not vice-versa. An association and a title on a visiting card makes the most rational sports lover into an official caught up in bureaucratic manoeuvres.

For me, India Empowered is when I am not Mr Anand from the land of snake charmers and mystic eccentricities but Anand from a country whose intellectual capital is coming of age. India is a country where in every household there is a lamp of ingenuity, intelligence and perseverance. Now the light is on us and the world is taking notice.

SHYAM BENEGAL
FILMMAKER

A Level Playing Field

My idea of empowerment is when there are equal rights for every citizen.

India cannot be called a truly empowered state until women, who constitute half of the population, do not enjoy the same rights as men. Also, in a vertically stratified society like ours, where the caste system still flourishes, we need to ensure at least basic human rights to the 'untouchable community'.

It's a fallacy that empowerment comes through reservation. The historical genesis for reservation was that the untouchables were not given basic human rights. In that era, it worked fine. But in today's context, reservation doesn't help, it hinders and creates inequality. It'll probably dis-empower people.

The best deal would be to concentrate our efforts on the untouchable community. Rest assured, the rest of the community will move forward since they already have a voice and the abilities to excel.

Another aspect that needs attention is the area of social security. We might be becoming a global player but we need to create a social security net for people who don't have equal opportunities.

One way we can achieve this is by extending education at the grassroots level. Education is a crucial tool to empower people. But it has to be worthwhile education. We have to formulate a clear policy on education which will take us forward as a society.

All these things that I've pointed out aren't just the responsibility of the government. If it is, then it means we're dependent on the government and that's not empowerment.

The whole idea of empowerment is to help every citizen realise his potential. The government can provide opportunities so that people can come into their own. The ability to express that power then rests on the individual.

We, as Indians, can do all this. What stops us from being fair and providing basic human rights to a marginalised community or giving equal opportunities to women? Governments always take the easier way out by distributing largesse or money. What does the government do when there's a disaster anywhere in the country? It just distributes money. The government doesn't create safeguards so that the disaster doesn't happen again.

It's up to us, the citizens of India, to take up the cause of our country.

HARSHA BHOGLE
SPORTS COMMENTATOR, COLUMNIST

Put Sports on the Fast Track

Dear Dr Singh, I am addressing my contribution to this wonderful series, a series you felt was important enough to contribute to yourself, to you as the Indian I admire the most, the finest agent of change we have had in recent times.

21 years ago, in a classroom at IIM Ahmedabad, a professor teaching us a course called Fiscal Policy and Business, stopped his lecture to wonder when India would have its first 1,000-crore company. Later I discovered that India's total advertising spend that year was no more than Rs 450 crore. We would probably have been stupid, or dreamers (and I wonder why the two go together sometimes!), to imagine that *Business Week* would carry an 80-page cover story on India as one of two emerging global powers.

It sets me thinking. 20 years from now, can *Sports Illustrated*, or the *Times* of London, or indeed *India Today* run a cover story on India being the next global sporting power? Is that a stupid thought? Am I dreaming? Is that a pig flying?

In your glory years as finance minister, you merged India with the world, you backed India to stand on its feet. By inculcating the spirit of competition, you allowed excellence to infect India's private sector and, in course of time, some pockets in the public sector as well. You empowered India, you liberated Indian enterprise. If it could happen to India's businesses, to India's economy, why can't it happen to Indian sport? You highlighted my definition of empowerment—giving people the freedom to excel. In Indian sport today, an individual may dream of excelling but the system will not give him the freedom to do so.

Few things galvanise a nation as much as sport does. In that theatre of human emotions, only unscripted drama rules. Look how excited we are about Sania Mirza who has fifty other girls better than her at the moment. We are excited because an Indian is competing with the world.

So too with Narain Karthikeyan who fills us with joy when he competes with the symbol of India on his helmet. When Rajyavardhan Singh Rathore won an Olympic medal many like me stood up and clapped like we hadn't for years.

But our federations do not like empowerment. It is a terrifying word for them for it conjures up ghastly images. Words like excellence, accountability and passion haunt and imprison them. In this new India of freedom and achievement they are fortresses of feudalism and mediocrity. The chief of Indian hockey once said that paying match fees to players who work very hard to play for India is akin to bribery. That hurt. As much as it would to you if your successor enforced 98 per cent income tax, 400 per cent customs duty and nationalisation of Infosys and Wipro.

This is the ministry the sports minister has to run. But why should it be so? Would you make me your minister for defence? Would you allow me to run the All India Institute of Medical Sciences? Weren't you an outstanding finance minister because you had a passion for it, because you were a nationalist? Asking somebody to become sports minister today, as you know, is like asking a star centre forward to become assistant baggage man. Why? Why can't a sports minister be passionately in love with sport? Why can't you pick that kind of person? Why not Michael Ferreira?

Just as today's young boys and girls believe they can be the best software professionals in the world, so too must young sportsmen. They need to be empowered, not strangled. That is our dream. Can't we allow them that? Can't they bloom? Can we not even plant that idea in their head?

BHAICHUNG BHUTIA
FOOTBALL PLAYER

To Compete on the World Stage, the Hunger to Win

My life has been projected as a classic case of a small-town boy who has made it big and I tend to agree with it given the place I come from. I was born in remote Tinkitam, a very quiet and peaceful village nestling in the hills of Sikkim. We are a pretty well-to-do family and money was the least of our concerns. That, in a way, helped me do whatever I wanted to in life.

I picked up football very early, since it was the only game everybody played in our village. I loved the game but did not give it much thought at that early age. It was only after I joined the Sports Authority of India (SAI) that I began to take it seriously.

I was selected to play in the Governor's Gold Cup in 1992 at the age of 15 and it was during that tournament that Bhaskar Ganguly, one of India's finest goalkeepers, spotted me. The following year, I came down from the hills to the plains of Bengal to join East Bengal. It was only then I began to dream of making it really big and hence, chose to become a professional footballer.

It's very difficult in this country to be a professional footballer unless you are really good at it. Many good players from Bengal have taken up jobs, because they are not confident about their future in the game. But I was always sure about what I wanted to do.

I continued going to school at the Assembly of God's Church, but couldn't continue for long since it clashed with my playing schedule. The club paid me a stipend of Rs 5,000 per month and within a year I settled down in the cutthroat world of Maidan football.

The turning point in my career came in 1995 when I was picked for the national side. The Uzbek coach Rustam Akramov gave me a new direction in life when he switched my role from that of a midfielder to a striker. I began to enjoy the game a lot more since I was getting more opportunity to do what I liked best—score goals.

I moved to JCT, played for a long while with East Bengal and then Mohun Bagan but somehow I wasn't happy. I had seen all there was to be seen at the highest level in this country's football and I needed a change. I wanted to see the world, to see how football is played elsewhere.

In 1998, I went to give trials with the New England Revolutionaries in the US and it really opened my eyes to a new world. I knew I had to play abroad if I were to improve myself as a player and as an individual. I began looking at options and the following year I went to play for Bury FC in England. I remember people saying it was mission impossible succeeding in English League where it was a lot more physical; but I still needed to test myself.

When I came back to India, I was a changed person. It had been the most enriching experience of my career. Money wasn't a factor since I wasn't getting much more than I would have in India, but everything else was a plus. You have to live with them, eat with them and play with them to know what the game is all about. I began to understand what professionalism really meant. I also learnt about the administrative and marketing aspects of the game.

Having returned to India, I was very restless, since the taste of foreign flavour remained with me. I went to Malaysia to play with Perak FC and now, although I have signed for East Bengal, my quest for excellence hasn't ended. I will continue to better myself but then, it seems, I am just one of a kind.

What has been most disappointing all these years is that none of my colleagues have shown the zeal to discover themselves. Their attitude is all wrong, they are too casual, too happy-go-lucky. They don't have the hunger, the willingness to strive for that something extra. They are happy earning whatever they are and being wherever they are. Their attitude has to change. The same goes for the federation and the clubs.

India has had several fine footballers, but very few with the knowledge required to run the game's administration. We need to hire professionals to run the game in this country.

As a footballing nation, we are nowhere and unless we change our attitude right from grooming footballers at the nursery level to running the administration professionally, we will stay where we are. It's so frustrating to know that so much can be done and yet no one has come forward with the right motivation. If I had my way, I would scrap everything and start anew. I would hire the right people to get things started in a much more professional manner. I still dream of seeing India play the World Cup and I am certain we can do it if we go about it the right way.

To me, India empowered is when sports will be run and marketed professionally with players having the hunger and incentive to compete with the best in the world.

KAPIL DEV
CRICKET ICON

Roads to India's Progress

India's social and economic policies have brought a phenomenal boom in almost all areas: education, telecom, IT, media, entertainment, pharmaceuticals, automobiles, manufacturing, exports and agriculture.

The movement of the Sensex, investment and easy housing schemes in the last few years also point to a new category of Indian—he is now asking questions, becoming bolder and willing to take chances.

Aspirations of the middle class are being met through the 'reach all' policies of the banking industry. A family of four who roughed it out on a two-wheeler can now look at a second-hand car at a cost almost similar to that of a new two-wheeler! The same story repeats itself in mortgages.

Could one ever imagine having multiple options to travel by air in India? Cheaper travel for long distances was always by rail. But it never meant shorter travel time. With the Shatabdis and Express trains, that too has become a myth. Despite these developments, the slow development of roads and connectivity has slowed down the overall improvement in life.

In major cities, where growth has been organic, suburbs are competing: the concentration on road development has begun but suburbs are not developing as fast as they should.

In the last four-five years, lifestyles and family structures have changed across all income levels, probably because of purchasing power. Our country manufactures food but 30-40 per cent is wasted because it doesn't reach destinations fast enough.

People are keen on self-economic growth, men and women are joining the workforce in almost equal numbers, they are eating out more, going out more on family holidays. In other words, there is far more movement than there was earlier. But given the fact that travel time, essentially by road, is extremely slow and taxing, efficiency and manpower utilisation is shrinking.

It's a vicious circle: if movement becomes difficult or cumbersome, there will be no growth. Suburbs around cities will come up but not get inhabited, there will be no investment and it will contribute to the overall slowdown of the economy. Rural areas will not develop and general advancement will be affected.

Look at the connectivity between Pune and Mumbai or even between Delhi and Noida. At one point, journeying between these cities was arduous. With the development of expressways and flyovers, the suburbs are developing at a very healthy pace and so are the rural areas around them. What use is improvement in air travel if reaching the airport becomes a nightmare!

Growth in any nation comes if its people start moving. Efficiency of a nation comes when its people can optimise their time constructively. I agree we have a hugely increasing population but that's the reason why connectivity is so important—to make possible an even and balanced outward growth around cities rather than 'clogging' the already crowded areas.

If we are unwilling to 'venture out', there will be stagnation. Road infrastructure is like the blood vessels of a human body—they sustain all the other organs. According to me, improvement in all spheres will come if we concentrate on developing our road network—to ease pressure on people and to encourage them to move forward and thereby, grow and progress.

ANJU BOBBY GEORGE
ATHLETE

Do Justice to Our Talent Pool

I should consider myself lucky in more ways than one. For me, everything has started falling into place ever since I won the bronze in Paris in 2003. Still, I think we need to do a lot of things on several fronts, more so in sport, if we want to be among the top sporting nations. The day it happens, we can feel proud of being a nation empowered to achieve all that a developed one would.

To me, empowerment does not mean winning a medal here and winning another there. It's not even the case of one individual doing it or a couple of others. It has to be on a consistent level by most of us at almost every major international meet. An Olympic medal is what we have been craving for all the time, particularly in track and field events. We are not doing justice to the proportion of talent and population we have if one looks at the number of Olympic medals we have won so far.

But I am happy there were at least two occasions when we came close to fulfilling our long-cherished dream: once when the all-time great Flying Sikh Milkha Singh gave us a glimpse of what our athletes are capable of at Rome in 1960 and, 24 years later, when P.T. Usha lost the bronze by one-hundredth of a second in Los Angeles in 1984.

Even by recent records, the gap seems to have been narrowed down, thanks to Leander Paes and Lt Col Rajyavardhan Singh Rathore because our first Olympic medal was way back in 1952 when K.D. Jhadav won a bronze at Helsinki. Since then we have come a long way and when I say we have narrowed the gap, I mean Paes' bronze-winning performance which came in 1992 at Barcelona and Rathore's which won him the silver at Athens in 2004. This itself is an achievement and goes to prove that we have the talent and are right up there.

We can reach the top but there are some hurdles on the way: lack of infrastructure, training facilities, dietary concerns and sports medicine expertise. It's easy to say that despite facilities athletes are not winning much, but no one realises the hard work an athlete puts in to reap the benefits of long hours on the track and field. Similarly, the hard work by coaches and support staff does not even get a mention. One failure is taken as the end of the road for athletes while the cricket team—mind you, it's a team game and rarely has it won because of an individual's performance—even if it chases 150-odd runs against a mediocre team, is hailed as something out of the ordinary. But in an athlete's case, winning a medal is what counts; not cutting off a fraction of a second or improving by a millimetre. In fact, the difference between winning and losing a medal is just that.

Now coming to the facilities available in the country, let me tell you about my problems. I am allergic to dust and can easily catch a cold. But unlike most, I can't go to a chemist and buy any medicine to cure myself.

I have to consult a doctor and his prescription has to be precise—the medicine that I take has to be without any banned substance. But we don't have the luxury of such sports medicine experts in India.

Every time I cannot run to Delhi or another city searching for the right kind of doctor. In fact, I suffered for three months in early 2005 before getting the right medicine from abroad. Well, I could do it because of my contacts but what happens to those who cannot afford it?

I've also been lucky in getting the sports ministry's help for training abroad but there are several who can't even approach the ministry officials.

I had some problems abroad when I lost my passport and money during training a couple of years ago. But some good friends in the media, the sports and external affairs ministries helped me out before a major meet.

These are impediments that need to be taken care of, particularly at the ministry level, so that the athlete can go about his or her training without hindrance. Luckily, my husband Robert and the entire family has been behind me in what I have achieved thus far. This is not possible in every case. Today, the George family has every bit of information about me—from my first medal at school to the last one in the World Athletics Finals.

My only disappointment so far has been not winning a medal at Athens despite being at my peak. I'll strive hard to make amends at Beijing.

Meanwhile, if we could only create the right environment for athletes, the day is not far when we will see India reaching the pinnacle of glory.

SATISH GUJRAL
ARTIST

Look After Art, the Keeper of a Nation's Soul

It's a time when Indian art and artists are being greatly discussed. Indeed, there have been some interesting reports of the fantastic prices Indian works have fetched. Our policy of public art spaces has done much to keep alive the spirit and creativity of a fledgling artist. Look how booked are some of the capital's galleries at the Lalit Kala Akademi, India Habitat Centre or India International Centre. This is in contrast to the west where several artists die unsung, only because of the lack of places that encourage art, regardless of whether it makes money or not.

Certainly, much has gone right with the way art has been patronised and nurtured in our country. Some, like myself, have reaped the benefits of it. But I can't be oblivious to those who couldn't and the reasons behind it.

As an artist, I feel those forces that go into the making of the cultural fabric of our country need to be strengthened. I will start with the museums because it is museums through which art reaches people. When India became free, this need was felt and it was proposed that apart from a national museum, there should be museums in our states. It was a worthy idea. But 50 years since this idea was conceived, we see that its implementation leaves a lot to be desired. Most museums do not have budgets even to whitewash their walls. As for their collections, the less said the better.

For example, I am a Punjabi and have contributed considerably to the development of art in my state. Yet the only time the museum in Punjab required any work from me was 40 years ago and this too for free. I agreed to donate a work as the then curator M.S. Randhawa, made a personal appeal for it. Since then I have never heard from the museum.

Our national gallery in the capital doesn't fare much better. About ten years ago, when I was chairman of the purchase committee of the gallery, the total yearly budget was Rs 30 lakh. Much of it went on travel by members of the committee. That situation remains. In those days, when the budget was Rs 30 lakh, no painting of a leading artist could be acquired for less than Rs 5 lakh. This ratio is manifold now and there is hardly any increase in the budget. No thought is given to solving this problem.

In countries like the US and those in Europe, the problem was solved by inviting private enterprise. Any individual or corporation could donate a painting to a museum and in case the committee appointed by the gallery found the donated work worthy of being in the gallery, they made an estimate of the market price of that work. The donor was issued a receipt. This receipt could be used for income tax exemption. The result of the scheme is that western museums are full of art works. They are other ways too. The committee, every year, decides that it will acquire the work of a certain artist. The donor then has the choice to donate such a work.

I proposed the same system here but it didn't get much consideration. Someone said it could open a window to corruption, which is totally irrelevant. The committee thus appointed, like all committees of museums, is reshuffled from time to time. They are not more vulnerable than any other government committee. In the west, museums compete with each other to acquire old and new works.

The second proposal that the founding fathers made was to open academies in our states. Besides the patronage they get from state governments, they are also funded by the national academy—Lalit Kala Akademi.

It was supposed such academies would promote artistic activities and help needy artists. But what it has bred is gross nepotism and corruption. According to one estimate made a few years ago, 80 per cent of the budget of the national academy was spent on administration alone and the rest was taken care of by the staff.

I was on the committees of these academies for many years and finally came to the painful conclusion that there was simply no need for them because they only ate into the national budget without doing any worthwhile service for the promotion of the arts.

Then come cultural fests. This is another shoddy activity and achieves nothing. They forget that every traditional festival is cultural and we don't need to invent festivals. But it seems they are gaining supremacy rather than being folded up.

What disturbs me is that most of the good art is being hoarded by NRIs (contrary to opinion, actual foreign buyers or international media attention are yet to arrive). Galleries, by rigging prices and creating hype, have made it a fashion to judge an artist's value by the price he/she fetches. Mere merit seems to have taken a backseat.

Behind these practices lie the exploitation of artists, whose work is hoarded by galleries at a pittance of its authorised price. Artists get little out of it. If my proposal had been accepted, we would have filled our museums with the best work of our artists, and they would have got their rightful share.

All of this may sound like lamenting, especially when you read every morning about the astronomical prices artists are getting. Even if that were true, what I want to emphasise is that artists should get a share of that high price. The UNESCO has laid down this norm long ago. I am afraid this often doesn't happen with private galleries and artists would rather not complain for fear of losing favour with the galleries.

More than just being a pleasure for the soul, art is a vital keeper of a nation's culture. It is important we look into the issues I've raised. Wouldn't it be truly wonderful when families, friends, students can include a tour of our museums as their weekend plan and emerge refreshed and inspired?

BHUPEN HAZARIKA
MUSICIAN, BALLADEER, FILMMAKER

It Is Music that Binds a Nation

Way back in 1939, I wrote a song in which I said I was just a small spark of the age of fire, but even then I wanted to build a society where there would be no space for traders in religion and untouchability, where walls of discrimination would crumble and a paradise of equality would be created on earth.

That incidentally was my second song. In 1964, I felt that the sky had given me wide vision, storm, tremendous energy, thunder, a loud voice, courage and reason—with which I would sing songs of humanity in a sea that was in the grip of pirates and provide the silent masses a spark of life.

Music is power. Music is empowerment. Remember how those great lyrics had set the entire subcontinent on fire and provided such a great momentum to the freedom struggle? Have you ever met a person who would say he does not like music? Have you ever found a doctor who would ask his patient not to listen to music? Music is communication, very effective communication. Why do you give a coin to the blind singer on the pavement? Not because he is blind, but because he can sing.

What did Rakesh Sharma tell Mrs Gandhi when she asked him how India looked like from space? Saare jahan se achha!

I had always dreamt of an India where every individual would acquire knowledge and skills of communication. Look how strong our tradition has been since the ancient times. A two-letter word—Om!—and you acquire such unbelievable energy. It is divine power and divine energy in the form of music that kindles the fire within an individual.

In 1976, I sang about inter-caste marriages, in which I told a couple who came to seek my blessings: this is the age of mass communication through satellites in outer space. This is the age of nuclear energy, of snatching away that energy from the evil forces and using it for the benefit of the common man.

India is a vast country. Very few people have been lucky enough to have criss-crossed this country. I am one of the few who have had the opportunity as a singer and film-maker. Whether it is the illiterate sarkari gaon-burra (village headman) in Dong, the village on the easternmost tip of Arunachal Pradesh where the sun's rays first fall on Indian soil, or the broker in Dalal Street in Mumbai, all are bound by the same music that is India. One hundred crore souls. It is not a matter of joke. Imagine their potential. Gandhiji did. We are fortunate our president A.P.J. Abdul Kalam understands it. Prime Minister Manmohan Singh understands it. You have to be in touch with the people at the grassroots to be able to kindle the fire in them. You can do that with music. India, after all, is a wonderful mosaic of musical traditions, which can be transformed into musical power.

But I often feel sad when I notice a lack of confidence among the people, especially in the north-east. I will not blame the young men for taking up arms. We must accept the fact that the benefits of development have not trickled down to the last village. There is a huge communication gap. The rights of the common man to enjoy the benefits of development have been usurped. It is good that the Right to Information Act has come into force. But have we told the masses about it? Have we, as the world's largest democracy, been able to evolve an effective communication model, a two-way model that would make every citizen a partner in our dream to become a developed country by 2025?

SHAMMI KAPOOR
BOLLYWOOD LEGEND

Let the Net Gain Count

Empowerment basically means to be able to do things on your own. As I see it, education is the basic pre-requisite of doing things on your own terms.

An educated country has the best chance of thriving. If people are aware of their rights and duties, they can help in nation-building. Education is actually a way of living. India should provide free education to each and every child. It should be made a citizen's basic right. More than anything, a well-educated democracy is much better than an uninformed one.

And in today's time, I feel, education is created by technology. Internet is a driving force of communication and we must utilise it in India.

I'm a high-volume internet user. I use it for information and not infotainment. Though there's nothing wrong about the latter, I just like the power of information. These days, I blog a lot. Every day, I learn something new about the world and it is a big high.

I feel our education system is very outdated. We need to update it but according to the global movement. Our studies are too theory centric. We should be telling our children to come up with their own theories.

The idea should be to make learning more innovative and fun. We should go in for e-books and new ways of imparting knowledge. The thrust should be on students to tell their teachers something new that they've discovered.

Computers are the need of the day. In fact, students should be given computer classes from the first standard. It's my dream to see a computer in every house in India. But for that, they need to provided with electricity first. But that's another thing entirely and I'm sure the government is well aware of that.

But the picture isn't so bleak. I'm amazed by today's youngsters. They're really very aware and well-versed with everything new. Even in the film industry, our technicians know the latest software and techniques. It's a very heartening thing to see this. But very few people can avail this right to information. That's where I think the government can come in. Basic education should be given to every child in India at his or her doorstep.

SHAH RUKH KHAN
ACTOR

Put a Smile on Every Face

As far as I am concerned, India is 100 per cent empowered. Maybe if you take a high view, then you may feel that our country is still to be empowered. But I'm an optimistic guy, I view the whole thing from the mindset of Indians.

You've got to know that for any regular guy from Ulhasnagar, getting good products at affordable prices is an index of the country being self-sufficient and empowered. The ideology of India has always been to create its own. Maybe we can make cheaper versions of cars or mixies but we never look outside.

As I see it, our grass is as green as anyone else's. That's why I won't ever do a Hollywood film. Rather I'd like to do a Hindi film that does the business of a Hollywood film.

I'm a semi-young Indian who has never been to a mall in India. The other day I was talking to my friend, Juhi Chawla, and she told me that the malls are just as good or bad as in any other country. That's great.

Things are wonderful in India. The economic structure is rising, technological advancements are making headlines and social consciousness is also pretty encouraging. We've made progress in all spheres. Be it malls in Gurgaon, irrigation in Punjab or computer advancement in Hyderabad: greatness is happening every day. We're unaware of it but we're definitely not worse than what we were 50 years ago.

Disinvestment and the removal of Foreign Exchange Regulation Act (FERA) show that all this is an educated process. And we aren't just following any monkey business. We're empowered in thought and that's crucial.

Personally, I've a problem with the power of information. I'm not an authority on it but I think somewhere down the line, information has been a huge downside. We can access information anytime but we don't know what to do with it. So, information creates bottlenecks. We create a flyover to Nehru Place but forget to connect it to Surya Hotel. Likewise, information as a tool is good but its utility is still unclear. Give a person what he wants but don't bore him. Make avenues for him to use that information, give him the opportunity to make his life better with that information.

Talking about my field, I feel real life inspires cinema. All the headlines we read in the papers become stories on screen. The newspapers tell us how a police officer behaves or what a social worker looks like. Whenever we try to tell people anything, we go over the top. Cinema tells the picture in colour and empowers people in the sense that everyone can take home what they want.

For me, cinema is all about entertainment. And if I can empower within the framework of cinema then I'm content. It's very simple: if I want to make a TV film for children, I will do something like PlayStation. Why not? Kids have a right to be entertained.

I don't expect kids to become a Nehru or Gandhi but I want them to know their country. The thought should be: give them what they want at the right stage. Every story has one theme: triumph of good over evil. It might be Jesus saying it or Prophet Mohammad or The Incredibles.

I empower people with smiles. As long as I can provide two hours of complete fun, I'm happy. Maybe I only reach inside, make you mushy or soft with emotion but I promise to make it so basic that it gets conveyed. I love to be sweetly mushy and want all my audience to smile in relief, at inane stuff or just smile. If for two hours, I can make them forget that they had to wade for two hours to reach home during the Mumbai floods, I'm happy. I've done my job of empowering them to smile.

Make no mistake, I stand for empowerment through escapism.

SANIA MIRZA
TENNIS PLAYER

Gender No Deterrent

It's startling but true that, despite being born in an era quite different from my ancestors, the average person's thoughts about women—particularly the girl child—haven't changed.

Girls are in no way inferior to boys and, given encouragement and support, could excel and do India proud in all walks of life. Believe this, if I found success it was only due to my parents' support and nothing else. Hard work to me was elementary. I had to defy all odds to first convince those around me that a woman was capable of bringing name and fame to the country. I guess all this needs to change if India wants to see many more Sanias, not just in tennis but in other fields as well. What I feel needs to change most is one's mindset, particularly towards women.

It's strange that a girl child is considered a curse by many in our society, in both villages and cities. This came as a rude shock to me two years ago when I was appointed the brand ambassador of the girl child by the central government.

How can people be so cruel? It's difficult to digest that a child's future is just in males. Without women, the world would cease to exist! My heart bleeds when I read that there are some areas in our country where almost seventy out of 1,000 girls fail to see the light of day. Worse still are people in our society who sympathise with and actually support this female-male ratio imbalance.

The figures for female foeticide and infanticide are chilling and the fact that we have not been able to check this is alarming. An end to this barbaric act or stringent measures to check female foeticide to me would be India empowered.

While female foeticide remains a burning issue, I would also like to highlight that women are no longer cut out for just household chores. Every child I feel should be given adequate and equal opportunity for education.

Education is the first step to building confidence, to tap potential, to be independent, and to speak one's own mind. It's only when we recognise this and act on it that change will be seen. Once again it is disheartening to learn that when a girl is born her future is pre-determined mainly due to the warped attitudes of parents, relatives and traditionalists who themselves have had limited education.

Let us all join hands in educating people or in doing whatever it takes to totally cleanse our society of such misconceptions. Whoever said or believed that women are not the future are surely not those who think of empowering India.

It's a fact that in a country starved of champions—for whatever reason—there are restrictions aplenty, which is probably why India still hopes and waits for its next hero.

For me to see India without poverty may be a huge thing to ask, but it sure is something that I hope the generations to come can see. There's no doubt that India does possess talent. There are examples in abundance to prove that, but what remains a mystery is the fact that women still fail to enjoy 'equal opportunity' status. What is it that women cannot do?

What I dream of in an empowered India is when a child, whether male or female, is allowed its freedom to do what he or she wants, which—with the guidance of parents—includes sport too.

One has to remember the adage 'All work and no play makes Jack a dull boy' which does put things in perspective, particularly for those who simply think education and not sport can build one's future. Education is necessary, but so is sport. It builds character and creates an alternative platform. But before that I feel it is very necessary to educate ourselves and believe that an empowered India can only be achieved through concerted effort. Let's do it India.

DHANRAJ PILLAY
HOCKEY OLYMPIAN

Village Youth Must Get a Platform

Remember Ajit Pal Singh Kular? He captained India to its World Cup gold in Kuala Lumpur in 1975. He was not from a big city. He came from Sansarpur, a village just outside Jalandhar cantonment which has produced over a dozen Olympians.

Look at Michael Kindo or at the current India hockey captain Dilip Tirkey. The biggest sporting icons and the best players have not come from the big cities. They've worked their way up from anonymous villages, struggling to even get to a tournament where they may be spotted by the big daddies of the game.

I myself belong to a humble town called Khadki, a short distance from Pune, where I first played the game on kuchcha surfaces. When I came to Mumbai, all I knew were the rules. I had speed, but didn't know how to cash in on it. So, if I got this far, its because of my hard work and dedication, but also because I was lucky to get an opportunity to learn and improve early in my career.

That opportunity—to play with the trained city teams, to contest at higher levels, to learn from the stars—should be available to every lad with a hockey stick in his hand. If he's good, he deserves that opportunity. That, to me, is India empowered.

And that, I think, is still a faraway dream as far as hockey is concerned.

Take Maharashtra, for example. Kolhapur, Solapur and the adjoining areas have an abundance of talented youngsters keen on hockey. But they don't have school championships, no talent scouts visiting remote villages, no chance to ever be spotted and picked for a state's side or even a local club.

Then there's the yawning gap between infrastructure that global stars enjoy and the sorry excuses we make do with at home. There are only a couple of Indian centres—Hyderabad's Gacchibowli Stadium and Chennai's Mayor Radhakrishnan Stadium—that have world-class hockey facilities, including comfortable rooms, sufficient training space, a swimming pool and all the things that go into the making of a global sporting centre. All other centres, even those in cities that have produced big stars, have grossly under-utilised resources. If hockey is to be empowered, at least two astroturf surfaces in every city are a must.

Then there's the question of how to empower players dealing with the Indian Hockey Federation (IHF). Over the years, the IHF has been run by a handful of people, autocracy style. Everybody sees senior players; stars and even Olympians stay mum while big bureaucrats who run the game are around. Where's the transparency in the selection process?

Earlier, in the mid-nineties, people like me, Pargat (Singh) and other senior members conferred with the officials when a team had to be picked. That trend has ground to a halt.

All countries that take their sports seriously, and certainly their national game, stress on professionalism in management, training, infrastructure, marketing and development of the game. India Empowered to me is when Indian stars can sign on the dotted lines of contracts with foreign clubs knowing they're satisfied with the terms and conditions, that they negotiated the best deals themselves, knowing they did not sell themselves short. Why does the IHF have to play go-between every time a foreign side shows interest in one of our young stars?

Injured players need to be looked after, with assistance for surgeries, top quality medical aid and a concrete recuperation programme. Rajeev Mishra, a fine centre-forward from Varanasi, another small town, was lost to Indian hockey thanks to one such injury, and to poor care from the IHF.

The IHF also needs to make attempts to rope in better and more corporate sponsors. Endorsements are a great option—after all, hockey players like Viren Rasquinha, Gagan Ajit Singh, Kanwalpreet Singh are handsome young men and can peddle brands as well as cricketers or movie stars. What they need is to first become recognisable faces, for which the IHF should permit some level of interaction with the media. A blanket ban on talking to the press is ruinous for the game.

What I dream of is an empowered India where every village boy has a platform to showcase his skills, where every good player has a fair chance of making it big, where every star has a youngster to mentor and a mentor to thank.

GANESH PYNE
PAINTER

Freedom to Make Unbiased Choices

Born in the pre-Independence period, I lived through the glorious days of the freedom struggle. Young and impressionable then, the unfolding of events, the tumultuous years of struggle followed by the jubilation of being 'free' at last, all this had a tremendous impact on me.

But gradually I grew up to learn that we are a Third World nation, cast away as the 'darker' side of the world. Today we have come a long way with the world acknowledging us as an emerging economic superpower. But more than half a century later, the questions that crop up in my mind are: are we actually free? Are we empowered? Is empowerment all about money power? I confess that the current scenario leaves me disillusioned.

We talk of the economic boom and simultaneously read disturbing reports about starvation deaths in remote villages. We talk of big investments and big money which does not trickle down to the lower rungs of society. The rich are getting richer by the day, while the poorest of the poor are sucked into the vortex of poverty. Is that the empowerment we proudly boast of?

Empowerment to me is not the glaring disparity in lifestyles we see today. Rather, it is a nation where citizens enjoy equal privileges, where the common folk are educated and aware enough to make unbiased choices on their own, where the people are true representatives of the Gandhian way of thought.

Isn't it a shame that numerous cases of tax evasions go unchecked while bankrupt state treasuries are unable to spend on development? And somehow we commoners have lost the will to protest and speak out. Isn't it tragic that a nation as rich in resources as India is still stagnating at the bottom and all we do is lament about what could have been done? I feel helpless when the administration throws up its hands and candidly declares 'we are sorry for the time lost, we should have done this but have failed.' Can we commoners be hopeful, if the bureaucracy with all its machinery is basking in complacency?

Empowerment is also about the strong political motivation to make a positive change, to steer the citizens to the goal of common welfare. At times, the cynic in me can't help but doubt the ulterior motive of the people at the helm. Perhaps the poverty-stricken, uneducated masses serve their selfish needs better.

When will political parties forget mutual rivalries and unite to work for the betterment of India, a nation which does not deserve to languish in absolute abjection? I, as a citizen of the largest democracy in the world, do not have much faith in this democracy. The entire process of election, however exaggerated it may sound, is a farce. Do we really have a choice? A choice where we can actually 'choose' between ideologies and are not forced to opt for a corrupt or fascist regime.

Empowerment is only possible when today's bright and erudite young men and women do not make a conscious decision to stay away from active politics which makes way for musclemen and goons to call the shots in legislative assemblies and the parliament.

Today, quite disappointingly, the executive has been rendered ineffective and paralysed and the judiciary has to take up the cudgels on its behalf, with its timely intervention when situations go out of hand. It is an unfortunate trend and only reconfirms one's forebodings about the prevalent administrative system.

But autocracy can never be the alternative. What we need to do is to mobilise the masses at the grassroots and make them aware about their potential, their power to change things for a better life. Only then can we be truly empowered. I am still hopeful.

RAJYAVARDHAN SINGH RATHORE
OLYMPIC SILVER MEDALIST

As Many Sports Centres As Malls

India has a glorious historical and cultural past; the country is endowed with rich natural resources, its geographical location, human resources make the conditions ideal for the country to launch itself into a bright future what with the opening up of the economy and globalisation.

In the field of sports, the past has not been bright, except for hockey. The few bright performances have not culminated in due recognition.

To me, India empowered means our bright brains not only shaking the world of IT and technology but through its application bringing about change in our day-to-day functioning: getting rid of musty files, babudom, corruption and a decadent mindset.

Empowered India will have snazzy cars zipping on highways, malls buzzing all around, spick-and-span public utilities, hospitals, railway stations, all indicators of a growing economy. But more important, the gap between the rich and the poor should not widen and per capita availability of all goodies must improve. And this should all reflect in our human development index.

A poor farmer, a labourer should get a decent share of all economic indicators. The fruits of globalisation should percolate to the downtrodden. Technology should enable a villager to get legitimate returns on his hard work.

The greatest strength that this country has is family bonding. No wonder an Indian may earn anything abroad, but would like to settle in India. This bonding should extend to society and the country as a whole. We should not do outside our own house what we do not do within our house. Such a culture will empower India and bring it at par with more advanced countries.

Being a sportsman, I cannot imagine the country knocking for a place in the top league without the right sporting ethos. Sporting excellence is linked to the empowerment of a country. Sports culture should go hand in hand with other indicators of development. Per capita availability of sports fields, tracks, courts, pools etc. should keep pace with, say, malls and mobiles, and become evenly spread in cities and the countryside.

By sports culture, I mean that some sporting pursuit should become an integral part of the daily routine of all Indians, be it a professional, a doctor, a shopkeeper or a farmer. A sporting pursuit could be playing a game, swimming, walking or, if nothing else, encouraging near and dear ones to take to any one of these activities and and applauding their achievements, however small.

This would improve the health of Indians, so essential in all spheres of human endeavour. We are health conscious—the popularity of yoga and related exercises proves it—but when it comes to aerobics and activities requiring strength, we tend to shy away.

This interest should be extended to organised sports activities. Medals and international recognition will automatically follow. All those complaints about selection, politicisation of sports, and so on, will automatically vanish with the flood of sports enthusiasts.

MALLIKA SARABHAI
DANSEUSE, SOCIAL ACTIVIST
KARTIKEYA SARABHAI
ENVIRONMENTALIST

Where the Mind is Without Fear

How often has Tagore's wonderful and inspiring poem been quoted in this very series: where the mind is without fear . . . and yet we are afraid. Today, 58 years since we became independent, we are still afraid, afraid of being ourselves. Afraid of our own identity. Afraid to chalk out our own development path. Afraid to lead rather than imitate. Afraid of breaking imposed rules. Afraid to look at our own heritage. Today we are still trying to throw off our colonial complexes.

We are afraid of not being a part of a herd, be it a herd defined by religion or community, village or language. We hide behind masks of gotra and kul, afraid to own up to our thoughts, afraid even to countenance that we have or can have thoughts that might be different from others of our clan, afraid of the ostracism that we might face if it is known that we think or dare to think differently.

We are afraid of our own tradition and need others to approve of it before we own up to it. Otherwise why would the popularity of yoga increase after the United States adopts it, and why would we suddenly be using products made of neem and haldi after others have tried to patent them for their importance?

We are also afraid of change and demand adherence to those strands of tradition or perceived tradition that are convenient—'don't question passed down knowledge as it is disrespectful' (but who checked from whence it was passed down, and if it was valid then or is valid now?). The diasporic parent who sends the child to college so that he is more in tune with the adopted country but still insists on a traditional, parent-imposed marital choice.

We are afraid to ask questions because that might invite the wrath of those questioned, of those in authority. How can we question a teacher's information, even though we know it to be incorrect? Won't that lead to the teacher failing us in anger?

When hellish forces take over governance and unleash untold misery and corruption, we are afraid to speak out against injustice: for, in the real world, that can lead to reprisals, to violence, to being targetted.

We are afraid to innovate, to choose our own path to development which might be more sustainable, because we are more comfortable following the already trodden path of the west. What if we fail? What if we get laughed at?

And worst, perhaps, we are afraid to dream a dream, afraid to believe that it can be achieved.

An India empowered will be an India free of these fears. Where to quest will not be seen as revolting; where to disagree with the mainstream will not bring reprisals; where to follow your own tune will not lead to lynching; where to speak your mind will not lead to torment; where to be a woman will not be to invite rape; where to be classless and casteless will not mean being disenfranchised; where to walk your own road will not mean being gunned down; where difference will enhance the mix, where divergence will increase the tastes, where tolerance will augment the bouquet, where birth, name, colour and sex will count for nothing as far as opportunity concerned.

Then and only then will we be empowered.

GULAMMOHAMMED SHEIKH
PAINTER

Kala and Vidya Are Two Faces of the Same Coin

I wonder if there is any nation on earth as culturally rich as India. Having learnt to live in multiple times and cultures, we have imbibed a continuous interweaving of ideas and practices of diverse origin, traditional and contemporary, local and external in every sphere of life, spilling out on to our streets in kaleidoscopic complexity. Like the mythical Speaking Tree, the Indian subcontinent is made of hundreds of visual, aural and literary cultures exemplified in its myriad languages and dialects.

Pupul Jayakar once remarked that the number of practitioners of the visual arts in rural India was equal to the entire population of Australia! To extend the assumption further, one could say that every home in India harbours a potential artiste. Consider this. Scores of women in south India (and perhaps elsewhere) make animated patterns of varying designs: kolams/alpanas/ rangolis at their doorstep every day. Kharak women in the Bhavnagar region of Gujarat and Meena women around Kota in Rajasthan decorate the walls, floors and courtyards of their hand-plastered huts and houses every season.

In the late sixties, artist Bhaskar Kulkarni, an employee of the handicrafts board, was encouraged by Mrs Jayakar to investigate such practices in drought-ridden Bihar. Deeply disturbed by the unimaginable poverty he saw in Mithila, one of the most backward regions of Bihar, he initiated women to make paintings to earn a livelihood. Knowing they painted images in traditional bridal chambers called kohbar he persuaded them to make similar things on the paper he provided. These were sold through the handicraft sector and a phenomenon called Madhubani painting was born. Hundreds of women found expression for their inherent creativity in addition to a means of livelihood.

Artistes like Sita Devi, Mahasundari Devi, Ganga Devi, Baua Devi and many others emerged as outstanding practitioners of this reinvented tradition.

Ganga Devi's instance is exemplary. Cast away by her husband and living in abject poverty, she strove to empower herself through art. Narrating her own life story she introduced new dimensions into the 'traditional' repertory of Madhubani painting. She was later conferred the Padmashri and a road was named after her in her native Mithila.

Artist Haku Shah encouraged a housewife in Ahmedabad named Saroj to make appliques and she now creates an array of lively designs reminiscent of the paper-cuts of Matisse. He also initiated Ganesh, a folk singer from Rajasthan, into making drawings resulting in unusual renderings of the singer's life-experiences. In suburban Anand, Santokba watching her art student son paint got the urge to paint at her late age. She painted literally thousands of feet of Mahabharata stories commissioned by the Indira Gandhi National Centre for Arts. In a rare achievement of empowering the itinerant community of performing and visual artistes, Rajeev Sethi initiated the establishment of a collective township at Shadipur on the outskirts of Delhi.

Interestingly, a majority of these practitioners are women, often unlettered, but visually highly literate in contrast to their urban counterparts. In a society ridden with the age-old caste system, art practices too are viewed in hierarchical terms. Defined as 'craft' and generally marketed through the handicrafts sector these are valued far below products of urban origin. The example of Australia is important in this context, where the art of its aboriginal population has provided the nation the means to earn a unique identity, prestige and market in the international art circuit. Aboriginal artists like Rover Thomas or Clifford Possum are regarded as national icons of Australian art. It is difficult to equate a Ganga Devi with an M.F. Husain in our situation.

In the urban sector, a vast pool of unorganised labour is involved in making cultural objects: a toy or a kite sold in the bazaar, the massive effigies of Ravana for Dussehra or tazias for Muharram. The Durga puja and Ganesh chaturthi pandals present an incredible inventiveness of design and execution. In 2004, in a Dussehra procession outside Delhi, I saw an amazing image of a massive Hanuman floating in air with hands moving and body levitating. It made the entire area turn into a magical site. The anonymous makers of such objects however rarely figure in the category of artists despite their professional expertise or inventiveness; regarded 'kitsch', their designs do not figure in the handicrafts sector either.

The numerically small, 'minority' culture of urban modern art is like an extended family with a sizeable number of women practitioners, functioning around the circuit of art galleries and museums through a system of exhibitions held most of the time in metropolitan cities. This culture, grown out of half a dozen art schools (the rest being hidebound and conservative), was limited to a few cognoscenti and remained almost invisible until the eighties when a phenomenon called the 'art market' happened. It became visible when rising prices of art in auctions and the mushrooming of galleries began to attract media attention.

The fact that an artiste, if successful, can now make a decent living has, however, not resulted in an upgrading of art schools or succeeded in recognising the importance of art in school or university education. The handful of art schools with a liberal system of education continue to face the same financial crunch as before and the culture of public collections of contemporary art has not yet taken root. The unique experiment in this direction that was initiated in the early eighties has suffered a severe setback.

Bharat Bhavan in Bhopal was established with state funds as a multi-arts centre serving the needs of a region (Madhya Pradesh) with a national/international outlook, its philosophy broadly in tune with our federal polity. It included two museums: one housing the art of the rural-tribal region of Madhya Pradesh and the other of contemporary modern art of India (with a section on the urban art of the state); a poetry library of Indian languages; indoor and outdoor auditoria for performing arts; a documentation programme and workshop facilities for visiting artistes. It initiated awards for excellence in various disciplines of art at the national level and published multiple journals on arts, cinema and literature in Hindi. Conceived and realised by poet-bureaucrat Ashok Vajpeyi and artiste J. Swaminathan, it was (and still remains) a blueprint for the rest of the Indian states to emulate. It attracted the artist community from all disciplines and set standards of excellence in every sphere of its operation, including awards. In the absence of passion and commitment once the two pioneers retired, Bharat Bhavan has become victim of national neglect facing a bleak future due to lack of funds, leadership and political interference.

The seven zonal cultural centres established during the Rajiv Gandhi regime and provided with enormous corpus funds running into crores by the state governments seem to have performed little to justify their existence for all these years. The central Lalit Kala Akademi has been a hotbed of internal intrigues and manipulations with hardly any hope of redemption. The Indian Council for Cultural Relations is meant to be our window to the world. Except for receiving a few, and for the most, nondescript exhibitions or sending similar ones abroad (along with dignitaries and official functionaries) it remains in slumber most of the time. The National Gallery of Modern Art too seems to be content in performing little beyond the tasks that officialdom deems necessary and permissible.

The work of contemporary modern artists has, however, reached the most competitive venues in the world art of today despite the absence of institutional support. The lack of understanding in supporting the vibrant art scene reflected in official attitudes has led to the generation of support systems through private sponsorship and collective ventures. As a result, contemporary Indian art has become far more visible in the international circuit than it has ever been.

On the outskirts of Delhi, the corporate house of Apeejay has established a well-equipped new media centre for visual arts. Khoj, an exemplary artists' collective, has managed to organise a series of international art workshops in Delhi, Mysore and Mumbai. Individual exhibitions sponsored by private galleries have become far more professional in display and publications. Significant exhibitions abroad like the Century City (London/Tate Modern), the Edge of Desire (Perth/ The Art Gallery of Western Australia, New York/Asia Society, Mexico City/Tamayo Museum) with a sizeable representation of contemporary Indian art curated by Indian art critics have been noticed in the international fora. The works of young artists are handpicked by high-profile galleries abroad and by curators of international biennales.

In 2002, a retrospective of Bhupen Khakhar, the first ever of an Indian artist abroad, was held in one of the most prestigious institutions of the western world: the Reina Sofia museum in Madrid. Art critic Geeta Kapur was invited to be on the international jury of the Venice Biennale. All these events however do not make news and remain outside the concerns of the Indian cultural officialdom. For the media, culture has come to mean film, fashion or food, (all that money can buy?); it does not however miss an opportunity to report the price index of the latest mega purchase at auctions.

The reasons for this state of affairs are not far to seek. These rest in the social mind-set and attitude towards art, inculcated and reinforced by an imbalanced system of education. Viewed as a soft discipline, art till recently was either equated with hobby or entertainment, rarely with vocation or profession. Little wonder that schools in, for instance, my hometown Baroda offer no education in liberal arts, let alone in the fine or performing arts. The spiralling art market and possibilities of art as investment might now convince parents of the wisdom of art as a prospective career for their children but the respect that scientific disciplines, IT or management evoke is rarely offered to the arts.

I recall an observation of a high functionary of the university where I taught. He was appalled that the status and salary of a mere musician was equal to that of a scientist within the university. Vidya maybe sought and respected, but not kala or creativity. This attitude has deprived generations of young adults of an adequate understanding of art practices, let alone the opportunities of developing informed connoisseurship. Located in verbal disciplines, our institutional education leaves little room for aural or visual literacy. Even vidya is often limited to information, rather than knowledge, which seems to counter the old adage of *Sa vidya ya vimuktaye*, or knowledge that liberates. Ideally speaking, vidya proposes analysis, processing and understanding of information leading to gnana, to the realm of ideas. Another ancient saying drives the point in while defining the art-less individual as a brute sans horns and a tail! We are yet to learn the potential strength of our plural cultural practices.

Nowhere in the world does there exist and flourish the variety of cultural manifestations initiated by the people, individually or collectively, as in India today. Extending the experiment of Bharat Bhavan further, we may think of museums and art centres on holistic lines including all aspects of urban and rural cultures rather than dividing them into caste-like categories. Despite having witnessed an appropriation and distortion of cultural beliefs and practices by fundamentalist forces cutting at the very fibre of a basically liberal and multicultural society in recent times, we continue to treat culture with tokenism.

Sadly, however, it worries few, least of all our rulers and policy makers, that our apathy in matters of culture has left many a national institution without professional leadership. The National Museum, the IGNCA, the ASI, the Crafts Museum (so vibrant when a scholar like Dr Jyotindra Jain headed it), in the capital, the Bharat Bhavan in Bhopal, the Museum and Picture Gallery in Baroda and umpteen others elsewhere have remained headless for several years and are administered by bureaucrats. Would this happen to scientific, technological or even management institutes, this sidelining of professionals and professionalism? Do bureaucrats have the master key to deal with any discipline? And since there is no professional accountability, it matters little if names like Ananda Coomaraswamy or Binode Behari Mukherjee are not heard of in the corridors of the department of culture.

The India of my dreams is without want on every front, a fair and just society without discrimination on grounds of caste, religion, gender or race, but I place its soul in the creativity of its arts. I visualise a change of heart of our educational system with vidya and kala deeply embedded in it. For if vidya liberates, kala humbles and humanises. I see no better antidote to the brutalisation and violence we are plagued with these days than a combined dose of vidya with kala.

MILKHA SINGH
THE FLYING SIKH

Revenue Sharing for Sporting Excellence

It has been close to 60 years since we gained independence, yet we are struggling to produce world-class sportspersons. To date we have just had five athletes who made it to the Olympics finals—Gurbachan Singh Randhawa (Tokyo, 1964), Sriram (Montreal, 1976), P.T. Usha (Los Angeles, 1984), Anju Bobby George (Athens, 2004) and me (Rome, 1960). This aptly reflects the standard of sports in the country.

I think we lack planning and sincerity. It would be better if we have clear-cut plans for result-oriented training. Let there be a timeframe for coaching—be it eight years, twelve years or twenty years. The government should fix accountability on coaches and players alike. We cannot hope to win medals in the international arena in the absence of any planned approach.

Look at China, we should follow its footsteps. Back in the 1950s, Chinese athletes were no match to us even at the Asian Games level. Today China is a superpower in the field of sports. They have academies for various disciplines where budding sportspersons are brought in young. Each academy is entrusted to an in-charge on whom lies the onus to produce results. Failures are viewed seriously and those responsible for it are penalised for their laxity. The Chinese have shown to the world that with dedication and planning, results can be achieved.

I propose that training of sportspersons be handed over to the Indian army. I am a product of the army's training, and so is Lt Col Rajyavardhan Singh Rathore. This is important because only the army can instill discipline and dedication among sportspersons which is lacking in other spheres. Moreover, the army is really keen to undertake such a project. The Army

Institute of Sports (AIS) has already been set up in Pune where the best equipment and coaches are being provided to talented players.

The Union ministry of sports, the Indian Olympic Association (IOA) and all national sports federations/associations should join hands to prepare a blueprint to raise the overall standards of sports. Everyone should work in tandem to realise the dream of winning medals at the Olympics, Asian Games, Commonwealth Games and world meets. Office-bearers of sports federations/associations should also rise above petty politics and work with conviction to make India a nation with a great sports culture.

I won't say that India is lacking in infrastructure, funds and exposure for sportspersons. Things have improved phenomenally if we compare it to yesteryears. We had not even heard of basic facilities like running shoes, tracksuits and coaches during our times. Today, top-class equipment, good sport outfits and state-of-the-art infrastructure is available to our young sportspersons. All they need is to train with honesty and sincerity. The country has nearly 27,000 coaches now.

The budding players should make most of the opportunities provided to them. I would also comment on the shortcut methods adopted by sportspersons to win medals like the use of performance enhancing substances, concealing their ages to compete in lower age groups and defecting to other states for pecuniary benefits. They forget that nothing is greater than winning honours for the country. Jobs, rewards and awards come much later. The youngsters should think beyond smaller gains and train diligently to shine at the highest level. Not only that, they should also make winning a habit. A good athlete should dominate for at least 10-12 years.

I would also quote the example of Italy where soccer has a cult following and is its biggest money-spinning sport, just as cricket is in India. But the top soccer clubs in Italy put in at least 30 to 40 per cent of their profits in running other sports in their country. Therefore, the Board of Control for Cricket in India (BCCI) should also be generous enough to give up some of its profit for managing other disciplines. The sports ministry and IOA should take up this issue with the BCCI for the overall improvement of sports.

In the end, I will also say that Indian sports bodies should make a concerted effort to be at the top of the medals' tally in the 2010 Commonwealth Games to be held in New Delhi. We will be spending crores of rupees in organising the Commonwealth Games, but it will all go waste if we fail to finish among the top five in the final standings, particularly in athletics (I was the last man to win a gold medal in athletics in the Commonwealth Games held in 1958 at Cardiff). We can justify spending that much money only if we have medals to support our claims. The government, IOA and other sports bodies have another five years. It's time we fixed our targets to be on top of the world.

TABU
ACTOR

Define Yourself by What You Do

What empowers me is the ability to take decisions and stick by them. Then you can take complete responsibilty for your action. I feel empowered when I see a decision of mine through with conviction. That's very special because in our culture, we are trained and conditioned so that our decisions often have to meet the approval of everyone around us—our family, peers and friends.

When I take that initiative, no matter what people say (because people will always say something or the other), it's very empowering to see the outcome of your decision. It's your own, it's your baby, your achievement, your folly, your mistake.

In this phase of my life and career, this is what I feel. This is the sum total of the past few years. I have noticed that my best moments, my moments of strength have come from realising that this is what I have done—nobody can take the credit or the blame.

The whole idea of empowering women is really a paradox because it doesn't really need to be that way. Nothing from the outside can empower a woman, she's all about power herself. A woman is empowered when she understands, acknowledges and applies her own power. The last is the problem because you are very rarely told all the things that are good about you. We have to practise our power, apply our strength.

I practise it in my work, the strongest area of my life—it's more important to me than anything, even love or a man. It's bound to be, after all I have been working since I was sixteen, it's occupied half my life. It's my voice, the strength of an actor's voice.

I don't think we actors use our voices well enough. We don't realise how powerful the echo of our voice really is. What you communicate, what you could give and what you are giving, it's a great responsibility. When I was doing all those roles, people said they are so powerful. I didn't realise what they meant, for me it was just a good role. But now I understand how you can use or misuse the power that you have.

I really didn't know how far our work reaches until I was in New York for two months. I took a lot of taxi rides and everyone knows 95 per cent of taxi drivers there are Indians or Pakistanis. Every time I sat in a taxi—and I'm sure every star has had that experience—they would refuse to take money from me and they were so moved that someone who's on screen was actually riding in their cab.

I met people from all parts of India—from Punjab to Kashmir. They spoke about anything, from terrorism to extramarital affairs, and they had an opinion on the work I had done and how it impacted their lives.

It was so empowering to be away from home and meet people who admire you and pray for you. You could easily get overwhelmed by that, but when I tell this to my mother or my friends they say I you should feel strong.

It's very empowering to encounter all that—it makes you understand the strength of your work, the power of your work. How one single person can reach out to so many people. I'll never ever forget those taxi rides.

Of course, as people that the audience loves and looks up to, you have a great responsibility. What you say and convey through your roles is what you stand for. I don't know if I have come to that stage yet—I've portrayed many immoral people too, but I'm glad I did these roles because that's all part of society and the people in our lives.

I know what I don't stand for but I still haven't come to fully understand what I stand for. When I figure that out, that will be empowering. For now, I stand for my work, that's what defines me. People are defined by what they do—I'll always want to have something to do to define me. I would like to be known through my work, something with any kind of relevance. I'll always have to be doing and engaging in something that I feel is important for me. What follows is only the offshoot.

It's this conviction, that I am responsible for what I do, for much of what happens to me, which makes me believe that change in India— more employment, better infrastructure, better schools—will come only if we and the government work jointly. In fact, what will empower us Indians most, is to stop our constant blame game and look within. Everyone has to take responsibility for the country—just as we all take responsibility for ourselves. Because we make the government what it is.

P.T. USHA
ATHLETE, OLYMPIAN

Looking for New Icons

These days there is one thing that often strikes me when I take off my jogging shoes and stretch tiredly back with the newspapers every morning. Headlines that invariably say how India is looking up, how its economy has perked up, how the growth graph is promising to go through the roof.

Good news? Well, it should be, even for sports. After all, we now have more money to nurture our immense talent pool, get them set for the international arena, raise India's sporting pride a few notches every year. Not like the time when I started off.

I sincerely wish all that would happen. I don't want to sound pessimistic, but look at what is happening now: each year, the government is quietly cutting down its actual budgetary allocation for sports. It was Rs 237 crore in 2004-2005, it is Rs 301 crore in 2005-2006. Don't be fooled into thinking there is an increase. The government had spent Rs 1.18 per capita to develop sports last year, but it is actually spending 30 paise less this year.

Now, if you say that the government's spending 88 paise per capita to develop sports sounds good enough, think again. The biggest chunk of the allocation—60 per cent—is spent in paying an army of sports officials their salaries and allowances, another 20 per cent for maintaining existing infrastructure, 10 per cent is spent on the benefits for sportspersons (scholarships and incentives). So what are you left with to actually develop sports? Just about 10 per cent of the piddly allocation.

Now look a little farther, at China. The government there is already training kids for the 2016 and 2020 Olympics—scientifically, strategically, systematically, giving them complete backing and financial security, even vouchsafing for their future.

And here? I hate to say this but we have a government and a huge bunch of sports mandarins running our various sports federations and associations who apparently think it is their duty to crush or steamroll any effort even by committed individuals to do something for the cause of sports.

I don't want to elaborate on the theme, just look up the newspapers over the last couple of years. I find that most sports bodies in the country are run by the same people who were running them when I first came into sports. There's hardly any infusion of new thinking or initiative, no meaningful talent hunting.

I am actually ashamed that people like me and Milkha Singh are still considered sports icons in our country. Both of us never won anything more than fourth places in the Olympics of our time. Is it not a reflection of where India still stands in the international sports arena?

I often hear people saying that athletics in our country is where it is because cricket has caught the popular fancy. That is hogwash. I still recall some newspaper headlines from 1983 to 1986 when I was at my peak and fresh from the Los Angeles Olympics performance, and India had just had its defining moment in cricket, winning the 1983 World Cup. Stalwarts like Kapil Dev, Gavaskar and Ravi Shastri were being quoted saying that athletics was getting a whole lot more media attention than cricket!

The fact is, even today, athletics is the best bet for India in sports, no matter whichever way you look at it.

It still has a huge market here. Consider this: an average district athletics meet still draws about a thousand contestants, and their number is still upwards of a lakh and a half each year, countrywide. This is because athletics is a community sport that brooks no class or other differences. You can still run barefoot and win a race, without strapping on unaffordable gear.

And do we really have exceptional talent coming up? Well, the only record of mine that still stands is the one I clocked in hurdles at Los Angeles in 1984, all the rest have been vanquished.

I have also found more to be happy about. I now run a sports school that I have founded in my hometown. I would say without risking exaggeration that four of my wards are great Olympic material. But they need to be provided with what I could never dream of in my time: advanced scientific training, international facilities, complete State backing, and yes, financial security for the future.

If we have those in place, I am confident that India will begin winning three to four track medals in each Olympics from 2012. More importantly, we need to see that there is no narrow bias, no class, creed or parochial considerations when we pick our young sportspersons to be groomed. Unfortunately, it is often not so now.

There is also a dire need for some attitudinal correction among our sportspersons. I have observed that many talented young ones look at sports as just a vehicle to get them jobs or some money. That really has to change. Sports can't be just that if you are to really make your presence felt internationally.

I'll sign off with what I think are the crucial things India needs to do for its sports:

- Our sports promotion and control systems need a thorough overhaul. They should be doing what they are supposed to.
- Give our young ones all the facilities that their peers have in developed countries. Equally important is strategic planning of their development. The first four years of serious induction into sports are crucial for developing their general qualities. The years after they turn sixteen should be devoted to clearly planned development in their specialisations. Right from honing the basics at Level 1 to preparing them for a specific big event at Level 4. Hardly anything of that kind happens now.
- Give them enough live competition exposure. This is an area where we are still miles behind many countries even now.

Equally vital is giving them financial security for their future. When you get off the starting block, giving everything you have for your country, you need to be sure that the country will take care of your future, whatever happens.

VOICES FROM THE ARMED FORCES

M.P. ANIL KUMAR
FORMER FIGHTER PILOT

The Disabled Must Be Self-Sufficient

As was the wont, I called on my old teacher N. Balakrishnan Nair during a visit to my alma mater (Sainik School, Kazhakootam, Kerala) in the mid-1980s. He told me in the course of our chat that the school had benevolently admitted twenty-five needy students from Bihar that year.

I scanned our alumni website to ascertain where these students, some from the boondocks of Bihar, had stationed themselves in life. Officers in the army, navy and customs, journalists, doctors, engineers, research scholars, lecturers, executives—all doing well and shinning up the totempole. I could not but wonder where these schoolmates would have been had they not obtained quality education? Flotsam and jetsam perhaps.

Roughly a century ago, Shri Narayana Guru, sage and social reformer, had an uncomplicated solution to nudge the oppressed masses of Kerala to unfetter themselves from their social and economic subjugation—education. Unlike the self-styled modern messiahs, Guru never exhorted violence or grabbing as means to amelioration. He foresaw education as the stairway to salvation. It reaped rich dividends.

The above illustrations epitomise the capacity of education to catalyse the upward mobility of the straitened strata of the society. At the risk of luring opprobrious epithets, I would aver that the time has come to defenestrate the reservation policy based on castes. It has failed to meet its exalted objectives. Its beneficiaries are the ones with political leverage and the well-heeled SCs, STs and OBCs, not the needy ones.

Instead, the government should focus on their education, books, meals and groundwork for competitive exams; building top-notch schools to provide first-rate education to impecunious students; sponsoring the higher education of the bright among the indigent lot. Unimpeded access to quality education will aid them to make the grade through open competition, instill self-esteem and self-assurance among them, breed role models to emulate and prod their social and economic elevation.

I know my impassioned pitch for skirting the beaten track will fall on deaf ears as no government will have the gumption to groom them that way. It cannot beget instant results and tangible fruition will take decades; hence it will be a political hot potato. Nostrums like reservation, and more reservation, are sly remedies to con the electorate. I boldly believe that empowerment through education is the sure-footed path to pull off the durable uplift of the downtrodden masses. Education is the one-way highway to empowerment. There is no short cut.

I was a fighter pilot in the IAF until a mishap 17 years ago snapped my cervical spinal cord, rendered me quadriplegic and condemned me to a wholly dependent life. From my vantage point aboard a wheelchair, the world looks a markedly different place, nay, a different planet. Disabled persons—variously seen as wastrels, counterfeit coins, eyesores and laughing-stocks—are indisputably at the nadir of the food-chain. Though there are excellent exceptions, lip-service and pity are what we get in abundance. Our parliament passed the Persons with Disabilities Act in December 1995 after much goading. Equal opportunities and non-discrimination, its cornerstones, have been flung to the winds. Why not? The disabled community is not an attractive, exploitable votebank.

'Disabled persons will never be true citizens until they are defined by their contributions, not needs,' bemoaned Sam Sullivan, a Canadian alderman and a quadriplegic. Our society has chosen to be a moral one in which no one should be in need. In a welfare state, the need of one confers a right to the resources of the rest. 'Needs assessment' is the bedrock of our social support system. The classic mechanism of the welfare state is to identify large numbers of similar needs and to assign means to agencies devoted to solving or mitigating them. Alas, people are earmarked by their needs, not by their talents and assets. Think of friendships: they are always based on assets and contributions; no one develops friendships based on what's wrong with the other person.

In sum, we need to one our skills and talents; we need to make our communities aware that everyone, regardless of disability, has vital contributions to make. Communities prosper when all their citizens contribute.

Rehabilitation, that catch-all mantra chanted by the government, means more than just equipping people with crutches, prostheses, wheelchairs, etc. Livelihood is the crux, not handouts. Governmental props, regrettably, enslave the recipients, stunt their talents and abet corruption. Besides, the sundry arms of the jumbo bureaucracy customarily work against one another to nix well-meant welfare programmes. Yet, the imperative of the State joining forces with the society to enable a delivery system needs no emphasis, but we need a novel paradigm to expedite the deliverance of disabled people from the yoke of destitution. Ergo, I believe that a slick public-private tie-up is the avenue to redemption, as demonstrated by the polio eradication drive launched jointly by the government and Rotary Club. Apart from access to transport and buildings, the disabled people want to be made employable and find employment opportunities where they live.

Since unemployment is a curse worse than impairment, a two-pronged initiative to boost employability and employment cannot wait. The education model (with an accent on vocational training) I broached above is the key to making disabled people employable. Since the 3 per cent job quota pledged in the 1995 Act has not increased employment, a robust blueprint to fuel employment needs to be devised. Everything being equal, an employer will always favour a non-disabled candidate. As the private sector will not do it pro bono, why not borrow the German policy of stipulating incentives? Like, higher the number/ratio of disabled workers, higher the tax incentives for the employers. The disabled community will be empowered when the support apparatus facilitates them to stand on their own feet, move on their own steam.

Lastly, India will be empowered when the state of affairs is conducive for her citizens, especially the underprivileged lot, to realise their full potential and live with dignity.

ARUN PRAKASH
FORMER CHIEF OF NAVAL STAFF

Dignity, Self-Respect for Those Who Guard India

The people of India solemnly resolved on 26th November 1949, in the preamble of the Constitution, to secure for every citizen justice, liberty, and equality, to uphold the promotion of fraternity, and ensure the dignity of the individual. There could not have been a better prescription for the empowerment of a people and a nation. 56 years down the line is a good time to undertake a reality check and to perhaps re-order our priorities.

Living in Lutyens' Delhi, I guess I am on weak ground, but let us first talk about the dignity of the individual. Just as nations are empowered by their standing in the world, human beings are empowered by a sense of personal dignity and self-respect. Take these away and you have an abject amoeba. But that is exactly what happens daily at daybreak, when millions of our brothers, sisters and children awake in slums, in degrading shelters of bamboo and plastic and squat for ablutions beside railway lines, footpaths and public drains.

I have been in cities across the world where if you stand at a vantage point, all you can see is row after row of drab, grey housing blocks. Unsightly they may be, but they signify a national resolve to ensure that no citizen will sleep on the footpath. Why do we not empower our citizens by evolving a national consensus that providing basic housing and sanitation, and restoring their dignity as human beings, is an issue of top priority?

While abroad, an Indian walks proudly, with his head held high, because he knows that the world knows his worth. Back at home he scurries: eyes averted, nose covered, avoiding piles of uncleared garbage, unruly traffic and stray cattle. It will not be long before the world too sheds its polite reticence and remarks loudly at the conundrum of India's economic resurgence and intellectual excellence, co-existing with physical slovenliness.

Every one of us feels diminished at our country's civic neglect, filth, squalor and urban decay. So why do we not empower ourselves by ensuring that the taxpayer's money is spent on enforcing basic civic laws, cleanliness and order on the streets, and in getting the ubiquitous garbage off our streets? Let us talk of justice and equality before the law. The common man feels vastly reassured and empowered when the rule of law is upheld and his environment is safe. But he is continuously watching to see if those who break our laws get their just deserts. He is also looking to see if the enforcers of the law respect it themselves. Swift dispensation of justice, no matter how exalted the delinquent, is another issue that bothers the citizen.

Why can't the guardians of the law be selected and trained so that they inspire confidence and respect? Why can we not house them decently and pay them a salary that will give them dignity and self-respect and protect them from petty temptation? By raising their status in society, we empower ourselves.

Swift justice today is a distant vision, and unless some radical measures are adopted by our esteemed judiciary, the vision will keep receding as cases pile up.

It has often been pointed out that as individuals we have quadruple standards of conduct. One for ourselves and one for others; one while in India and another while staying abroad. If our children do not learn civic conduct and a sense of values in their homes, our educational system should step in to fill the void. Here again we have a conundrum. Our institutes of higher learning are right up there with the best in the world, but our primary and secondary education is in shambles. Let us really empower ourselves by investing in our children. By devoting funds, and more importantly, focusing attention on basic education.

What about fraternity? The greatest gift that the founding fathers of our nation could have bequeathed us is the precious right of universal franchise, which we have exercised with regularity since independence, come hell or high water. There can be no greater empowerment of a citizen than this. But let us pause a bit here and remind ourselves that elections are not an end in themselves, but only a means to an end— which is the upliftment of the common man and betterment of our society. In unity lies empowerment of India. Let fraternity and brotherhood amongst our people not become a casualty of the rough and tumble of our sacred democratic tradition.

Lest I be called a hypocrite, let me add in conclusion that the vast sums of money that we spend today on 'guns' could certainly be better spent on buying 'butter' for our children or achieving much of what I have said.

However, if history has taught us anything, it is that security through strength, not weakness, empowers a nation and also engenders development in the long run. But when utopia comes, we shall certainly be ready in the biblical tradition to 'beat our swords into ploughshares'.

J.J. SINGH
CHIEF OF ARMY STAFF

Safety Principle As Article of Faith

For me, India is a civilisational concept. It was the cherished dream of our forefathers, a journey towards that dream for us and finally the realisation of that dream by our children. India is an idea of perfection, an idea of completeness and an idea of the very best synthesised in the crucible of humanity. India empowered is the essence of this dream.

An empowered India can no longer be transgressed and trespassed. The sentinels of the nation are no longer merely seen as the mighty ranges in the north and the deep waters around us. India's strength would be reflected by a strong economy and a powerful military machine which is both professional and modern. This strength would come about with the indomitable will of its people and the insurmountable resolve of its soldiers.

Empowerment will be achieved through a conducive atmosphere for growth, ingenuity, education, enlightenment and ideas flourishing in an environment of safety and security. An empowered nation will carry both opportunity and prosperity to the far-flung corners of the country, thereby bridging divides and building relationships of faith and unity.

This can only happen if we retain our core strength by relentlessly defeating forces of divisiveness and encouraging centrifugal tendencies to join the mainstream. This concept of participative and unifying collective security should be the national security policy for an empowered India.

No country has achieved greatness on the strength of a part of its population; no people have broken the shackles of mediocrity through the genius of a few; no army has won a war merely on the strength of its generals. This can only be achieved in an India free from internal conflicts. This, for me, is the cherished goal that I would like the country to achieve

368   J.J. SINGH

because an ailing part of the body is bound to impact its overall health and efficiency.

Jammu and Kashmir has reinforced our traditions of moderation, secularism and peaceful co-existence. It gave us the concept of Kashmiriyat which in essence is the very basis of our nationhood. Similarly, the rich cultural heritage of states like Manipur, Tripura and Assam augments the idea of a multicultural and proud society that the country represents. Our strength is our diversity, our diversity is our identity and our identity is our intellectual ability. Our collective aspirations need our collective will and our collective genius. Therefore, for me, empowerment lies in this diverse, yet collective genius and the solidity and homogeneity of a rock formed by molten metals, crystals and earth.

Our journey towards progress, modernisation and poverty alleviation will not be a journey free from hurdles. No nation has achieved greatness without surmounting challenges—India is unlikely to be an exception. Our needs include forever increasing energy resources a peaceful neighbourhood which is vibrant and stable. Thus, the ability to achieve our modernisation goals can only be fulfilled if and when we are capable of thwarting challenges from potential adversaries. Though this is often considered the task of the government and the armed forces, this is a journey that all of us must undertake as a nation, as a people and as a dream that we all have envisioned for ourselves.

For centuries ideas, ideals and ideologues have shaped our journey. Today slowly yet steadily, the realms of reality are taking their final turn towards India's tryst with its destiny. After years of hard work and sacrifice, the time has finally come to share the fruits of our endeavours. This sustained effort has seen us substantially enhance our ability, our confidence and our resolve to achieve results in an atmosphere of global competition. The country has seen rapid industrialisation driving the people and the country towards the road to prosperity and self-reliance.

India ranks amongst the developed countries in its expertise in space technologies, information, bio and nanotechnology. For me, an India does not exist at the bottom end of the technology chain; it shines at the very top and our ascent towards that top has already begun. For this, we need collective advancement in the burgeoning knowledge economy. The currency of power in the 20th century was deterrence, the currency of power in the 21st century will be knowledge.

It is also my firm belief that an empowered India will only achieve its destiny if we can individually and collectively help by taking up the challenge of helping the underprivileged in our society. An India empowered can truly become empowered when the divide between the privileged and the underprivileged is bridged. This will not only happen through the policies and efforts of the government, but by the small incremental efforts of each and every one of us through participative empowerment of children amongst the weaker sections of society. For me, empowerment is a collective dream that the haves and have-nots must see together. The haves should be 'more sharing and caring'.

Collective genius evolves from a balanced approach and thinking. Ideas emerging from that genius should be implemented by firm resolve. This resolve can only find fulfillment through equal opportunity and encouragement towards the attainment of equal benefits for men and women alike. Ours is a country which has traditionally accepted and encouraged the role of women in society, a country where there are numerous deities in the female form. It is a country where women have conquered space and proven that given the opportunity, they are capable of achieving the dreams of the nation. For me, the girl child must remain the focus of collective human resource management.

Finally, I see empowerment through the collective spirit of India, which can only manifest itself if we recognise and follow the very essence of being an Indian.

V. SOMASUNDAR
IAF MI-17 RESCUE PILOT IN J&K

Strong, in the Face of Disaster

Disasters cannot be stopped. The world over, whether it's Hurricane Katrina or the tsunami or the Jammu and Kashmir earthquake, this is a reality of life. But how a country reacts depends entirely on its advancement. Fortunately, we have a well-defined set-up in India. And we in the armed forces are at the cutting edge of the delivery system along with people on the ground and in the government.

When disaster strikes, as soon as we get the information, our commanders are fully empowered to put us on standby. In the case of the 8 October 2005 earthquake, our reaction was instant. Within three hours of receiving the alert, we had reached most affected areas, including Tangdhar and Uri.

By 2 pm, we had airlifted a medical team from Udhampur to Tangdhar. As a chopper pilot, there was a great sense of empowerment in being able to give the first visual assessment of the damage caused by the quake.

Flying above the areas, we were able to judge the kind of damage, whether material or human. Of course, in this case it was both. This is crucial because the civil administration's response is based on our assessment. There was human damage and material damage.

This is precisely why we initially prioritised rushing medical succour to the affected areas and evacuated casualties to field areas and hospitals. Once the injured had been rescued and given treatment, we began pumping in relief supplies in our second phase of operations.

And to its credit, the IAF had flown 497 sorties until the weather packed up on October 11 evening. The force established an air bridge between Delhi and the Valley as supplies from Haryana and Punjab, being sent on a routine basis, were picked up.

We had a fair idea of the areas worst affected and were in a position to make operations more detailed for the next phase of relief operations. Our choppers also stood by for night operations, which speeded up the overall effort.

I have witnessed the destruction of Bhuj, the tsunami and the snow tsunami. I can say now that our reaction time has decreased remarkably. This is a sure sign that we are maturing as an organisation and as a nation. However, I do believe that to be truly empowered, there are important decisions our political class can make at every level.

Real empowerment is when the country's resources are available for whoever needs them at whatever time and in the best possible way. We have a country that produces graduates by the thousands every year. Apart from the NCC, is it not possible to have batches of educated youth attaching themselves to the army or other units, to be given a valuable once-over on reacting to crisis situations?

One of our biggest problems is that we desperately need a credible reporting system on the ground. Such trained youth would be invaluable in such a situation. Empowerment will then be the seamless cohesion of the armed forces, the government, the political class, the administrations and the people, at all levels and at all times.

SHASHINDRA PAL TYAGI
CHIEF OF AIR STAFF

Lessons the Armed Forces Teach Us

Empowering India, the way I see it, has two aspects. The first is an empowered India in the comity of nations. The second aspect is to empower its people. Empowerment is about the giving of authority; it is an index of freedoms—of thought and action for the people; and about 'true' sovereignty as a nation. If people are empowered, then the nation they form cannot but follow suit and in quick time. Freedom and sovereignty are indeed the bounty of a strong and prosperous nation, built on the honest efforts of its citizens. I do believe that the wealth of a nation lies not in material things, but in the integrity and courage of its citizens.

The question, therefore, is how much are we empowered. India has progressed admirably on counts of self-reliance, essential infrastructure, economic indices of growth and GDP, science and technology—including space—and nuclear capabilities and indigenous R&D, the strength of its armed forces and production of food and essential commodities. We are a regional power poised to play a greater role in world affairs.

Despite such significant achievements we do also have a downside. Our human development index is low, as is the per capita income. Corruption, lack of good governance, slow justice, outdated laws, wide inequities between rich and poor, illiteracy, unemployment and social injustices of various kinds persist. In other words, the fruits of progress are effectively denied to a wide majority of our people. Perhaps our current maladies are on account of a general drift away from character and ethics. Can we remedy that?

The character of a nation, mirrored in its institutions and actions, is a reflection of the strength of character of its people and their adopted value systems. Character is a sum total of many qualities such as integrity, honesty, ethics, conscience, loyalty and courage. Strength of character will help us rise above the 'self' and the 'immediate' for the common good. Truly, ethical values provide the foundation on which civilised societies exist. Do we have a good measure of civic sense?

This debate is not new; 'values and character' invariably lose out to two simplistic arguments. The first, of impractical idealism—utopia—and the second, 'that you can't preach morals to the starving'. The first argument is but a convenient excuse to continue 'with things as they are', and the latter condition would automatically improve if 'real' social justice is practised by the 'empowered'.

Though not perfect, we in the armed forces have traditionally laid great emphasis on values and are proud of it. The core values to which servicemen pledge their allegiance are, 'Service Before Self', brotherhood, camaraderie, esprit de corps and a readiness to sacrifice if required. Intent is also translated into practice in fair measure. We have remarkable cohesion and a 'one' family 'ethos', enabled by the absence of caste, clan, income, status and religion based distinctions. Yes, some of these values are wrought by regulations and discipline. I recommend these values and methods for all.

It is do-able, if each of us is able to introspect, develop and act ethically. The family is a most important establishment, where examples set would speak louder than words. Teachers and leaders are the other agency that can bring about such a transformation in a variety of imaginative ways. Then again, 'there is nothing like a pat on the back administered often enough and low enough to build character'. Weak laws that satisfy all can rarely serve their intended purpose. I am convinced that if we act out of strength of character, on a universal value system, our people will be empowered and so will India.

YOGENDRA SINGH YADAV
PARAM VIR CHAKRA, HAVILDAR, INDIAN ARMY

Seize the Moment for a Brighter Future

If India is to be empowered, the first thing, the most critical thing, the government must do is ensure that every youth gets an education. Our future is bright but imagine how bright it will be if 99 per cent of our youth are educated. And if they infuse in themselves the spirit of sacrifice, India's future as an empowered nation is assured.

We must not worry about the past or our enemies. Every citizen's ideal must always be the interest of this country. I can tell you every soldier has a dharma, a philosophy towards the country. It may take time for that dharma to spread evenly.

Our culture is ancient, perhaps the oldest in the world. Yet we are helpless as we watch our youth drift towards a way of life introduced by the west. In a sense, the core of our culture is threatened by these new ideals. India has always been open, outward-looking. So if we are to keep our culture adequately safe, this is the time to ensure that something so ancient, so rich is never lost.

Let us stop pointing fingers, worrying about the deeds of others. We must seize the day, look at ourselves, attend to our own lives. Half the problems in this world are because people and countries have failed to look at their own lives first.

Culture apart, India must take advantage of its new-found place in the world of technology to empower its people. If we make good use of technology, we can be a fearless people, take ourselves and the nation forward.

As we move ahead, we must analyse why we still attach so much importance to caste, creed and religion. We are humans first, all from a single source. In a country so diverse and complex as ours, how can we turn to any one religion? All religions are the same. The country is god, the matrabhoomi. You can't look at it any other way.

Isn't it unfair when our politicians, who are supposed to keep the country united, appear to be so divided at times? There are good men and women in our political system too but their number is going down. How I wish there was a way to ensure that the entire country is looked after and not just constituencies.

We talk of an egalitarian society. Yet we deny education to our women. Society is built around the woman, she is the janma mata. She created it, she can destroy it. Women must be given much more power, jobs that men do. They can get rid of so much evil.

On the issue of women, think of how we are going wrong in tackling the population explosion. Just how many more people can our country take? If we are to be a modern society, we have to think of ways to check this furious rise in numbers. If we are unable to handle this problem, we can achieve very little. In whatever we set out to do, we must put our heart and soul. That's the thing to remember. Because money and stature do not count for much.

(Yogendra Singh Yadav of 18 Grenadiers received the country's highest gallantry award for his heroics at Tiger Hill during the 1999 Kargil conflict)

List of Contributors

OMAR ABDULLAH, *20 August 2005* 28

L.K. ADVANI, *17 August 2005* 30

ANU AGA, *12 September 2005* 231

MANI SHANKAR AIYAR, *28 September 2005* 33

MUKESH D. AMBANI, *2 October 2005* 234

VISHWANATHAN ANAND, *14 December 2005* 313

GHULAM NABI AZAD, *7 December 2005* 36

SUBROTO BAGCHI, *24 September 2005* 236

RAHUL BAJAJ, *7 September 2005* 239

A.B. BARDHAN, *14 October 2005* 39

SHYAM BENEGAL, *23 October 2005* 315

BUDDHADEB BHATTACHARJEE, *27 September 2005* 42

DIPANKAR BHATTACHARYA, *31 October 2005* 45

HARSHA BHOGLE, *28 August 2005* 317

BHAICHUNG BHUTIA, *22 November 2005* 319

KUMAR MANGALAM BIRLA, *27 October 2005* 242

MICHAEL F. CARTER, *18 October 2005* 244

SOMNATH CHATTERJEE, *16 August 2005* 23

B.K. CHATURVEDI, *25 August 2005* 49

P. CHIDAMBARAM, *18 December 2005* 53

MEGHNAD DESAI, *1 September 2005* 181

NANAJI DESHMUKH, *29 October 2005* 183

KAPIL DEV, *15 November 2005* 322

Y.C. DEVESHWAR, *8 October 2005*   247
MAHASVETA DEVI, *11 December 2005*   186
SHEILA DIKSHIT, *30 November 2005*   56
DHANANJAY DUBEY, *20 December 2005*   189
PRIYA DUTT, *15 December 2005*   58
GEORGE FERNANDES, *15 October 2005*   60
GOPALKRISHNA GANDHI, *10 December 2005*   63
ANJU BOBBY GEORGE, *8 December 2005*   324
K.P.S. GILL, *1 November 2005*   66
NARESH GOYAL, *13 November 2005*   252
I.K. GUJRAL, *18 August 2005*   69
SATISH GUJRAL, *12 November 2005*   326
WAJAHAT HABIBULLAH, *10 October 2005*   72
BHUPEN HAZARIKA, *24 October 2005*   329
BHUPINDER SINGH HOODA, *18 November 2005*   76
KANCHA ILAIAH, *11 November 2005*   192
A.P.J. ABDUL KALAM, *21 December 2005*   3
K.V. KAMATH, *10 September 2005*   256
SHAMMI KAPOOR, *29 November 2005*   331
KIRAN KARNIK, *6 December 2005*   259
SHAH RUKH KHAN, *24 August 2005*   333
JAGDISH KHATTAR, *17 November 2005*   262
NAINA LAL KIDWAI, *16 September 2005*   265
M.P. ANIL KUMAR, *8 November 2005*   361
NITISH KUMAR, *23 November 2005*   79
R.C. LAHOTI, *5 December 2005*   18
ANAND MAHINDRA, *29 September 2005*   267
ARUN MAIRA, *2 December 2005*   270
R.A. MASHELKAR, *22 September 2005*   195
MAYAWATI, *13 December 2005*   82
SANIA MIRZA, *16 November 2005*   335
U.S. MISRA, *28 October 2005*   84
SUNIL BHARTI MITTAL, *20 September 2005*   273
MEHBOOBA MUFTI, *25 November 2005*   90

378 LIST OF CONTRIBUTORS

PRANAB MUKHERJEE, *2 September 2005* **93**

BRIJMOHAN LALL MUNJAL, *20 November 2005* **276**

N.R. NARAYANA MURTHY, *16 October 2005* **280**

A.M. NAIK, *11 October 2005* **283**

G. MADHAVAN NAIR, *23 August 2005* **197**

K.R. NARAYANAN, *10 November 2005* **95**

FALI S. NARIMAN, *5 September 2005* **97**

JAYANT V. NARLIKAR, *22 October 2005* **199**

KAMAL NATH, *3 November 2005* **99**

NANDAN M. NILEKANI, *6 September 2005* **286**

P.R.S. 'BIKI' OBEROI, *20 October 2005* **289**

R.K. PACHAURI, *20 October 2005* **102**

M.K. PANDHE, *5 November 2005* **105**

DEEPAK PAREKH, *8 September 2005* **291**

PRAFUL PATEL, *6 November 2005* **108**

MEDHA PATKAR, *26 September 2005* **200**

NAVEEN PATNAIK, *4 November 2005* **111**

VIVEK PAUL, *4 September 2005* **293**

SHARAD PAWAR, *4 October 2005* **114**

DHANRAJ PILLAY, *7 November 2005* **337**

SACHIN PILOT, *13 September 2005* **119**

SAM PITRODA, *7 October 2005* **299**

ARUN PRAKASH, *17 October 2005* **364**

AZIM H. PREMJI, *23 September 2005* **296**

GANESH PYNE, *19 December 2005* **339**

S.Z. QASIM, *13 November 2005* **204**

SUBIR RAHA, *26 October 2005* **302**

VASUNDHARA RAJE, *29 August 2005* **121**

N. RAM, *6 October 2005* **129**

ANBUMANI RAMADOSS, *14 November 2005* **134**

RAJYAVARDHAN SINGH RATHORE, *14 September 2005* **341**

ARUNA ROY, *17 December 2005* **208**

SYED KALBE SADIQ, *21 November 2005* **137**

P.A. SANGMA, *1 December 2005* **140**

MALLIKA-KARTIKEYA SARABHAI, *12 December 2005* **343**

JYOTIRADITYA SCINDIA, *17 September 2005* **142**

SRI SRI RAVI SHANKAR, *18 September 2005* **211**

P. SHANKAR, *16 December 2005* **144**

M. SHANMUGHAM, *4 December 2005* **213**

RAKESH SHARMA, *9 September 2005* **148**

KIRAN MAZUMDAR SHAW, *30 August 2005* **304**

GULAMMOHAMMED SHEIKH, *19 October 2005* **345**

BHAIRON SINGH SHEKHAWAT, *31 August 2005* **11**

DEVI SHETTY, *11 September 2005* **215**

KAPIL SIBAL, *12 October 2005* **151**

AMARINDER SINGH, *24 November 2005* **154**

J.J. SINGH, *3 September 2005* **367**

JASWANT SINGH, *1 October 2005* **158**

MANMOHAN SINGH, *15 August 2005* **16**

MILKHA SINGH, *3 December 2005* **351**

K. NATWAR SINGH, *27 August 2005* **160**

V.P. SINGH, *19 August 2005* **166**

RAGHUVANSH PRASAD SINGH, *3 October 2005* **162**

V. SOMASUNDAR, *13 October 2005* **370**

VENU SRINIVASAN, *9 November 2005* **306**

SUSHMA SWARAJ, *5 October 2005* **168**

M.S. SWAMINATHAN, *21 October 2005* **217**

TABU, *27 November 2005* **353**

B.B. TANDON, *22 August 2005* **170**

RATAN TATA, *25 September 2005* **308**

NARESH TREHAN, *30 September 2005* **221**

S.P. TYAGI, *21 September 2005* **370**

P.T. USHA, *20 November 2005* **355**

SADHGURU JAGGI VASUDEV, *19 September 2005* **224**

P. VENUGOPAL, *15 September 2005* **227**

MULAYAM SINGH YADAV, *26 November 2005* **173**

YOGENDRA SINGH YADAV, *26 August 2005* **374**

SITARAM YECHURY, *9 September 2005* **175**